Countervocalities
Shifting Language Hierarchies on Corsica

Studies in Modern and Contemporary France 12

Studies in Modern and Contemporary France

Series Editors
Assistant Professor Siham Bouamer, Sam Houston State University
Professor Denis M. Provencher, University of Arizona
Professor Martin O'Shaughnessy, Nottingham Trent University

The Studies in Modern and Contemporary France book series is a new collaboration between the Association for the Study of Modern and Contemporary France (ASMCF) and Liverpool University Press (LUP). Submissions are encouraged focusing on French politics, history, society, media and culture. The series will serve as an important focus for all those whose engagement with France is not restricted to the more classically literary, and can be seen as a long-form companion to the Association's journal, *Modern and Contemporary France,* and to *Contemporary French Civilization*, published by Liverpool University Press.

Countervocalities

Shifting Language Hierarchies on Corsica

ALEXANDER MENDES

Liverpool University Press

First published 2023 by
Liverpool University Press
4 Cambridge Street
Liverpool
L69 7ZU

This paperback edition published 2025

Copyright © 2025 Alexander Mendes

Alexander Mendes has asserted the right to be identified as the author of this book in accordance with the Copyright, Designs and Patents Act 1988.

All rights reserved. No part of this book may be reproduced, stored in a retrieval system, or transmitted, in any form or by any means, electronic, mechanical, photocopying, recording, or otherwise, without the prior written permission of the publisher.

British Library Cataloguing-in-Publication data
A British Library CIP record is available

ISBN 978-1-83764-439-1 (hardback)
ISBN 978-1-83624-550-6 (paperback)

Typeset by Carnegie Book Production, Lancaster

For Margot

Contents

Acknowledgments	ix
Transcription Conventions	xi
Images	xiii
Preface	xv

1	Introduction: Tightropes	1
	Introduction	1
	§1.1 Corsican, Briefly	2
	§1.2 Beyond the Central Periphery	7
	§1.3 Italo-Multilingualism?	12
	§1.4 Balancing Acts	15
	§1.5 Approaches and Outline	19
2	Pearls	27
	Introduction	27
	§2.1 Ethnography of FLE	28
	§2.2 Setting the Scene	34
	§2.3 Pearls	37
	§2.3.1 The Q Episode	39
	§2.3.2 A Parent	47
	§2.3.3 Eyelids	53
	§2.4 Globalizing Surges	56

3	ABCs		61
	Introduction		61
	§3.1 *Abécédaires*		63
	§3.2 *Abbiccì dì*		65
	§3.3 I Spy		71
	§3.4 Mirrors		81
4	Stories		91
	Introduction		91
	§4.1 Language Stories		92
	§4.2.1 "Une langue assez … rigolotte"		96
	§4.2.2 "Ils ne vont pas te comprendre"		101
	§4.2.3 "My weakness was my strength"		108
	§4.2.4 "Elle est morte, elle est finie"		114
	§4.2.5 "Il n'y a pas de petites langues"		123
	§4.3 Mediation		133
5	*For(z)a*		139
	Introduction		139
	§5.1 Corsican Linguistic Landscapes		140
	§5.2 Reading rue Droite		142
	§5.2.1 The Bus Stop		143
	§5.2.2 "The True Faith"		146
	§5.2.3 Multilingual Fragments		150
	§5.2.4 *Arabi forza*		156
	§5.3 *For(z)a*		160
Coda			167
Bibliography			177
Index			191

Acknowledgments

I am grateful for the blessings and privileges I have had in pursuing this project of learning, for the various paths I have been able to take, for the gifts and joys and failings.

I respectfully acknowledge the Corsican, Patwin, Ojibwe, Muscogee, Cherokee, and Haudenosaunee, Lenape, Osage, and Shawnee communities on whose traditional homelands this work has been carried out.

I offer this work in grateful remembrance of two of my teachers, Lenora Timm and Alexandra Jaffe, champions of the French regional languages Breton and Corsican, respectively.

I am most grateful to those who have participated in this research over the years, on Corsica and beyond, for their graceful patience, help, and insights, for the opportunities to dialogue and listen. To Michèle Andreani and colleagues at the Académie de Corse, colleagues and students of Bastia-area middle schools, the Teaching Assistantship Program in France (TAPIF) through the Cultural Services of the French Embassy in the United States, Antonu Marielli and A scola corsa, Ghjuvan-Liviu Casalta, Christhel, Erik, Lilian, and Ugo Uribelarrea, Emilie, Dominque, and Christian Mikdjian, Marie-Paule and Bruno Lancry, Marie-Pierre and Antoine Marchini and the Centre régional de documentation pédagogique/CANAPÉ de Bastia, Marie-Line Flori, Corrine Luiggi, Marylena and Ghjuvan-Francescu Giamarchi, l'Associaziò Cantu in paghjella, Paule Bevaraggi, Catherine Leforestier, Gabrielle Mattei, Brigitte Paolacci, Pascal Tabanelli, Annick Lamy, Patrick Delvarre, Muriel Donati, Xin Demarchi, Sonia Moretti, Michelle Crowell, Anna Palmqvist, Ahmed Idrissi, Noelia Gómez Sambuco, Rawley Crews, Aurora Marchi, Bethany Powell, Alix Issakhanian, and Céline Orenga. And to those I'm surely forgetting. *Vi ringraziu assai*!

To Marcellu Fortini and the Centre méditerranéen de la photographie, whose work from the *Abicidì fotogràficu corsu-francese* appears in Chapter 2. The original pedagogical workshop was directed by Valérie Rouyer, *chargée de mission en pédagogie* at the CMP, François Rusjan Biaggini, *infirmier réfèrent* at the Maison des adolescents de Haute-Corse, the UPE2A class (Unité pédagogique pour élèves allophones arrivants) and Gabrielle Mattei and Brigitte Paolacci, teachers of *français langue étrangère*, and Luce Giacomoni, *documentaliste* of the Collège de Montesoro—Bastia. The CMP project was financed by the city of Bastia with the support of the Maison des adolescents de Haute-Corse and the Collège de Montesoro—Bastia.

Many thanks to Frédérique Bertrand and the Centre culturel Una Volta, especially Santa Ortali and Juana Macari, for graciously allowing art from *Abbiccì dì* to be reproduced in Chapter 2.

To Chloe Johnson, Sarah Davison, and the entire team at Liverpool University Press for their untiring support and guidance. I am also grateful to the anonymous reviewers whose generous engagement with my drafts has enormously helped me in my thinking and writing.

Many thanks to my colleagues and students who have provided me guidance and inspiration, especially Will Lombardi, whose concept of the postlocal has been a favorite of mine to ponder, and Guilherme Von Streber, whose work has challenged me to learn more about translanguaging. To my professors and colleagues at the University of California, Davis and Emory University. To those whose generous feedback has been invaluable in improving my work, especially David Gramling, Christina Higgins, Katy Highet, Cheryl Yin, Chris Palazzolo, Piergiorgio Mura, Christine Ristaino, and Margherita Heyer-Caput. Thanks as well to Lamia Mezzour-Hodson and Noah Guynn for their kind assistance with translations in Chapter 5. And to my colleagues at Duolingo, especially Bozena Pajak, Jessie Becker, James Leow, Sharon Wilkinson, Emily Moline, and Kate Barker.

I cannot repay the kindness, patience, and skillful teachings—academic and otherwise—of my mentors, Vaidehi Ramanathan, Julia Menard-Warwick, Hiram Maxim, Valérie Loichot, and especially Julia Simon. To those whose friendship has sustained me in heart and mind over the years, especially Sarah Coniglio, Julie Hassna, Siobhan Mulreany, Carmen Castaldi Gómez, Alexandrine Mailhé, Chelsea Escalante, and Chad Córdova. To Valérie Teisseyre and Marc'Andrìa Mattei, as always, for their friendship. To my parents for their unwavering love and support. And to Jacob and Kyle, for everything.

Transcription Conventions

,	short pause
.	longer pause
…	longer pause
( )	quiet speech
xxx	unclear
[[	overlapping speech
(( ))	description
italics	insistence
?	rising intonation
–	interruption

Images

3.1	*Ghjucà* (to play). Credit: Frédérique Bertrand.	67
3.2	*Zinzì* (sea urchin). Credit: Frédérique Bertrand.	68
3.3	*Diavule* (devil). Credit: Frédérique Bertrand.	69
3.4	"A—Museu di Bastia—Palazzu di I Guvernatori—Musée de Bastia—Palais des Gouverneurs" (tree, air, friendship). Photo credit: Marcel Fortini, Centre méditerranéen de la photographie.	72
3.5	"L—Mediateca di u Centru Culturale Alb'oru—Médiathèque Centre Culturel Alb'oru" (book, high school, secularism). Photo credit: Marcel Fortini, Centre méditerranéen de la photographie.	76
3.6	"U—Scale di Santa Chjara—Rue Sainte-Claire de Bastia" (urn, university, utopia). Photo credit: Marcel Fortini, Centre méditerranéen de la photographie.	79
5.1	Bus stop sign, "Arabi fora" (Arabs out). Note the small drawing of the suitcase and coffin toward the bottom right. Photo credit: author.	144
5.2	Bus stop bench. "Arabi fora rentre chez toi Arabe" (Arabs out, go home Arab). Photo credit: author.	145
5.3	Display of Jehovah's Witness pamphlets in Arabic and French. Photo credit: author.	147

5.4	Corsican-language clean-up flyer, "Rispettu, pulizia, circulazione, u vulemu fà u primu passu? A mo cità, a tengu cara" (Respect, cleanliness, mobility. Do we want to take the first step? My city, I love it). Photo credit: author.	151
5.5	Street name plaque, "Ex rue Droite rue Chanoine Letteron" (Former Right Street Canon Letteron Street). Photo credit: author.	153
5.6	Jesuit fountain plaque, "Fons urbis praefecto Petro Giovellina restitutus anno domini MDCCCVI imperj Napoleonis Magni secondo" (City fountain restored by mayor Petru Giovellina in the year of our Lord 1806 and in the second year of Emperor Napoleon the Great). Photo credit: author.	154
5.7	Old shop sign, "Régal'Ad Snack" (Feast Snack Bar). Photo credit: author.	155
5.8	Graffiti palimpsest, "Arabi forza" (Arabs strength). Photo credit: author.	157
C.1	Yvan Colonna graffito, "omu eri populu ti si fattu" ([you] were a man made of [your] people). Photo credit: author.	168
C.2	Graffiti palimpsest revisited, a new "A" for "for(z)a." Photo credit: author.	169
C.3	"Bastia è basta" (Bastia and that's it) → "Pulenta è basta" (Polenta and that's it). Photo credit: author.	170

Preface

Todas las lenguas están muertas
Muertas en manos del vecino trágico
Hay que resucitar las lenguas con sonoras risas
Con vagones de carcajadas
Con cortacircuitos en las frases
Y cataclismo en la gramática.

All the languages are dead
Dead in the hands of the tragic neighbor
We must revive the languages
With raucous laughter
With wagons of cackles
With circuit breakers in the sentences
And cataclysm in the grammar. (Huidobro, 2003: 75)

Qu'est-ce que vous allez faire de votre week-end? (What are you going to do this weekend?), I call on a female student. *Je vais au village* (I'm going to the village). The air in the room seems to get tense. *Oh, lequel?* (Which one?). Ghisonnaccia. A town on the eastern littoral. Other students glare on, unimpressed. I flounder, trying to carry on the conversation with the group of middle schoolers, but their arms are crossed and faces stoic. Had I said something wrong? I'm relieved when the bell finally rings.

I spent a long time trying to interpret exactly what happened in this exchange. At the time, I had been teaching for a few months at two local schools and had learned the push-and-pull rhythms between cities and villages. In Corsica, it is common for people to spend the week in the city and retreat to a family home in a small village for the weekend and longer holidays. You can now even buy t-shirts that proudly proclaim, *Je peux pas, je monte au village* (I can't, I'm going to the village). When you tell someone where you're from, you name the village where your family home is located, not the city where you live and work during the week. The *au* in the expression *au village*, can be understood as "to the village," "in the village," or "to my village," the latter revealing an implied possession in the Corsican sense of retreating to one's family space. The absence of an explicit articulation of a possessive adjective, *mon* (my), is suggestive of an ambiguity in claims to place.

The student who had told me she was going to Ghisonnaccia was of North African descent. The eastern littoral is known for having been a hub of repatriation of French North Africans in the 1960s, where they played a large role in agricultural *main d'oeuvre*. The area was also the scene of the *évènements d'Aléria* (events at Aléria) wherein Maghrebi repatriates were accused of practicing chaptalization, doctoring wine in the fermentation process by adding sugar, leading to an eruption of violence between Corsican regionalists and French armed forces. The other students seemed to scoff at the girl's claim that she was going to "her" village—non-Corsicans don't have villages.

Several years later when I returned to Bastia for my doctoral fieldwork, I rented an apartment near the *vieux port* (old port). Upon arriving, I chatted with the landlord who greeted me and explained he would be spending the months that I rented the apartment *au village*. I knew that he had a French, not Corsican, last name, and wondered if he was one of many people who return to Corsica because of family ties after one or two generations of their family being *sur le continent*, in France. Which is your village? I asked. A bit abashed, he explained it was not actually his, but his Corsican girlfriend's, another instance of a non-Corsican deploying the expression of going "to the village." I was fascinated.

By way of things like this particular example, *au village*, I became interested in the ways that non-Corsicans learn to display their knowledge of being in a culturally specific place. I experienced this myself, though perhaps less self-consciously at first, when I ventured to speak Corsican, and someone would ask me how I'd learned a particular pronunciation. Perhaps it was from the grandparents of another student I tutored in English, who had learned of my interest in Corsican and made me recite the days of the week or proverbs or count. In any case, I had inadvertently learned this display as well, reflecting to Corsicans a localized knowledge linked to a particular place. But, whereas my (an American student from the University of California) use of particular forms of Corsican was praised, the young Maghrebi student only got blank stares when mentioning her village.

And the village still beckons. Throughout my work, colleagues (on Corsica and abroad) have suggested on several occasions that research on language would be much better carried out *au village*. To them, it made no sense to attempt to study language on Corsica in an urban setting since "real" Corsican language and culture could not be found in cities. But, I continue to ask myself, surely Corsican-ness exists in cities, too? What are the interactions between allophones, immigrants, foreigners (like me, and others), and the Corsican language and culture—even if not in a village? A tricky question.

Teaching middle school is a joyful kind of chaos. I spent the 2012–13 school year as an *assistant d'anglais* (English teaching assistant) working in middle schools in Bastia, in northern Corsica. My experience was, of course, colored by the fact that I was living and working in a country and language that were not my "native" context. The *salle des profs* (teachers' lounge) was one of my favorite spaces for the happy shouting and camaraderie (in French and Corsican) that ensued in intense bursts between classes—sharing snacks, offering to pay for colleagues' drinks at the coffee vending machine, and commiserating about the latest quotidian dramas. With students, on the other hand, it took time for me to learn the song and dance of working with adolescents as I adjusted to the role of a novice instructor, not without growing pains. I was unsettled by the fact that students unrelentingly addressed me with the formal *vous*, though I now understand this as the institutional expectation, the way that children address adults in schools. I had been mesmerized by teachers' commentary aloud to the entire class as they passed back papers, critiquing each student's work to the whole group—*à refaire, c'est mieux, la catastrophe* (redo, better, catastrophe). I froze on the spot when, after having completed a one-on-one exercise with students in a class, the teacher asked me to stand in front of the room and tell her how each student did and perform this same sort of evaluative monologue in front of everyone. I was petrified. For everyone else in the room, though, it was banal. My shock was the fun part for them.

Upon my return to the same school years later for my doctoral fieldwork, I observed the newly arrived immigrant students in the French as a second language (FLE) class struggle with other seemingly ordinary practices, for example the intricacies involved in maintaining one's school notebook (*tenir son cahier*). What should be written where on the page? On the same page or a new page? In what color? When given a worksheet, how should one properly cut and paste it onto a page in the notebook? Whereas "normal" students who had been doing this for years were able to carry this out automatically, FLE students usually asked, often for each individual task, how they should transpose what was going on in class or on the board into their notebooks. If they didn't ask, FLE teachers sometimes explained, remembering the need to be explicit. On several occasions, students asked me if I had an extra four-colored pen or glue stick, so I bought extra to have with me for when I went to class with them. With these practices and tools, we were learning what the expected performance of good language learning looks like in France.

My own studies of the Corsican language—attending adult language classes and community events and sitting in on middle school classes—have been exhilarating, if at times uncomfortable. I was constantly referred to as "the American," and sometimes *un ami* (a friend) interested in the language, this outsider identity awkwardly foregrounded to local students as if to assert, if he can do it, you can, too. Although there were other foreigners in the classes (German, Belgian, Moroccan), our teacher singled me out as *le petit doué* (the little gifted one). At one point, our teacher, an older man of the activist generation of the 1970s went on a tirade, saying some locals didn't take kindly to outsiders. Upon seeing my shock, he assured me in front of everyone, *pas toi Alex, t'es adorable* (not you Alex, you're adorable). Shaken and confused became a theme.

Our teacher eventually suggested I attend an additional Corsican class in order to have more exposure and varied instruction. My first day in that class was a whole new kind of strange surprise—I was asked to present myself and the room burst into excitement, people were filming me on their phones, aghast that an American had waltzed in and spoken a couple of sentences in Corsican. If I was often a bit nervous in class, my ease of access to these spaces was facilitated by my nationality. Over the years, I have gotten the sense that it would be much more difficult for a French person, for example, to do what I (an American) was doing—weaving through Corsican circles to learn about the local culture and language. Much more difficult has been attempting to explain my interest in multilingual dynamics on Corsica, which is usually regurgitated back to me as an interest in *intégration* (integration). I have had to navigate this linguistic and cultural minefield and have, like some of my research participants, admittedly struggled to make myself as inconspicuous as possible, to try to fit in—or to stick out less, or to stick out in the right ways—as I attempt to study multilingualism on the granite island. What follows is my attempt to consolidate these stories.

I offer these vignettes as an opening onto the rest of the book. Similarly, each chapter begins with a vignette to contextualize, to set the scene as it were, and introduce the central themes of the different sections. They are a welcome opportunity for me to further insert my voice and subjective experience as researcher, and a reminder that these accounts are necessarily partial and by no means completely objective.

Chapter 1

Introduction

Tightropes

Introduction

Corsica is located in the northwestern Mediterranean, the fourth largest of the region's islands after Sicily, Sardinia, and Cyprus. Throughout its history, Corsica has traded hands between Pisa, Genoa, and Aragon, and even enjoyed a brief bout of independence in the mid-eighteenth century. Corsica's colorful past is attested by statue menhirs depicting early warrior populations, ruins of the Greek settlement at present-day Aléria, and the cliffs at the southernmost point supposedly visited by Odysseus. The legend of princess Davia, a young Corsican beauty taken by pirates who went on to become a favorite of her Moroccan sultan, persists in local lore. Symbols of Corsican culture point to a violent past, as in the Moor's Head flag, a disembodied head on a white background said to represent the rising against Saracen invasions and chosen as a symbol of independent Corsica. Unique linguistic histories are reflected in Corsican vocabulary, as seen in the two contemporary words for "dog," *cane*, from Latin *canis*, and *ghjàcaru*, perhaps related to Italian *sciacallo* (jackel), which apparently comes from a Sanskrit root. What can seem to be an amalgam of exaggerations and contradictions, Corsica is a kaleidoscope of heritage.

   This chapter aims to familiarize the reader with the contemporary Corsican sociolinguistic context by outlining important milestones, trends, and policies throughout the island's history. My intent is not to write about the Corsican language in isolation. Nonetheless, in order to explore language use and ideologies on the island, one must understand the linguistic context on the ground, which recent policy and scholarship have primarily approached with a focus on revitalization of the local language. I seek, rather, to more holistically explore Corsican *and* other languages. That is, my focus is on Corsican's relationship (or potential relationships) to other codes, language ideologies, and *combinations* of languages that arise in various contexts on the island as well as discourses and representations of linguistic heterogeneity, broadly conceived. These competing conceptualizations of linguistic multiplicity are what I am calling countervocalities, for example when I say "multilingual" and someone counters insisting on "bilingual." In this way, I respond, however partially, to recent calls for further work on multilingualism on Corsica with regard to "managing linguistic and cultural diversity" (Quenot, 2020: 147), a broadening of our understandings of multilingualism on the island as well as ways in which various practices and policies contribute to language reclamation projects (Leonard, 2011). I first offer a brief history of language dynamics on Corsica, particularly highlighting the shift to French since the island's annexation and efforts to revitalize the regional language since the 1980s. I then discuss theories pertinent to the study of linguistic minorities and globalization, with careful attention to center-periphery dynamics in the case of European minority language communities and Corsica. I close by situating my approach to language work in critical ethnographic sociolinguistics and outline the chapters that follow.

§1.1 Corsican, Briefly

Language is, today, a central pillar of what is variously referred to as the Corsican question, the Corsican situation, or the Corsican problem.[1] The politicization of the Corsican language is not straightforward and should be understood as a dynamic process of political strategies and alliances rather than a lineage that descends from Corsican nationalism as we understand it today (Fazi, 2020). Prior to the island becoming a French territory in 1769, after centuries of Italianate rule (Genoa, Pisa), a diglossic division existed between Corsican, as the language of the home, and Italian (Tuscan), as the language of learning and government. Since its annexation, the shift to French was at first quite slow. Even in 1915, after the institution of free, secular, and obligatory

---

1   See also *La nouvelle question corse* (Fourquet, 2017), "The End of the Corsican Question?" (Serrano, 2011).

education in French by the Ferry Laws of 1882, intergenerational transmission of Corsican was rather high, at 85 percent (Fazi, 2020: 126). France's participation in the world wars led to a striking decline in the number of speakers of French regional languages; intergenerational transmission of Corsican dropped to 30 percent in 1935.

Mobility has played a key role in the decline of Corsican, specifically in Corsicans' participation in French military service and colonial projects, both carried out in French. Camus (1957) depicts Corsicans' participation in colonial administration in the character of Balducci, the gruff *gendarme* in his short story *L'hôte* ("The Guest"), which tells of the complicated relationship between the colonizer's footmen and the colonized. Indeed, Corsica has been (is) considered colonized, put to the service of the French State as a sunny vacation spot while it otherwise lacks economic and infrastructural growth as a periphery, what Robert Lafont (1967) has called internal colonialism. Postwar development initiatives on the island resulted in tensions between locals and those newly repatriated from North Africa (Albertini, 2018: 59–67), exacerbated by the emigration of large numbers of Corsicans to the continent seeking economic opportunities.

The latter half of the twentieth century brought important policy measures for the promotion and protection of Corsican.[2] The Deixonne Law of 1951 (and its subsequent iterations, particularly in 1974 to include Corsican) marked a turning point for regional languages in France, allowing for their teaching, if minimal, in schools. Importantly, this was only considered possible once the national standard and its concomitant unforgiving monolingual ideology were firmly established. Having supposedly eradicated *patois*, an unwavering francohegemony (Mendes, 2022) seeped through France and its territories. Corsican language activism surged in the 1970s alongside other regional movements in Brittany, Catalonia, and the Basque Country. This moment, known in Corsican as *u Riacquistu* (the "reappropriation"), sought to revalorize local forms of cultural and linguistic expression and foreground these in francophone institutions.

With the French decentralization laws of the early 1980s and the establishment of the Territorial Collectivity of Corsica and the Corsican Assembly, Corsican began to be introduced into domains

---

2 For thorough treatments of language policy on Corsica, see Blackwood (2008) and Adrey (2009).

previously occupied by French (and before that, Italian), notably in education. Though the Corsican Assembly has voted for co-officiality of Corsican and French on the island and continues to support this status, this is seen by France's highest courts as unconstitutional since the language of the Republic is French alone. There has nonetheless been some success in securing use of Corsican institutionally with various policies achieved by decades of activism. Though often associated with "nationalist" sentiments *vis-à-vis* the protection and promotion of traditional heritage, the Corsican language today enjoys widespread support from across political parties and voter demographics (Fazi, 2020).

The Corsican language and its relationship to local culture are often subsumed (if not conflated) in the idea of the Corsican *patrimoine* (cultural heritage or legacy). A dynamic assemblage of the island's artifactual, immaterial, and even biological resources, the *patrimoine* figures prominently in discourses of Corsican language maintenance and revitalization. Despite decades of revitalization initiatives, Corsican monolingualism today is obsolete. Everyone who speaks it also speaks French,[3] the majority language of everyday communication on the island. Vast ranges of estimated numbers of speakers help us to think about what counts as speaking and to whom. Colonna (2020b) has observed that, contrary to its prior restriction as the "Low" language in a diglossic divide, Corsican is well established today in education, literature, and the media. These institutional uses, however, may mask a lack of more quotidian use; that is, "representational" uses and accompanying positive discourse about Corsican have recently tended to exceed other communicative practices (Colonna, 2020b: 96).

Linguists in the latter half of the twentieth century, notably Jean-Baptiste Marcellesi and his colleagues, fought for the recognition of Corsican as its own language, rather than a dialect of Italian (Blanchet, 2020). This work led to important developments in sociolinguistic theory that countered formalist approaches that more often than not extracted language from lived contexts of use and the community concerned. Primary among these is the concept of *polynomie* (polynomy), "le concept phare" (the flagship concept) of Corsican language studies (Di Meglio, 2020). Polynomy, in contrast to

---

3   On Corsican Regional French, see Jaffe (1999).

the strict, neat divide established by the logic of diglossia, is constituted by an inter-tolerance among varieties of a language and a refusal to ascribe to a language-dialect dichotomy (Thiers, 2020: 39). Polynomy thus offers a unity-in-diversity orientation to language that does not require linguistic standardization in the normative sense, allowing instead for variation to play out in practice, for example, between different varieties of Corsican used in a single conversation.

Ideologically groundbreaking in its conceptualization of a plural alternative *vis-à-vis* a monolithic national standard like French, a polynomic approach as it is endorsed on Corsica today "change le rapport aux normes, le rapport à la langue, le rapport à l'autre. Il contribue par-là à réfléchir à une citoyenneté culturelle ouverte et généreuse" (changes the relationship to norms, the relationship to language, the relationship to the other. It thereby contributes to reflection on an open and generous cultural citizenship)[4] (Di Meglio, 2020: 63). This approach to the intermixing of language has led to the broader conceptualization of Corsican society as *bi-plurilingue* (bi-plurilingual) (Di Meglio, 2020; Quenot, 2010), that is linguistic diversity understood as that between varieties of Corsican, Corsican and French, and Corsican and other Italo-Romance varieties (e.g., Tuscan, Sardinian) (Jaffe, 2020: 70). In this way, we see that while polynomy is indeed a counter-ideology to linguistic domination, it is nonetheless not neutral (Jaffe, 2014). That is, the foregrounding of Corsican-French *bi-plurilinguisme* is not disinterested and may overshadow other kinds of multilingualism (Mendes, 2021). As Jaffe (2020) observes, "all language ideological frameworks—even those which recognize diversity—impose particular criteria and give value to some ways of speaking and being over others" (70).

Polynomy challenges the treatment of languages as bounded, separate codes (a kind of precursor to translanguaging, see below). However, in the Corsican case, linguistic diversity as the widely upheld ideal of *bi-plurilinguisme* can seem to fall short of an open, holistic understanding of language repertoires given its privileging of Corsican and French. Indeed, Tamazight-[5], Arabic-, and Portuguese-speaking immigrants, among others, are often erased in the wider imaginary of linguistic

---

4 All translations are mine unless otherwise noted.
5 Tamazight is an indigenous language of North Africa also referred to as "Berber." The label "Berber" is one that some members of the Imazighen community reject as pejorative. Throughout the chapters, when I refer to this

multiplicity on the island (Mahdi, 2014; Géa, 2016; Blackwood & Tufi, 2015), not to mention other languages of tourism and trade such as German, Italian, and English. Where are these languages? When and how are they visible or audible on Corsica? In what discourses are they used, or in what ways are they talked about, or not? I am interested in these disparate conceptualizations of what linguistic multiplicity is and means, the competing "homogenizing and heterogenizing discourses" on the island (Jaffe, 2020: 80). Exploring the question of language on Corsica is walking a tightrope: a dynamic act of balancing multiple languages and their baggage—Corsican in all its varieties, French as the State language, and the languages of immigrants, tourists, and the wider global economy.

My focus on language beyond the revitalization of Corsican gestures to translanguaging as a lens with which to approach these questions (Di Meglio, 2020: 56). Translanguaging views language use as free from the confines of separate, named languages to consider linguistic repertoires as holistic ensembles (Canagarajah, 2018: 31; García, 2009). What's more, translanguaging understands linguistic signs as only one part among many mobilized in meaning-making practices; it is a "multimodal social semiotic[s]" (Li Wei, 2018: 22) inclusive of various "resources and modalities" (Canagarajah, 2018: 31) recruited in communication and subject formation. Studying language dynamics on Corsica from a translanguaging perspective allows for an opening between the various languages involved as well as a foregrounding of visual, material, and spatial components that accompany their use. In my data, this is illustrated by instructors consciously teaching via multiple languages (the linguistic; Chapter 4), students learning to "correctly" shape their handwriting in French (the visual/embodied; Chapter 2), and graffiti that appear in an immigrant neighborhood (the material/spatial; Chapter 5). As Li Wei (2018: 23) explains, "From a Translanguaging lens, multilingualism by the very nature of the phenomenon is a rich source of creativity and criticality, as it entails tension, conflict, competition, difference, and change in a number of spheres, ranging from ideologies, policies, and practices to historical and current contents." Walking the metaphoric tightrope, then, is

language, I use "Tamazight" but retain "Berber" when quoting participants or other scholarship that uses this term.

not merely treading a neat path between two points (e.g., French and Corsican), but dancing beyond them.⁶

§1.2 Beyond the Central Periphery

Recent theorizing of the sociolinguistics of globalization has focused on the themes of mobility, complexity, and unpredictability *vis-à-vis* language dynamics in the contemporary neoliberal world, what Blommaert (2010: 1) calls "the capitalist present." Blommaert (2010, 2013) explains that sociolinguistic phenomena can be understood as occurring polycentrically on multiple scale levels. That is, speakers orient to different centers and peripheries depending on context. For example, speakers may make use of particular forms (accent, spelling, vocabulary), either adhering to or deviating from standards or other language varieties according to the situation. As a reaction to the "reifying legacy of structuralism" (Blommaert, 2014: 3–4), there has been a push to focus on "complexity" in sociolinguistic inquiry, a perspective that does not entail complete chaos, but rather a "complex, non-categorical, non-equilibrium, and nonlinear form of order" (Blommaert, 2012: 9). Sociolinguistic analysis, it is argued, should thus "aim at interpreting instability, rather than looking for stability where there is none" (Aronin & Jessner, 2016: 7).

In attempting to operationalize some of these approaches to language, the global economy, and complexity, sociolinguists interested in linguistic diversity and globalization have drawn heavily on the concept of superdiversity, "diversity within diversity, a tremendous increase in the texture of diversity in [globalized] societies such as ours (Vertovec, 2007, 2010)" (Blommaert, 2013: 4). Jaffe (2016: 15), however, clarifies that nothing is inherently superdiverse or not superdiverse. Rather, she argues, "superdiversity [is] a function of what scales of differences get mobilized or made relevant in varying ways" (5). Pavlenko (2018) pushes further, arguing that the superdiversity trend is not only insufficient, but has failed: the idea is over-romanticized as "relentlessly optimistic and bright" (147–8) while in reality it does exactly what it purports not to do by "reifying

---

6 As Li Wei (2018) asserts, "Translanguaging is not simply going *between* different linguistic structures, cognitive and semiotic systems and modalities, but going *beyond* them" (23; original emphasis).

languages as emic units" (158–9). Perhaps most concerning, she asserts that only western scholars benefit from such discourses of diversity (162). "Peripheral multilingualism" (Pietikäinen & Kelley-Holmes, 2013; Pietikäinen et al., 2017) offers an alternative lens with which to approach the study of linguistic minorities and globalization.

As in other "small" language communities, Corsica is often understood in a binary center-periphery relationship *vis-à-vis* continental France. In the wider sociopolitical imagination, Corsica (the periphery) is viewed as pitted against anything and everything French (the center), the island culture defined oppositionally as not French, not continental. Pietikäinen et al. (2017) have explored the situated nature of such dynamics in Corsica, Ireland, Sámiland, and Wales. As attested by these "small languages in new circumstances" of late modernity, they explain, central and peripheral are mutually constitutive and relative categories that require constant negotiation. The sites they analyze attest to a predominance of the rural in discourses of linguistic and cultural authenticity; the urban-rural divide on Corsica is particularly illustrative in this regard.

Urban areas on Corsica—larger coastal cities like Ajaccio and Bastia—are considered watered-down cultural spaces, since it is here that "authentic" Corsican culture is in contact with the outside (continentals, immigrants, tourists). The village is the locus of authentic Corsican culture (Jaffe, 1999). French dominates in the urban coastal centers as the language of everyday communication, commerce, and education. The village, and what it represents culturally and linguistically, exists in an oppositional relationship with the city: *in paese* versus *in cità* (village versus city), interior versus exterior, authentic versus illegitimate. The mountain-coastal division on Corsica further enforces the urban-rural divide geographically and helps construct an internal insularity: "'culture' [is] located upwards and inwards from the coast" (Pietikäinen et al., 2017: 140). This orientation to the Corsican interior as the locus of cultural authority is what Jaffe (2019) has called "the central periphery" of the island. A "central periphery" (the Corsican village), I posit, also implies a central center (e.g., Republican Paris), a peripheral center (e.g., Parisian *banlieues*), and a peripheral periphery (e.g., urban or immigrant Corsica).[7] Contemporary Corsica

---

7 As Luciani (1995) calls immigrants in Corsica, "la minorité de la minorité" (the minority of the minority).

is characterized by such competing centripetal and centrifugal forces (Ottavi, 2013: 140). Importantly, Smith (2019) asserts the need to address more than just colonizer-colonized (e.g., France-Corsica) relationships when making use of center-periphery heuristics:

> [I]mmigrants' understandings of language use and abilities in a postcolonial context should be taken into account by theorists who explore present day notions of center versus periphery. For these theorists, it might be worthwhile to have a less restrictive definition of what it means to be a member of the center or the periphery as well as to investigate how the center versus periphery model maps onto different situations. To further develop the center versus periphery argument, a relationship between the former colonizer and the colonized is not the only dichotomy worth discussing. (42–3)

Beyond the urban-rural dichotomy, immigrant and transnational perspectives are crucial to furthering an understanding of shaky and shifting center-peripheral dynamics on Corsica.

Corsica is, as I'm attempting to show, fraught with multiple ideological orientations to language. The study of language ideologies is concerned with "socially, politically, and morally loaded cultural assumptions about the way that language works in social life and about the role of particular linguistic forms in a given society" (Woolard, 2016: 7). Das (2016) explains that "Whether they are explicitly asserted or implicitly immanent through cultural practices and worldviews, language ideologies are always formed through semiotic processes and naturalized by historical narratives, institutional practices, and state policies" (16). On Corsica, orientations to language range widely from an (implicit) upholding of French as the State language to the foregrounding of Corsican in "nationalist"/separatist movements to rooting for Corsican-French bilingualism as a path toward a more inclusive future. As Ottavi (2013: 154) succinctly puts it, "la situation est mouvante et contradictoire" (the situation is dynamic and contradictory).

Corsican sociolinguistics today explicitly positions itself as a linguistics of *minoration* (minoritization), not unlike the focus on linguistic conflict in work on Catalan, and is characterized by its pragmatic and emancipatory orientation to language and power (Colonna, 2020a: 7; 2020b). As such, confronting linguistic hegemony is a core tenet of Corsican sociolinguistics (Blanchet, 2020: 10). Drawing from Gramsci's (2007 [1948]) formulation, Blanchet (2020: 19) explains that in the case of minorities facing linguistic domination, hegemony is the process by which speakers of minoritized languages are led to consent to the dominance and seeming goodness of a language other than their own. Hegemonic languages are thus those that "seem to be socially neutral, universally available, natural" and that "often rest their authority on a conception of anonymity" (Woolard, 2016: 25). I use the term "franco-hegemonic" to refer to the anonymously authoritative and implicitly (and explicitly) dominant position enjoyed by French in France and its territories (Mendes, 2022), its "national monolingual mononormative linguistic ideology" (Blanchet, 2020: 19).

In this same vein, we can think of various sociolinguistic contexts on Corsica as their own micro-hegemonies, "restricted, 'niched' hegemonies that coexist with others in polycentric environments" (Blommaert, 2010: 62).[8] The idea of the micro-hegemony can be understood as a unique sociocultural ecology unto itself. Within other broader hierarchies that exert forms of social, political, and economic control, a micro-hegemony nuances the scope and content of what counts as dominant. For example, the micro-hegemony of the French as a foreign language (FLE) classroom (Chapter 2) upholds French over all other languages, while the micro-hegemony of Corsican alphabet books (Chapter 3) promotes Corsican. The conceptualization of Corsican society as bilingual (*bi-plurilingue*) could be understood as another kind of micro-hegemony. Particular linguistic repertoires are valorized in particular contexts while other forms of heterogeneity are ignored, minimized, or erased (Mendes, 2021; Jaffe, 2020). In these competing conceptions of linguistic multiplicity, what I'm calling "countervocalities"—"a heterogeneity of multilingualisms and their epistemic commitments" (Gramling, 2021: 143)—languages are constantly rearranging in variously imagined hierarchies.

Corsican today is arguably the most successful revitalization case among France's regional languages. Given that the island experiences immigration rates per capita that approach those of the Paris region (INSEE, 2015), we might ask, what is the interaction between immigrants and the regional language? While much work has

---

8   See also Fourquet (2017: 13) on "la construction de l'hégémonie culturelle" (the construction of cultural hegemony) on Corsica.

addressed the contemporary Corsican sociolinguistic situation (Jaffe, 1999; Blackwood, 2004, 2008; Ottavi, 2012; Cotnam-Kappel, 2014; Colonna, 2020a *inter alia*), substantially less work has addressed that of immigrant language communities on the island (Madhi, 2014) or the interaction between the two (Géa, 2016). That is, there has been relatively little research on the interface between the speech community of the regional language (Corsican) and those of immigrant groups (Portuguese, Arabic, Tamazight, and so on). What the study of Corsican and immigrant languages has in common is the central preoccupation with power and linguistic domination. Additionally, the study of Corsican and immigrant languages on the island help us to think about the relationship between language and place. Indeed, other European minority languages are sometimes referred to as "indigenous," as in the case of Welsh (Coupland, 2012), underscoring a sense of rootedness in a particular territory. This contrasts with what Phipps (2013: 99) refers to as unmoored multilingualism, a loss of anchoring to geographic and personal touchstones in multilingual dynamics.

The Corsican speech community is not one understood as mobile,[9] unlike those of other groups on the island, for example arabophone immigrants from North Africa. In this mobile-immobile dichotomy, Corsican is constructed as local and "anchored" (Mendes, 2021) while Arabic (or any number of immigrant languages) is understood as foreign. Corsican is endemic, whereas Arabic is uprooted; the former must supposedly remain in place to sustain itself, while the latter is apparently dissociable from its geographic place of origin, with speech communities throughout the world. These orientations to language share a sense of heritage that draws from traditional notions of authenticity which point to origins (Woolard, 2016). I approach Corsican's relationships to other languages while foregrounding questions of mobility; indeed, "Mobility and multilingualism exist symbiotically" (Smith, 2019: 141). Immigration rates and the island's booming tourism industry reflect how Corsica "receive[s]" mobility (Pietikäinen et al., 2017: 30). Movement in the form of the population's historic exodus and this kind of received mobility are indeed key factors that contribute

---

9 Though the Corsican diaspora is well known, there are not, to the best of my knowledge, established communities of Corsican speakers outside of Corsica itself, aside from perhaps small pockets of enthusiasts or language activists in continental France.

to various formations of linguistic and cultural diversity on the island. The question of place is thus of primary importance: how do physical spaces become meaningful places (Johnstone, 2011: 211)? How is place discursively constructed on Corsica in light of linguistic heterogeneity and globalizing forces? In what language(s)? My exploration of multilingualism foregrounds a concern for the relationship between language and place on Corsica with a focus beyond the "central periphery." In short, the further destabilization of notions of center and periphery (Pietikäinen et al., 2017: 194) alongside the reclamation (Leonard, 2011) of various minority languages is what is at stake in studying multilingualism on Corsica.

§1.3 Italo-Multilingualism?

The Corsican sociolinguistic situation resembles those of other minoritized language communities in Europe such as Gaelic (Scotland), Basque, Catalan, and Galician (Spain), and Bosnian, Croatian, and Serbian (former Yugoslavia). These situations reflect linguistic multiplicity and reclamation movements of non-dominant languages, and have historically also experienced internal colonialism, à la Lafont, due to the economic weakness or exploitation of a given region (Toso, 1996: 31–2) and/or cultural or socioeconomic oppression (Toso, 2008: 29). An interesting parallel to draw with the case of *langues régionales* in France is that of so-called dialects and regional languages in Italy, a terminological division that at its best can provide legal protections and at its worst can potentially cast a dark shadow and deprive a community of valuable resources. The preservation of minoritized language varieties in Italy, as in France, was only considered feasible once national linguistic unification in Italian was established (Parry, 2002: 54–5); "State law 482 of 1999 on the protection of minority languages, recognized as such 12 languages: French, Provençal, Franco-Provençal, German, Ladin, Friulian, Slovene, Sardinian, Catalan, Albanian, Greek, and Croatian" (Coluzzi, 2008: 215). These are thus protected at the national level in Italy. An important "challenge to multilingualism" in the Italian context, Parry (2002) explains that "what was, and remains, controversial is that the [law] includes some linguistic varieties traditionally considered to be Italian dialects (namely Sardinian and Friulian), but excludes the large majority of these, regardless of prestige or the number of speakers," such as Piedmontese (49).

Indeed, language varieties referred to as dialects are not afforded the same resources or protections as "regional languages." Coluzzi (2004) analyzed corpus, status, and acquisition planning efforts of one legally recognized regional language, Friulian, and one so-called dialect, Western Lombard/Milanese, to illustrate discrepancies between the two categories in maintenance and revitalization efforts. Newer laws have appeared at the local level, such as Law no. 8/2007 in Veneto, which aims for the "Protection, development and promotion of the Venetan linguistic and cultural heritage" (Coluzzi, 2008: 222). As Coluzzi explains, "The absolute novelty of this law is that Venetan is called a regional language, not a dialect, which may allow its inclusion amongst the languages protected by the European Charter for Minority or Regional Languages at some point in the future" (ibid.). Multiple political structures (local, national, supranational) are implicated in these kinds of language policy efforts, which can render things more complicated. But lack of planning efforts, can lead to further shift to the national language (Coluzzi, 2004: 31). One important void is the "absence or very scarce presence of some form of teacher training and teaching materials" for regional languages and dialects in Italy (Coluzzi, 2008: 226); this could be said to be similar to the situation in France, where the institutional resources and time dedicated to regional languages are not at all on par with the national language. Parry (2002) observes that "It now seems to be 'politically correct' to support threatened languages, but the threat to the survival of the dialects as effective, living systems of communication is no less real" (55). He asserts that "national and regional legislation cannot guarantee [a language's] survival" and reminds us that "general support" is very different from "concrete commitment" to minoritized language varieties (56–7).

An illustrative parallel to the Corsican case from the Italianate world is its southern cousin, Sardinia. An autonomous region, the island is home to several local languages including Catalan, Corsican, Ligurian, and the main two varieties of Sardinian, Logudorese in the north and Campidanese in the south, among others (Mura, 2019a: 2–3). Indeed, as Toso (2008) explains "il sardo non si configura come *una* lingua minoritaria, bensì come un gruppo di parlate estranee al sistema dei dialetti italiani ma privo, tradizionalmente e nella realtà attuale, di una lingua-tetto di riferimento diversa dall'italiano letterario" (Sardinian does not amount to *one* minority language, but rather a group of language varieties unrelated to the Italian dialect system but lacking, traditionally and in the current reality, a top language of reference different from literary Italian) (104; original emphasis). Some scholars foreground the islanders' multilingual capabilities, such as Tufi (2013), who argues that "practically all Sardinians can be considered to be bilingual if not plurilingual" (146). Others highlight the challenges the language faces such as limited use in schools and other domains, leading to low vitality and risks to intergenerational transmission (Mura, 2019a: 3; Schjerve, 2017: 40).

Like Corsica, Sardinia has traded hands between several political powers throughout its history, from Pisa to Genoa and Aragon and enjoyed brief bouts of independence. Like other minority language communities, such as Corsican in France and Friulian in Italy, a Sardinian political movement grew in the 1960s with "una sensibilità autonomistica" (an autonomist sensibility) and special attention given to the linguistic and cultural specificity of the island (Toso, 2008: 103–4), which "served to articulate a local discourse of political emancipation" (Tufi, 2013: 149).

Sardinia has seen language policy measures similar to Corsica as the community grapples with maintenance and revitalization efforts into the twenty-first century, fueled by feelings of responsibility, urgency, and uncertainty (Tufi, 2013: 156). Mura (2019a) surveys language policy initiatives on the island while underscoring how these can coexist at odds with local beliefs and practices. For example, one of the most divisive and controversial questions is that of standardization of the minority language (Tufi, 2013), closely related to the selection of varieties to be taught in schools and how. While locals seem "inclined towards a plurilingual education on the island" (Mura, 2019a: 2), consensus on how to make this happen has yet to be seen. Aside from more practical problems such as needing teacher training programs for instruction in Sardinian, Mura argues "The dichotomy between standard and local varieties should not be underestimated. [...] the decision on which variety should be used could make school agents refrain from teaching Sardinian in the first place" (14–15).

Other policy initiatives, such as the promotion of Sardinian to be on par with Italian in the media, have yielded mixed results. In his close reading of Sardinian-language websites, Mura (2019b) found a breadth of practices ranging from only superficially using the minority language to more balanced representation. In making language-related decisions, some sites seem to consider other sociolinguistic realities of the island rather than prioritizing Italian-Sardinian parity, for example using English subtitles in news broadcasts to target migrant audiences, that is speakers of neither Italian nor Sardinian (32). Indeed, these kinds of European minoritized language communities experience language dynamics brought on by immigration, tourism, and the postnational economy. Relatedly, there was a recent allocation of nearly 650,000 euros to the Region of Sardinia for the teaching of Italian to migrants (Agenzia Nazionale Stampa Associata, 2019). The funds were given to adult education programs that aim to "to facilitate migrant integration into the social and economic fabric of the regions that host them" (ibid.). As regional counselor Filippo Spanu asserts, "There is no true inclusion without a full mastery of Italian, which favors dialogue and interaction and facilitates integration" (ibid.). It is notable that this discourse of integration, referring to outsiders in the regional context of Sardinia, focuses on empowering newcomers in the national rather than the local language (that is in Italian, not Sardinian). This harkens to the contrasts between Chapter 2, in which newly arrived students on Corsica undertake their studies of French, and Chapter 3, wherein the push for migrants to appropriate local language practices concerns Corsican. Discourses of integration and belonging in peripheral contexts are sites rich in tensions between national and local codes.

Not unlike the Corsican case, one of the main obstacles that the Sardinian community faces in attempts to maintain their language resides in the tension between strong emotional/affective value and weak instrumental value. This seemingly low "practical utility" (Mura, 2019a: 9) leads to the language being perceived as "a symbol of the past and an obstacle to social mobility" (Tufi, 2013: 149). Will the global market bring a sunset upon these Mediterranean island languages?

§1.4 Balancing Acts

Today, Corsica's sociopolitical climate is characterized by competing nationalist movements as the island grapples with the various struggles of our global present moment: the postnational economy, new and varied technologies, and the increased mobility of people, goods, and information. Three important events shaped the political moment in which I undertook my main fieldwork in 2016. They resulted in local and global reverberations and reveal ideological tensions at play in contemporary Corsican politics which serve to further illustrate the atmosphere on the ground. First, in December 2015, so-called "nationalist" parties won the majority of seats for the first time and secured the presidency of Gilles Simeoni in the Corsican Assembly. Former mayor of Bastia and son of the activist Edmond, Simeoni's party, Inseme per a Corsica (Together for Corsica), is the product of a careful allegiance between smaller autonomist and separatist parties that gave way to the historic victory. It has been argued that the vote was secured by clientelism in small *communes* throughout the island, illustrating a clan social structure based in rural villages that endures (Fourquet, 2017: 50). Support for autonomist and "nationalist" ideas is attested even among Corsica's youngest and most educated electorate (35). Simeoni was re-elected in 2021 and remains in office at the time of writing.

Next, in 2016, ultra-conservative Marine Le Pen of the Front National (FN) was on the campaign trail throughout France. Her platform was characterized, among other things, by vitriolic anti-immigrant rhetoric. Though she was supposedly refused service at a restaurant in Saint-Florent in northern Corsica while on vacation,[10] Le Pen went on to win the majority of votes from Corsica's two *départements* (administrative regions) in the first round of the 2017 French presidential election.[11] While Corsican leaders have insisted that far-right ideologies are brought to the island by continentals (for example, those stationed at military bases) (85), other have argued that historically there has been "[de] la bienveillance et [de] la compréhension de l'extrême droite continentale face aux actions violentes et xénophobes se déroulant sur l'Île de Beauté" (goodwill and understanding of the continental [French] extreme right faced with violent and xenophobic actions unfolding on the Isle of Beauty) (141). Corsican "nationalists" are careful to refute support for the FN. In this way, we see, aside from the competing autonomist/"nationalist" groups that merged to win Simeoni's election, competing nationalisms between Corsica and continental France.

10   See fr.soc.politique (2016); Dalpvia (2016).
11   She also won the majority in Corsica during the 2022 election.

Lastly, summer 2016 was rocked by the burkini scandal, which originally broke out in Sisco, just north of Bastia. Riots erupted, incited by locals' shocked reactions to a woman wearing a head-to-toe bathing suit (known as a burkini, from *burqa* + bikini) at the beach. The mayor of Sisco, followed by several mayors throughout France, banned the garment since it supposedly ostentatiously flaunted religious identity, sparking international outrage. This ban was later struck down by France's highest court, the Conseil d'État. It can seem ironic that Republican values like *laïcité* (secularism) be so passionately defended given that Corsica is supposedly fueled by defining itself in opposition to France. Was the mayor of Sisco another Balducci (Camus's Corsican *gendarme* in Algeria) carrying out a French agenda despite himself? These three events (the election of Simeoni, widespread support for Le Pen, and the burkini scandal) can be understood as representative of the central pillars of what Fourquet (2017) calls "la nouvelle question corse" (the new Corsican question): the maneuvering of clan social structures, "nationalist" ideologies, and immigration—a veritable balancing act.

Corsican politics reveals concerns that are at once central to the island's role as subsumed by the French State while also foregrounding its place as outside the Metropole and orienting to a wider Mediterranean geopolitical space. For example, while French-Corsican (linguistic) co-officiality continues to fail to be passed into French national law, other measures such as that recognizing Corsica as an *île-montagne* (island-mountain), a statute taking into account geographic constraints *vis-à-vis* proposed development projects, was passed and celebrated (Mari, 2016). While certain specificities of "the Corsican situation" are validated (special geographic considerations), other particularities (the further institutionalization of the regional language) are kept at bay. Corsica's liminal geopolitical status between nation and region, between overseas colony and Metropolitan cultural minority, has resulted in a generalized "malaise" (Pomponi, 1979: 353; see Serrano, 2011: 2). The island is neither French, nor its own nation-state. This evading of established categories to (attempt to) play by its own rules, as attested by the development of the polynomic approach to minority language revitalization for example, is indeed a trademark of Corsican sociocultural dynamics (Mendes, 2021).

The sidestepping of nation-state-level categorizations has been theorized by Smith (1992) as "scale jumping": "turning local into regional, national, and global movements, escaping the traps of localism, parochialism, and particularism through an expansion of geographic and political reach" (Jones et al., 2017: 143). Rozenholc (2014) characterizes what she observes in Tel Aviv as an example of such a scale jump; she finds that the urban spaces she studies foreground *méditeranéité* (Mediterranean-ness) rather than a national belonging to Israel, thereby escaping the confines of the nation to underscore a place in the wider region. This "option méditerannéenne" (Mediterranean option), she argues, is testament to a will to reposition and reorganize urban hierarchies "par la production de lieux en tension entre proche et lointain" (by way of the production of places in tension between near and far) (12). Similarly, participants in Evers's (2018) work on curricular language policy in Marseille asserts that while France is anchored in Europe geographically, the context "qui a une vraie cohérence" (that has true coherence) is that of the Mediterranean (448). Scale jumping extends even to the natural world: in his work on Spanish botanical gardens, Hartigan (2015) found that multispecies publics (humans and the more-than-human world) establish relations of care as they orient to regional biomes, that is to Catalonia's and Valencia's place in the Mediterranean rather than the Spanish State.

Akin to Rozenholc's near-and-far *méditeranéité*, Lombardi (2014) sees a simultaneity in global-local dynamics in what he calls the postlocal, "the experience of immediate, immanent placement that is nevertheless globally connected" (41). The postlocal, he explains, keeps "an enmeshed understanding of local/regional/global always in mind, but also [...] suggest[s] that places retain a resilient 'thickness' in everyday life" (43). In this way, I posit, Corsica can be interpreted rhizomatically as at once French-Corsican-Mediterranean-European-global, all while retaining a grounded Corsican-ness—a kind of postlocal *francophonie*. The productive tensions between scales (Rozenholc, 2014), the polycentricity (Blommaert, 2010) at play, and the shakiness of centers and peripheries (Pietikäinen et al., 2017) attested by these preferred alignments with the Mediterranean rather than the nation-state can help us think about how discourses of local and global are strategically mobilized by multilingual subjects. While the postlocal foregrounds spatial simultaneity, Blommaert (2004) has explored simultaneity from a historical perspective: "we have to conceive of discourse as subject to *layered simultaneity*. It occurs in a real-time, synchronic event, but it is simultaneously encapsulated in several layers of historicity, some of which are within the grasp of the participants while others remain invisible but are nevertheless present" (131; original emphasis). In this way, we see that discourse "is conditioned by, and refers to, several layers of historical material" (157). Spatial and temporal simultaneity in the discourses I analyze is revelatory of participants' local and transnational experiences with language and culture: handwriting that betrays foreign influence (Chapter 2), the use of Italian or Valencian while conversing in Corsican (Chapter 4), graffiti that transform local maxims to play with new meanings (Chapter 5). In the following chapters, I will draw from these concepts in my exploration of how global-local tensions are discursively constructed in multilingual dynamics on the island.

§1.5 Approaches and Outline

My study of multilingual dynamics on Corsica foregrounds the reclamatory (Leonard, 2020) clout of minoritized languages, namely Corsican and other languages' ability to destabilize francohegemonic language ideological orientations. Minoritized codes, though "small" (Pietikäinen et al., 2017) or "grassroots" (Blommaert, 2008), draw transgressive power from indeterminacy (Jaffe, 1999) and ambiguity (Candea, 2010) in their shapeshifting capacities as they confront "globalizing surges" (Ramanathan, 2013a, 2013b). That is, speakers adapt their communicative practices and transform societal discourses based on their experiences of globalization phenomena, often incorporating subjective experiences of/in non-dominant languages. This kind of "multilingualism from below" (Phipps, 2013) is one locus at which new multilingual subjectivities (Kramsch, 2009) can emerge.

My approach is qualitatively oriented to other work in linguistic ethnography (Smith, 2019; Das, 2016; Woolard, 2016; Blommaert, 2013; Heller, 2011; Hélot & Young, 2006; Jaffe, 1999; Rampton, 1995). I seek to explore power dynamics in language use with attention to political and material conditions, akin to Heller's (2011) critical ethnographic sociolinguistics of postnationalism. Critical sociolinguistics (Heller et al., 2018) is concerned with inequality and power as they are structured by and themselves structure situated social practices. A focus on political economy therein attends to processes that construct and maintain language ideologies and our material conditions, thereby shaping the ways in which we participate in the contemporary global economy. Studying language from this perspective means studying the "unresolvable entanglement between the material and the symbolic" (5).

My data collection, based in linguistic ethnographic approaches (Copland & Creese, 2015; Blommaert & Jie, 2010), consisted of participant observation, semi-structured interviews (a total of 12), and collecting other primary documents firsthand. These are complemented by fieldnotes, allowing for fruitful data triangulation. My interpretations are based on iterative readings of the data to establish themes, categories, and codes (Heller et al., 2018: Chapter 4; Saldaña, 2016: 119–24, 218–26), while the analyses are grounded in critical discourse analysis (Blommaert, 2004; Chouliarki & Fairclough, 1999; Fairclough, 1995) with a focus on language attitudes and ideologies. While in general my approaches for data collection and analysis are ethnographic and discourse-analytic, respectively, each chapter admittedly involves a specific nuance given that I draw from a rich array of data types in my exploration of multilingual practices on the island.

The social network for this study extends from schools to other district-level offices and local nonprofits, through which I have been able to recruit various participants. Throughout this work I have met with local educators and authors for interviews; attended cultural events and conferences sponsored by the local city government, nonprofits, and academic institutions; and volunteered at schools' English club events. In addition, my host family remains at the core of my experiences on Corsica and has helped shape my steps and my thinking. These experiences form the foundation for my approach in this work and greatly inform my interpretations and analyses.

Linguistic ethnographic approaches are apt for the study of complex sociolinguistic phenomena since they provide highly contextualized accounts across a range of data types and situate lived experience, including that of the researcher, at the heart of the sociolinguistic research endeavor. I foreground researcher voice and subjectivity—reflexive knowing—in my interpretive and analytical process in the study of discourse. While it has been argued that "in a sense, all ethnography, is self-ethnography" (Goldschmidt, 1977: 294; Reed-Danahay, 2009: 29), I will briefly explore autoethnography to clarify how my work might be understood. As Muncey (2010) neatly encapsulates, "Definitions of autoethnography question among many other things the idea of multiple layers of consciousness, the vulnerable self, the coherent self, critiquing the self in social contexts, subversion of dominant discourses and evocative potential" (50). Autoethnography, in short, is "a method that affords an *insider's* perspective on the practices, meanings, and interpretations of cultural phenomena/experiences (Goodall, 2000)" (Adams et al., 2015: 31; original emphasis). This kind of "native" approach can help challenge insider/outsider dichotomies to instead look to "shifting identifications amid a field of interpenetrating communities and power relations (Narayan, 1993)" (Buzard, 2003: 77–8). I am not, however, "native" to the context I study; as such, "autoethnography" is not an appropriate definition for the inclusion of subjective experience in my work.

Drawing from Bourdieu (1990), Burawoy (2003) proposes a reflexive ethnography: "an approach to participant observation that recognizes that we are part of the world we study. Reflexive ethnography presumes an 'external' *real world*, but it is one that we can only know through our *constructed relation* to it" (655; original emphasis). Madison (2012) builds from this clarifying that critical ethnography, unlike autoethnography, "is not my *exclusive* experience" (10; original emphasis). As she defines it, "*critical* ethnography is always a meeting of multiple sides in an encounter with and among others, one in which there is negotiation and dialogue toward substantial and viable meanings that make a difference in others' worlds" (ibid.; original emphasis). My positionality (Madison, 2012: 8) and experiences infused throughout what follows are thus perhaps better framed as reflexive research rather than autoethnographic.

Language dynamics of the urban Corsican public space are reflective of the minority language context as an ongoing and unstable project (Woolard, 2016); notions of multiplicity therein are not fixed and cannot be taken for granted. Though it may seem obvious that multilingualism be interpreted as inherently multiple and fragmented, through this work I have learned that "multilingualism" is not an agreed-upon concept or category. Indeed, the topics of my research were not always readily understood. I could never seem to spit out my interests (namely "multilingualism" and "globalization") in exactly the right way—the right way in order to be understood by my various interlocutors, or the right way for me to understand what I was (am) trying to do. Often, when I would ask about people's opinions regarding how Corsica or their schools were affected by globalization, I would stumble between *globalisation* and *mondialisation*.[12] On one occasion an interviewee abruptly stopped me to say that there was something wrong with the question, that it wasn't clear due to my French. As time has gone on, however, I have noticed that it is not a mere matter of a language barrier or vocabulary. Interlocutors make assumptions about and position one another in tricky ways, and people are sometimes hesitant to respond to this kind of question: they are talking to a foreigner, there are stereotypes about xenophobic locals, globalization involves money, the list goes on. Notions of mobility (more related to *mondialisation*) and economic factors (more related to *globalisation*) are salient to varying degrees in the data, especially apparent, for example, in interviewees' responses (Chapter 4). Similarly, physical displacement—of workers, teachers, resources—remains a constant theme, highlighting space and place as central concerns throughout.

When attempting to express my interests in language, "multilingualism" often proved to be intimidating or not quite the right word, as illustrated by this fieldnote recalling a dinner I attended: "two of her friends [...] were taken [aback] to hear the word I dared to use, multilingualism: *On n'est pas très bien en langues chez nous, tu sais* (eyebrows raised)! [We're not very good at languages here, you know!]" (fieldnote, March 28, 2016). Other participants understood "multilingualism" as an interest in the faraway or exotic and would begin talking about school projects on China or Africa. My fieldnotes include reflections regarding the divergence between what I thought I was asking and what people would respond, for example: "Her response to questions about globalization had much less to do with multiculturalism or multilingualism than I had expected, and much more to do with the (illusion of) material consumption, global brands, and objects" (fieldnote, June 15, 2016). Additionally, the word "multilingualism" often lures us into the trap of wanting to count languages, as if they

---

12 As Rozenholc (2014: 2) explains the distinction in the academic literature, *mondialisation* refers to "l'accroissement des mobilités et la tendance à l'unification de l'espace-temps" (increasing mobilities and shrinking of space-time), while *globalisation* is used "pour désigner l'universalisation des enjeux économiques, sociaux, politiques et culturels" (to designate the universalization of economic, social, political, and cultural concerns).

were neatly divisible. "Globalization" and "multilingualism" are not fixed concepts, but unstable and shifting.

Gramling's in-depth accounts of monolingualism (2016) and multilingualism (2021) offer insights into these far-reaching concepts which can somehow seem at once mundane and daunting. Conceding that he is "ultimately quite agnostic" about what multilingualism means (2021: 14–15), Gramling asserts that it is nonetheless "a meaningful and capacious idea, one with a promising, tumultuous, and flawed present – and a future worth caring for vigilantly in research and public life. Despite its terminological vulnerabilities and its technological instrumentalizations, 'multilingualism' is usefully able to encompass complex, divergent, and sometimes opposing experiences and ideas" (10). While myriad definitions and approaches to "multilingualism" abound, he explains that this is indeed part of the point in attempting to understand it: "One of the challenges of multilingualism itself is to accept and affirm this state of affairs as a methodological premise, and to suspect something is likely amiss when a comprehensive description is put forth too quickly" (53). Today, Gramling observes, ordoliberal economic tendencies (regulation-protection of the free market) increasingly contribute to the growth of multilingual technologies and language commoditization processes. What's more, neoliberal global markets have driven participation in discourses about multilingualism which have become, he argues, "an available strategic formula for re-empowerment among the already relatively powerful" (70). Multilingualism, while somewhat vague as an umbrella term, plays a role in structuring our economic (technological, political, and personal) realities in the twenty-first century.

As Duchêne (2020) carefully explains, although multilingualism has been lauded in sociolinguistics and beyond as a celebration of diversity, it is often co-opted by capitalist discourses, and its rise to trendy keyword should be understood critically:

> [M]ultilingualism is not neutral, but rather intrinsically embedded in social processes that inform who and what counts as a legitimate speaker, language, and practice. As such, multilingualism represents a site of struggle for access to and distribution of knowledge, resources, and status. Indeed, what constitutes desirable multilingual competence, a desirable multilingual speaker, and desirable or less desirable languages (*or combinations*

thereof) is part of the political economy of linguistic exchange; these highly variable factors are dependent on history, context, and the market within the capitalistic, patriarchal, and colonial logic in which we operate. (93; emphasis added)

Duchêne argues that we need to further probe how our understandings of "multilingualism" can structure social inequality, given that it is prone to "produce and reproduce exploitation and dominance" (95). Thus, "multilingualism" can serve only as a point of departure, not as an answer *per se* to questions related to linguistic diversity and globalization. There exist multiple accounts of linguistic heterogeneity on Corsica; like all language use, these accounts are not disinterested.

The overarching questions I aim to address include: How is linguistic multiplicity navigated on Corsica? What is Corsican multilingualism? How is multilingualism discursively imagined, represented, and mobilized? How does this linguistic diversity facilitate or hinder civic participation (Piller, 2016: ch. 6)? How do these dynamics vary across contexts? and What can this tell us about language and place in our global present moment? I analyze a range of data types and contexts to allow for an exploration of multilingual dynamics in all their productive tension—processes by which multilingualism is imagined, constructed, maintained—including issues of linguistic hegemony (dominance in policy and action), representation (print, graffiti, digitally), mobility (transnational or received), and affiliation (religious, political, national) as well as the permeating question of heritage (local or foreign, national or regional). The chapters I present are discrepant records of multiplicity which are not necessarily reconcilable. Competing notions of sociolinguistic heterogeneity in the cases I analyze underscore that distinct multilingualisms do not manifest (are not imagined) on equal terms. Exploring such countervocalities on Corsica sheds light on the ways in which difference and inequality are discursively created and maintained.

The following chapters explore different dimensions of institutional multilingualism, for the most part related to policies, practices, attitudes, and ideologies within and extending from educational settings as well as language in the public space. The chapters address reclamation, imposition, or erasure of different languages and variously arranged language hierarchies on Corsica. Throughout the book, I move from inside the school (Chapter 2) to artifacts from the schoolscape

(Chapter 3), to discourses about teaching (Chapter 4), to public spaces adjacent to the school (Chapter 5). I present an array of texts, alternating between interactional and artifactual data: transcripts from participant observation and interviews in chapters 2 and 4, and books and photographs in chapters 3 and 5. This productive alternation offers a cross-section of attitudes toward and representations of multilingual dynamics. The inclusion of different data types, which could at first glance seem quite disparate, has allowed for a fruitful expansion and extension of my previous work (Mendes, 2018a; 2018b, 2020, 2022) in order to bring various threads together in an attempt to paint a fuller picture of multilingual dynamics on the island.

Chapter 2 is a case study of newly arrived adolescent immigrant students in a French as a second language class (FLE) in a Corsican middle school (Mendes, 2018b). I analyze three speech events and develop a metaphorical heuristic, pearls, for their interpretation as multilayered and illustrative of the everyday influences of globalizing surges (unruly globalization phenomena outside our control) in the language classroom. Chapter 3 offers an analysis of two Corsican alphabet books, one of which was authored by the immigrant students from the previous chapter. While French dominates in the FLE classroom, the books illustrate the foregrounding of Corsican in other contexts like the print culture of picturebooks. My analysis shows that even in attempting to valorize linguistic and cultural diversity on the island, the scope of such diversity gets narrowed and ends up focusing mostly on Corsican.

Chapter 4 brings teacher voices to the fore in an analysis of interviews with educators from Corsica, Italy, Morocco, Sweden, and Spain. Focal participants' reflections on local language and cultural dynamics reveal subjective experiences of competing language hierarchies. Language teachers participate in shaping and enacting what is understood as multilingualism and globalization in their embodied orientations to place and time as they struggle to reconcile personal experiences in their search to establish a multilingual subject position (Kramsch & Zhang, 2018). Chapter 5 turns to public spaces adjacent to one of the focal school settings and offers a reading of the linguistic landscape (LL) of one street in Bastia. The particular neighborhood is known for being a immigrant hub and has a poor reputation among locals. I read divergent ideological orientations to language and place in the street's signage to illustrate tensions between competing discourses of belonging. While this LL analysis is not directly related to school settings, it has been argued that the Corsican LL plays a role in "public pedagogy" and the learning of the local language and culture (Cotnam-Kappel: 2014: 67); these kinds of texts can thus also contribute to our understandings of language teaching and learning dynamics on the island.

I offer these chapters as a meditation on multiplicity. This book is an exploration of competing language ideologies and orientations to place on Corsica that shows that "multilingualism" and "globalization" are not concepts that can be taken for granted. The tension that arises from countervocalities, disparate conceptualizations of linguistic multiplicity, is one means by which we can establish and foster multilingual subjectivities.

Chapter 2

Pearls

Introduction

I got off the bus and approached the gates of the Collège du Sud. I remembered the sprawling campus from my time as an English language assistant there three years previously, and was comforted that I knew my surroundings better now than before: which bus to take, where the copy room is, passing period rhythms. I was buzzed in through the gates and briefly interrogated by the *gardienne* (building manager) to whom I explained that I'd be working with the FLE classes. Upon meeting Emmanuelle for the first time, I realized I remembered seeing her at Sud during my time as an assistant in breaks between classes in the raucous teachers' lounge. She is bubbly and dynamic, as colleagues had told me.

My first days with the FLE students were filled with moments of intense curiosity. What was an American doing in class with them? They rambled to me, excitedly asking and sharing. Someone's dad had lived in Boston. Have you ever been to New York City? Someone dreamed of going to Hawaii, "le pays des rêves" (the land of dreams). Where is Sacramento (near where I was going to school) on the world map? I slowly learned more of their stories. One student came from Egypt the year before with little to no previous schooling. Another student, from Ukraine, lived with extended family and wanted to become a doctor. All of this amidst the everyday bustle of class—speaking over one another in different languages to debate the best Easter candies, admire a classmate's newly acquired public library card, catch up on recess drama. Happily dazed, I could hardly take it all in.

This chapter takes as its point of departure *français langue étrangère* (French as a foreign language, FLE) education as an example of institutionalized multilingualism and offers a case study of a class of newly arrived immigrant students in a middle school in northern Corsica. These foreign students are tasked with the learning of the State language, French, in a very particular setting—Corsica, with its own special circumstances, language, and culture. Immigrant students' experiences in Corsican middle schools provide a glimpse into a multilingual reality that illustrates competing sociolinguistic orientations: the island's French-Corsican bilingual society, the multilingual middle school curriculum, and students' fostering of their own home languages, all as they are "learning to learn" within the French educational system. Their experiences in FLE represent an intersection of the transnational in a particular regional situation; their stories shine through in distinct ways as they confront this unique cultural and linguistic context. Peripheral subjects (immigrants) in spaces already understood as "minority" (Corsica) help us to nuance our understandings of multiscalar and center-periphery conceptualizations of multilingualism (Blommaert, 2010; Pietikäinen et al., 2017; Smith, 2019) to push beyond the "central periphery" (Jaffe, 2019).

I first present the institutional context by explaining terminology and policies related to FLE education. I then introduce the research site and focal participants of the case study. Next, I offer a metaphor, pearls, for the reading of interactional data (transcripts and fieldnotes from class time) followed by discursive analysis of key episodes from the FLE class. I conclude with a discussion of globalizing surges—unruly globalization phenomena—as they come into play in language learning, particularly among minority (or peripheral or at-risk) groups such as immigrant youth.

§2.1 Ethnography of FLE

This section describes the central goals, terminology, and policies surrounding FLE teaching/learning as well as my ethnographic approach to the study of the FLE class at the Collège du Sud. Immigrant students in French schools are, today, referred to as *élèves nouvellement arrivés* (ENA). Previous terminology includes *primo-arrivants* (newcomers, which various social actors used when speaking to me of these students), *non-scolarisés antérieurement* (previously unschooled), or even *mal scolarisés* (poorly schooled) (Mendonça Dias, 2013: 162–3). These monikers highlight students' encounters with new environments—new cultures, languages, institutions—as well as varied educational trajectories which are often deemed to be lacking. During the 2014–15 academic year, there were 22,300 ENAs enrolled in French middle schools, 91 percent of whom benefitted from special classes or linguistic support, ranging from working with an educational aid to spending up to two years in FLE (Ministère de l'éducation nationale, 2015: 1; see Bonacina, 2011: §3.4.2 for a detailed overview). The proportion of these students considered academically "on time" is much lower than "normal" students (4). Often, immigrant students and those schools in "disfavored establishments" are conflated in policy into the same categories of inferior, remedial, or low-/nonachieving students (OECD, 2014: 6). Inequality among groups based on race, class, and nationality as well as language background hinders efforts to integrate students into the academic and social mainstream.

ENAs are placed in FLE alongside their home room classes after they have completed language and mathematical proficiency exams upon their enrollment in their new school district.[1] Ideally, ENAs take FLE to reach at least an A1 (CEFR) level in French before entering normal classes; policy dictates that FLE study should not exceed two full academic years. From allowing admission to normal classes with only an A1 level,[2] one could infer that integration supersedes the development of robust language proficiency. This integration is meant to be achieved via French linguistic homogeneity—a parroting of standard French which students may or may not be able to develop in their allotted time of intense language study. This leveling emphasis on French derives from a desire to adhere to Republican values of equality, and promotes sociocultural integration by way of mastering the single national language (Bonacina: 2011, §3.2.2; Lazaridis & Seksig, 2005;

---

1   Each district's CASNAV office (Centre Académique pour la Scolarisation des enfants allophones Nouvellement Arrivés et des enfants issus des familles itinérantes et de Voyageurs, the Academic Center for the Schooling of Newly Arrived Allophone Children and Children of Itinerant and Traveling Families) is responsible for the reception (*acceuil*) and monitoring (*suivi*) of ENAs.
2   Only some *académies* (school districts) provide the opportunity for students to test out of A2 or B1 proficiencies. This depends on local policies and resources.

see also Adrey, 2009 on Corsica).³ In short, the French language is "the priority of priorities" (Hélot, 2003: 267). However, one may wonder if ENAs admitted to normal study with relatively low linguistic proficiency (i.e., A1) are equipped to participate in the academic arena more than marginally.

Immigrant students come from heterogeneous backgrounds and vary in age, sociocultural upbringing, family context, conditions of arrival, language biography, relationship with the school, and written and mathematical proficiencies among others. Uprooted from their country and culture, often due to traumatic circumstances, ENAs' academic trajectories are inseparable from their transnational and sometimes fractured home lives. Often moving several times throughout their childhood, ENAs must adjust all at once to both the language and the approach to learning in each new school environment (Mendonça Dias, 2013; Rovera 2013). Their academic success is often framed with each new language and new institutional beginning as remedial since their previous learning cannot be seamlessly built upon. It is no surprise that seemingly random repertoires of language and knowledge result (Blommaert, 2010: ch. 4).

Situations like this are not exceptional among immigrant students; their linguistic backgrounds involve several languages and require consideration from multiple angles. That is, it is impossible to attempt to study multilingual practices in this population without considering traditional sociolinguistic categories (age, sex, educational background, nationality, etc.) alongside the stories of their global wanderings (Rampton, 1995; Hélot & Young, 2006; Blommaert, 2010, 2013). Though many immigrant students on Corsica are of Moroccan, Portuguese, or Romanian heritage (three of the largest immigrant groups on the island), their language backgrounds do not simply align with the national languages of these countries. Mobility becomes a defining characteristic in the FLE classroom, where students' personal histories take center stage in explaining the *mélange* of languages present.

---

3 "[L]'école est un lieu déterminant pour *l'intégration* sociale, culturelle et à terme professionnelle. Leur réussite scolaire liée à la maîtrise de la langue française est un facteur essentiel de cette *intégration*" (School is a decisive place for social, cultural, and eventual professional integration. Their academic success, linked to mastery of the French language, is an essential factor in this integration) (Ministère de l'éducation nationale, 2012: 6; emphasis added).

For example, Diego, a lusophone student in the FLE class under study, was of Brazilian descent rather than Portuguese. Aside from Portuguese and French, he spoke Italian (Tuscan and Bergamasco) and some English. The students' linguistic repertoires reflect eclectic transnational experiences, and their mobility can sometimes be attributed to strained economic and/or family situations (lack of work, financial instability, parental absence).

As the majority of contemporary linguistics scholarship on Corsica focuses mainly on Corsican revitalization efforts, largely at the primary level and/or in immersion, bilingual, or rural settings (Cotnam, 2012; Cotnam-Kappel 2014; Jaffe, 1999, 2010; Ottavi, 2008, 2012; Quenot, 2012), the study of immigrant students in an urban Corsican middle school is a unique context for the study of linguistic and cultural phenomena on the island. This type of inquiry is affected by the urban setting to the extent that FLE classes (and immigrant populations in general) are mostly concentrated in urban areas of the island. Importantly, there are no FLE classes in primary or secondary schools in the interior (CASNAV de Bastia, 2015).[4] The urban Corsican school setting presents rather complicated questions concerning immigrant students therein. For example, how does the multilingual student body (students of different cultural heritages and linguistic backgrounds) confront the multilingual curriculum (dominated by French, western European languages, and Corsican) all the while embedded within French-Corsican "bilingual" society, while society, institutions, and curricula seem to largely ignore the students' home languages?

The Académie de Corse (Corsican School District), though it is by and large considered to be a rural region, ranks among the school districts with the highest proportion of ENAs, nearing that of Paris.[5] The high incidence of immigrant youth in the district's secondary schools, clustered in the island's largest cities, is part of the unique

---

4 In the Académie de Corse there are 32 *collèges* (middle schools), six of which are in the interior. There are 11 *lycées* (high schools), two of which are in the interior. There are seven *collèges* and three *lycées* which offer FLE, all located in coastal towns (CASNAV de Bastia, 2015). The high incidence of schools in coastal areas makes sense since the island's population (Corsican and/or immigrant) is largely concentrated there, while the absence of FLE in the rural interior reinforces the idea that it is a strictly "Corsican" space.
5 0.8 percent in Corsica and 0.9 percent in Paris; see Ministère de l'éducation nationale (2012: 2–3; 2015: 2).

context in which ENAs on Corsica find themselves. Along with students' idiosyncratic personal backgrounds comes a wide variety of school schedules for the FLE teacher to juggle. This logistical multiplicity reflects the varied trajectories of the students. Students enrolled in FLE may frequently attend classes where mastery of French is considered less fundamental, such as PE, art, music, math, and other language classes (Ministère de l'éducation nationale, 2012: 5; Bonacina, 2011: §3.4.3.2). Because of their various ages, grade levels, and course schedules, ENAs may not consistently attend FLE class for any number of reasons, including other classes, internships, and fieldtrips.[6] For example, at Sud, several students attended additional FLE classes to get out of PE or study hall. Striking proof of the constantly shifting nature of the class: not a single hour of class time observed during my fieldwork involved an identical combination of students.

Adaptable features of the FLE curriculum include how many weekly hours students attend, which other classes they attend, which courses they receive grades for, and which standardized tests they take.[7] Even in day-to-day lessons, FLE instructors flexibly adapt the curriculum and policies as they apply to each student. For example, as I observed, students were divided into smaller groups based on French ability rather than grade level to collaborate on a given activity while others worked on either more or less advanced exercises. One of the clearest examples of the logistical difficulties in FLE is the need to be able to accommodate newcomers at any given time, as ENAs arrive and enroll throughout the school year. Sudden additions to the class are not uncommon: one student arrived from Morocco shortly before

---

6 As Bonacina (2011) explains, "In practice, this means that children spend some parts of the school day in their induction [FLE] classroom and others in their mainstream classroom, walking in and out of their induction classroom all day long. Furthermore, each child does so at different times of the day according to the timetable of his or her mainstream class[es]. As a result, induction teachers rarely teach the whole class at the same time and children have sometimes to put aside an activity they are conducting in the induction classroom to attend a lesson in [a] mainstream one" (65).
7 FLE teachers prepare students for the DELF (*diplôme en langue française*) language proficiency exam, the DNB (*diplôme national du brevet*), the diploma earned at the end of *collège*, and/or the CAP (*certificat d'aptitude professionelle*), the exam a student takes in place of the DNB if not planning to attend *lycée général*. Teachers perform important gatekeeping functions in deciding which exams students will take, if any.

my fieldwork began, and another arrived from Pakistan at the middle of the fieldwork period toward the very end of the school year. New arrivals often mean juggling disparate lessons for different students during a single class period, and teachers sometimes have to begin building a new student's French repertoire from scratch (i.e., learning the Roman alphabet). The nature of FLE requires creative flexibility.

Many kinds of trajectories make themselves apparent in the FLE classroom. While some scholars have used the term "itinerary" to refer to "a record of a route actually taken" (Woolard, 2016: 261), others use "trajectory" to mean "holistic process[es] of change and adaptation" (Kramsch & Zhang, 2018: 25). A trajectory is dynamic: it can be unexpectedly turbulent and tangential, rising and falling in arches that reach up and out from the nooks of the everyday to connect to global forces which bear downward in a web of interconnectedness. Whether one's journey is carefully plotted and carried out or completely transformed by unexpected obstacles and crises, the participants in my study reflect different kinds of adaptation to their current circumstances on Corsica. I use the term "transnational trajectory" to refer to an account of dynamic and nonlinear immigrant mobility inclusive of personal, institutional, and cultural factors (Woolard, 2016; Smith, 2019; Kramsch & Zhang, 2018). This angle helps us to holistically consider participants' various subjective experiences in space and time including their border crossings, family situations and relationships, academic and professional endeavors, socioeconomic backgrounds, and language repertoires—stories which are often readily incorporated into the daily life of the FLE class. The FLE class is thus a prime site for the exploration of ENAs' transnational trajectories, since these are often self-evident and are regularly incorporated into language learning and daily school life. That is, students' home-country/-culture knowledge is an integral part of their school experience as they encounter French/Corsican language and cultural practices.

Importantly, these students' transnational trajectories, their international mobilities connected with both their personal lives and language learning, have no a priori specified endpoint given that they constitute such a heterogeneous group. ENAs' presence "in France" is less goal-driven than one might assume, other than the nebulous desire to learn French and eventually find work. Studying ENAs and FLE education on Corsica allows for an exploration of the ways that globalization affects immigrant youth.

Upon learning of my proposed focus on multilingualism, it was in fact the principal at Sud who suggested I work with the ENAs and the FLE class. Though I originally had other ideas (working with Corsican language classes), this suggestion served as a humbling reminder that one cannot outright impose a research agenda. Not only was this an explicit reflection of the workings of power dynamics in ethnographic inquiry, I was, in the end, placed in a position identified by the institution itself as deserving of attention with regard to multilingual teaching and learning.

The fieldwork period, over the last four months of the school year, coincided with the class's anticipation of important moments related to language learning: preparation for the DELF language proficiency exam to test out of FLE, mainstreaming to normal classes, and/or transitioning to high school the following year. During my participant observation, I sat at the back of the classroom and took notes on the lesson, with particular attention to multilingual dynamics, global identities, and experiences of local culture (i.e., on Corisca).[8] Approximately one third of my observations are complemented by recordings and transcriptions. Fieldnotes, recordings, and transcriptions from classroom observations make up the primary interactional data, accompanied by other primary documents.

§2.2 Setting the Scene

I now turn to the school site itself in order to present the situated context of fieldwork. By describing the institutional setting in which the social actors work and study as well as some personal background of the focal participants in the FLE class, I push toward an understanding of the workings of globalization and multilingualism as they manifest in the microcosm of the urban Corsican middle school context.

The Collège du Sud (South Middle School)[9] is a large suburban middle school in northern Corsica. Part of the Réseau d'éducation

---

8   This portion of the fieldwork can be considered semi-participant observation (Bonacina, 2011: 121, 138), since I never acted as an evaluator (of teachers or students) in the classroom setting.
9   All names including that of the school are pseudonyms. Some identifiers have been purposefully separated or excluded to further protect participants'

prioritaire (Priority Education Network, REP), what we might refer to in the US as an at-risk school; the principal explained that it is considered *défavorisé* (disadvantaged), and that some of the families and children that make up the school's community live *dans une grande précarité* (in great precarity). He described the school as part of *les quartiers un peu plus populaires* (neighborhoods that are a bit more working-class), made up of Moroccan and other Maghrebi immigrants, located at an intersection of different peoples in the area. The school's official profile introduces the school, stating:

> Situé dans les quartiers sud [...] accueille aussi bien des élèves résidants dans des logements HLM, qu'en cité de transit ou dans des quartiers résidentiels. Classé en réseau de réussite éducative, l'établissement se caractérise par une relative mixité[10] mais la tendance socio-économique des familles reste défavorisée. (Académie de Corse, 2016)

> (Located in the southern neighborhoods [... the school] welcomes students residing in low-income housing as well as provisional housing or residential areas. Classed in the network of educational success, the school is characterized by relative diversity but the socioeconomic trend of families remains disadvantaged.

One of the largest on the island, the *collège* has to approximately 760 students. Various backgrounds are represented in the student body including Corsican/French students, those descended from immigrant families and raised in Corsica/France, and newly arrived foreign students. Middle school students from throughout the area who are enrolled in FLE attend Sud since it houses the middle school UPE2A[11] for the region (not every school has its own FLE program).

The FLE class at Sud during the time of my fieldwork in Spring 2016 consisted of 15 students across the four grades. Their time

---

identities. Some information is not included because it was either unavailable or unclear.

10 Though *mixité* (diversity) here refers to relative socioeconomic diversity, the presence of racial and/or (im)migrant populations can be understood implicitly as the neighborhoods south of the city center have the reputation of being immigrant hubs.

11 *Unité pédagogique pour élèves allophones arrivants* (pedagogcal unit for new allophone students)—that is, FLE classes.

of residence on Corsica ranged from over a year to less than a month. Though the majority of immigrants on Corsica are Moroccan, Portuguese, or Romanian, these nationalities account for only about half of the student body of the FLE class at Sud, who hailed from Albania, Brazil, Egypt, Morocco, Pakistan, Portugal, Romania, and Ukraine. Their languages included Albanian, Arabic (Egyptian and Moroccan), Pashto,[12] Portuguese (Brazilian and European), Romanian, and Ukrainian along with additional languages[13] including English, Greek, Hungarian, and Italian. None of the students had had exactly the same previous exposure to or study of French, and their proficiencies differed wildly. Some sounded very nearly fluent in French, others had trouble though they were already fluent in several other languages, while still others had difficulty reading or writing in any script. The students' transnational trajectories—how they ended up in Corsica, with whom, and why—were extremely varied.

While the majority of ENAs arrive in France with family members, four of the 15 students in the Sud FLE class were for various reasons without their families and living in the local girls' and boys' homes (*maisons d'enfants*).[14] These students are referred to as *mineurs isolés étrangers* (unaccompanied foreign minors, MIEs).[15] MIEs are sometimes sent by family to France to be educated in French with the hopes of better eventual economic opportunities. Upon reaching the inundated *maisons d'enfants* of the Paris region, children are often sent to those in more rural areas like Corsica. Corsica thus serves as a kind of overflow for the French mainland, further complicating the make-up

---

12   There was some disagreement as to the Pakistani student's language background, and no one at the school district offices seemed to have a clear answer. Unclear communication was compounded by the fact that his French was very limited.
13   These were in addition to their "first" languages, those they'd learned from a speaker in their family, from previous travels, or from school study.
14   Those living there are not all foreign children; they are for whatever reason under the protection of the child welfare system and are in various kinds of what were described to me as *difficultés* (difficulties).
15   "Un mineur isolé étranger (MIE) est un jeune de moins de 18 ans qui n'a pas la nationalité française et se trouve séparé de ses représentants légaux sur le sol français" (An unaccompanied foreign minor [MIE] is a youth under 18 years old who does not have French citizenship and who finds themself separated from legal representatives on French soil) (Rovera, 2013: 6). *Isolé* can also be understood as secluded, stray, lone, or segregated.

of the Corsican periphery and immigrants' place therein (i.e., Corsica at the service of the Metropole, France as "internally colonized"; Lafont, 1967). The director of the CASNAV office of Northern Corsica asserted that thanks to the tight-knit community (the school district, teachers and counselors, *maisons d'enfants*), they are better able to host MIEs compared to urban areas in continental France which are strained for resources. So, contrary to stereotypes of Corsicans as closed to outsiders, there also exists a proud notion of *acceuil* (hosting) in the attention given to these children, as reflected by high rates of success in academic retention and employment.[16] "Unaccompanied foreign minors" nonetheless experience FLE in distinct ways from their classmates as their ability to remain in France is tied to demonstrating French proficiency in order to either enroll in higher education or find work. Their case is one that illustrates the interconnected nature of language policy, curricular policy, and immigration policy among a vulnerable population (for a detailed treatment of the MIEs of the Sud FLE class, see Mendes, 2018b).

ENAs are learners. They are wild and wise adolescents. They are caught up in institutions and rules at the same time as being uprooted and wandering in new places, sometimes alone. They may be cheerful and carefree, or heartbroken and scared. Their struggles are real, and their successes are hard-won. Without painting too rosy a picture, I want to underscore that, for me, these students represent unbound ambition and potential.

§2.3 Pearls

I make use of metaphor in my reading of interactional data from the Sud FLE class. Metaphors such as distance, fluidity, borders, and edges have been widely used in the interpretation of sociolinguistic phenomena as well as their relation to globalization (Aronin & Politis, 2015; Catalano 2016: chs. 3, 11). Metaphor is useful in broadening our understandings of complex sociolinguistic phenomena (Blommaert, 2016: 247), and we need "new images, metaphors, and notions to cover

---

16 Synthesized from interviews with the school's *conseillère d'orientation psychologique* (psychological guidance counselor, COP) on May 24, 2016 and the local CASNAV office June 9, 2016.

adequately what we observe" (6). I propose the metaphor of pearls to nuance my discussion of globalization, a heuristic for qualitatively interpreting complex sociolinguistic phenomena (Mendes, 2018b). A pearl is a speech event in which multiple discourses collapse into a minute exchange. Interpreting such speech events requires deep contextualization. A pearl can be said to form when a language-related element necessitates the incorporation of personal experience such that these multiple components are understood as inseparable within the exchange.

In aquaculture, pearls are formed when an "irritant" enters an oyster, which is repeatedly layered with nacre. The language-related element (accent, spelling, word choice) serves as the "irritant" which spurs the formation of a pearl onto which other factors (cultural, economic, legal) are layered. Each pearl's distinct luster highlights the subjectivity inherent in interpreting such speech events; the hues we see in a pearl change with the light and with the perspectives of each person involved. These refractions might be similarly interpreted to what Pietikäinen et al. (2017) find in their work on minority languages of Europe, "a kind of metalinguistic and metacultural 'shimmer'—the brightly visible but unstable and shifting images of small languages that we have to deal with in the many peripheral spaces of late modernity" (69). The pearl metaphor also gestures to the seaside setting of the Collège du Sud, and helps to foreground relationality between language and place (Phipps, 2011; Mendes, 2020).

I make use of the pearl heuristic to discursively analyze excerpts from interactional data to interpret speech events from the Sud FLE class. The pearl metaphor captures the idea that these charged moments reveal underlying accounts of personal experiences with language, culture, and globalization. The pearl metaphor complements the ethnographic methodology undertaken, since it allows for analysis of micro-instances of language use to be interpreted considering wider sociocultural phenomena in a multilayered and emergent way (Blommaert, 2012: 5; Tusting & Maybin, 2007: 578). Like pearls inside oysters which occupy a small space, the speech events I present from the FLE class often have as their catalyst a small, seemingly insignificant detail, such as a single letter or word. The excerpts I present are notable for the ways in which language learning and pedagogy are not central as such. The content of the lesson at hand is less primary than experiences of various globalization phenomena, the metaphorical layering of nacre. I now present my reading of three pearls from data gathered during my observation of the Sud FLE class. Each episode will offer a synthesized presentation and analysis of the data with the goal of interpreting minute, concrete speech events in light of globalization phenomena.

§2.3.1 The Q Episode

Orthography[17] is a site of struggle for representation, apparent in many instances of language standardization/reform, for example Bosnian-Croatian-Serbian (Alexander, 2006), Moldovan-Romanian (Faucheux, 2006), and Turkish (Piller, 2016: ch. 8). Orthography is political for the way certain forms come to index specific speech communities and places, and thus reflect language ideologies, as in the case of Corsican micro-varieties (Jaffe, 1996, 1999: ch. 7). An orthography can be used to unify or distinguish, and is a learned practice significant to both users and viewers of the code—even in a standardized, national language and written in a "correct" sentence. Language ideology and the aesthetics of accepted literacy practices collide to expose transnational voices and global experiences—the layers of nacre in this first pearl. The following is a staging of "The Q Episode" as reconstructed via fieldnotes and transcriptions from recordings, presented alongside my own reading.

June 13, 2016, 10 a.m. class—The focal participants in this exchange are Diego, an energetic Brazilian student who loves soccer and is also fluent in Italian (having previously lived in Bergamo), and Bianca, the youngest and most talkative of the class, from Romania. Their teacher, Emmanuelle (from Corsica), had once mentioned to me that she thinks Greek and Latin should have a more prominent place in the curriculum. She is explicitly concerned with the FLE students' *intégration* (integration, into school and French society) by way of their acquisition of the French language. Magda, a Romanian classmate who often attends extra hours of FLE to get out of PE or study hall, chimes in occasionally.

---

17 I understand orthography as a system of spelling conventions, graphology as the study of symbols, and chirography as the study of handwriting. I refer to the written practices I analyze here as simply "handwriting."

In today's lesson, the class is reviewing a worksheet which targets the formulation of questions from *la vie quotidienne* (everyday life), for example making an appointment with a doctor or requesting directions to the post office. Emmanuelle, the teacher, has called Diego (Brazil) to the front of the class and is dictating to him the sentence they have collectively constructed, which he is writing on the board: "Bonjour, est-ce que vous pourriez m'expliquer comment fonctionne ce club de gym?" (Hello, could you explain to me how this gym club works?). Bianca (Romania) is surprised by how he has written the letter *q*,[18] and Magda (Romania) giggles as Bianca points out the horizontal bar Diego has drawn through the tail. Emmanuelle considers it and says, "Ah, oui, oui oui, c'est vrai, il est un peu:: étrange" (Ah, yes, yes yes, it's true, it is a bi::t strange) (turn 7).

Prompted perhaps by the attention given to the foreign characteristic of his handwriting, Diego suddenly jolts the conversation from discussing handwriting to aspects of everyday life in his Brazilian school in a rather confusing shift of topic (through turn 51). He shares seemingly banal details, perhaps happy to take center stage at the front of the room and talk about a cultural context on which he is the authority. He says that in Brazil they do not have whiteboards, like in Corsica, but green chalkboards. He says that the school is so close to the beach that students often go swimming for PE and are permitted into the school without shoes and simply in a bathing suit—to which Emmanuelle reacts, shocked: "Torse nu?! Non, c'est pas possible! C'est vrai?" (Shirtless?! No, that's not possible! Is that true?) (turn 26). So, the conversation hinges on expectations of the school space broadly:

18 Importantly, each time Bianca asks Diego about the *q*, she pronounces the name of the letter as in English, [kju]. This could be a simple difficulty with pronunciation, as the [y] vowel is notoriously difficult for second-language learners of French. A further possible explanation could be that she was trying to avoid pronouncing [ky], the "correct" pronunciation in French of the letter *q*, which happens to be homophonous with *cul* (ass). However, all the FLE students have had at least minimal exposure to English, and most are enrolled in English in school as well. It does happen throughout the fieldwork period that English is used in class for clarification of course content, so Bianca could also be resorting, in a sense, to English in the spirit of clarification or metalinguistic commentary. Bianca's use of English, if we interpret it as such, indexes her experience with English as an intermediary language with interlocutors of different linguistic backgrounds—one part of a larger holistic repertoire as understood in translanguaging approaches.

handwriting (the letter *q*), dress (no shoes, bathing suits), classes (swimming for PE), and material resources (chalkboards). Emmanuelle then asks him if this is the case in all Brazilian schools and he answers: "Dans les-dans les autres villes, je crois qui qui c'est comme ici, je sais pas, mais:, je sais pas parce que l'autre, où j'habitais? […] C'était plus, mm, um:, très pauvre, vraiment" (In the-in the other cities, I think that it's like here [in Corsica], I don't know, but:, I don't know because the other one, where I lived? […] It was more, um:, very poor, really) (turns 49–51).

In the very next turn, Bianca takes the discussion back to the *q*, probing Diego for an explanation no less than four times throughout the six-minute exchange as to how exactly *q* is written in Brazil. The example they continue to focus on, prompted by Diego's sentence on the board, is the way a lower-case *q* is written in France compared to in Brazil and in Romania. Emmanuelle offers her own interpretation of the different ways of drawing letters *vis-à-vis* French handwriting: "c'est en fonction de de du pays, d'où tu viens […] Mais du coup, après c'est vrai que quand on change de de de pays, eh? beh, ça devient illisible, p-pour un Français? C'est illisible. Personne ne peut comprendre, enfin, moi j'ai fini par le comprendre" (it depends on the country, you come from […] But actually, it's also true that when you change countries, eh? well, it becomes illegible, f-for a French person? It's illegible. No one will understand, well, me I understood in the end) (turns 57–9). Emmanuelle draws her own model *q* with the tail straight downward, prompting Bianca to also go to the board, where she very carefully draws her version, which has a small horizontal line at the bottom of the vertical tail that goes slightly to the right. The competition between the forms displayed on the board—three *q*s, French, Brazilian, and Romanian—orient the students to difference; they are learning how French speakers (or readers) identify what is not French.

The class continues to discuss ways of making letters, which leads to Emmanuelle drawing fancy, cursive capital letters on the board, explaining how upper-case letters in dictionaries are often elaborately decorated. She tells a student to get a dictionary from a cabinet on the side of the room saying that capital letters in dictionaries are "comme des arabesques" (like arabesques) (turn 69). She begins drawing an impressively elaborate cursive capital letter on the board, and there is general disagreement between the students as to which letter it is, *T*

42   *Countervocalities*

or *S*. Emmanuelle says it is, in fact, an *F*. She draws another letter to show them:

> 81. Emmanuelle: Nous, le t en français, le t en français, il se fait-en majuscule, eh? Il va se faire comme ça ((begins drawing elaborate cursive capital T on the board))
> 82. Bianca: [[non, ça c'est f, ça, je sais, mais je dois, c'est comme ça en France.
> 83. Diego: Mais, c'est vraiment très dessiné.

> 81. Emmanuelle: Us, the *t* in French, the *t* in French, it gets done-as a capital, eh?, It is done like this ((begins drawing elaborate cursive capital *T* on the board))
> 82. Bianca: [[no, that's *f*, that, I know, but I must, it's like this in France.
> 83. Diego: But, it's really very elaborately drawn

Emmanuelle continues to model dominant French cultural perspectives. Though this may seem unsurprising given that her job largely consists of teaching the national language, here the discussion goes beyond what is correct or incorrect in terms of grammar or pronunciation to the valorization of certain aesthetics regarding the appearance of written language. As the only native French speaker and French citizen in the room, she maintains her role as the sole authority on French culture. Emmanuelle clearly locates French as dominant in the hierarchy of languages present in the class, and her use of a dictionary (turn 69) functions as a tangible extension of State, institutional, hegemonic power to illustrate the points she makes regarding language.

Exclusive identity categories can be read in the grammatical personhood employed by the speakers. Emmanuelle's continued use of *nous* (we, for us) throughout the exchange puts forth an exclusive second person plural division, and further establishes her stance as the French authority as she compares the students' foreign handwriting. She also often frames her points using expressions like *chez nous* (for us, here in France) or *pour moi* (for me) (turns 59, 61, 69, 71, 81). Emmanuelle declares her own way of writing in French to be the correct way of writing in France. Consider, for example, turn 61, "nous, c'est comme ça" (for us, it's like this) or turn 81, when she draws an elaborate cursive capital *T*. Diego and Bianca counter her stance, adopting *moi* and *nous* in different places throughout (turns 62, 65, 91) to talk about the writing practices of their home cultures. Such markers reflect the clashes between the speakers' three different perspectives, as in the following, where Bianca and Diego demonstrate the formation of letters on the board, which is quickly glossed over by Emmanuelle:

84. Bianca: A mon avis c'est comme ça
85. Emmanuelle: Chez nous, c'est les majuscules qui sont-tu vois
86. Bianca: [[et
87. Emmanuelle: Le a, regarde, comme ça le a, tu vois
88. Bianca: Ah, mais lui il a, comme ça
89. Emmanuelle: Le b, tu vas le faire comme ça
90. Bianca: [[oui
91. Diego: Nous, les a, attends, on fait comme ça, c'est le ((he draws what is apparently a capital A in Brazil, it is round and circular))
92. Emmanuelle: Pour moi ça n'a rien à voir

―

81. Bianca: In my opinion it's like this
82. Emmanuelle: For us, it's capitals that are-you see
83. Bianca: [[an
84. Emmanuelle: The *a*, look, like this the *a* ((draws a capital A on the board, Diego is writing/drawing capital ABC on the board)), you see
85. Bianca: Oh, but him he has, like that
86. Emmanuelle: The *b*, you're going to do it like this
87. Bianca: [[yeah
88. Diego: Us, the *a*, wait, we do like this, it's the ((he draws what is apparently a capital A in Brazil, it is round and circular))
89. Emmanuelle: For me, that's nothing like it

Our three competitors remain at the board comparing handwriting. Emmanuelle shows them how to draw a cursive capital *A*, and then, moving on to *B*, directs Bianca explicitly, saying "tu vas le faire comme ça" (you will do it like this) (turn 89). Emmanuelle sanctions only French handwriting practices, dismissing what she does not recognize as French, as in turn 92: "Pour moi, ça n'a rien à voir" (for me that's nothing like it). Diego then rather unexpectedly reverts back to his discussion of Brazilian school life, offering further details regarding the socioeconomic context of his school, explaining that the teachers were volunteers. But, he insists, it is nonetheless a beautiful city and asks if he can show the class, motioning to the computer at the front of the room (turns 112, 116). Once Emmanuelle consents, Diego goes to the computer, followed eagerly by Bianca. In a whir, Bianca erupts excitedly as the internet search brings up photos of penguins—Diego says you can see them there (a zoo?)—the bell rings—class ends.

It is important to highlight how Diego's explanations of the day-to-day in his Brazilian school are interwoven throughout the discussion of handwriting (turns 4–51 and 112–18) rather than concentrated at only one point within the conversation. That is to say that the way that *q* is written in Brazil is one detail among many within the whole of the sociocultural context Diego describes. What is illegible to the French, according to Emmanuelle (that is, a *q* written with a horizontal bar through the tail), for Diego necessarily signals the many constellations in which the Brazilian school context is tied up, a layered simultaneity (Blommaert, 2004). As the conversation shows, the small bar of the *q* evokes swimming in the ocean, green chalkboards, a poor area, volunteer teachers, and a *très belle ville* (very beautiful city). Inseparable from the *q*, these details are the figurative nacre of this seemingly chaotic pearl, layer upon layer.

What Diego shares reaches up and out from the immediate context of the FLE class's discussion of handwriting, originally spurred by the drawing of *q*, and indexes various language and literacy practices, geographic mobility, and social class. Interestingly, though Diego expounds upon his experience in Brazil, he does not venture into talking about school culture or handwriting in Italy at all (recall that he had previously lived there). Perhaps he thinks it better than to delve into an exploration of Italian culture since it is not his "home" culture, or perhaps he has chosen to highlight his expertise on Brazil, much more exotic and further afield as opposed to neighboring Italy, whose islands are visible from the Corsican shore. In any case, Diego's personal experience and transnational trajectory allow him to posture as a cultural authority within this exchange. His perspectives are engaged with by Romanian and Corsican interlocutors, while the remainder of the class from various other backgrounds listen in.

Handwriting has shaped social formations historically. As a recent exhibit on the history of handwriting explains, "In the early modern period, learning to write was like learning a foreign language. French handwriting, for example, looked distinctly different from Spanish or German. [...] 'National' styles of writing played a significant role in expanding empires: handwriting became an important way to define cultural identity and impose bureaucratic and social order" (Newberry Library, 2022). It has been argued that words that change in color or shape can represent "a kind of code-switching going on through alternate typography"; a font can have "an aura of being local, of authenticity" which can reflect different values and identities in different languages (Gorter & Cenoz, 2015: 68). In the rejoinders of each interlocutor in this exchange, we can identify such competing displays of language. Diego proudly explicates the crossing of the *q*'s tail and Brazilian school culture at length, and thus displays a graphic identity derived from his Brazilian roots—a heritage handwriting. The entire exchange centers around his handwriting and explanations[19] of his life in Brazil. While Bianca displays and shares handwriting practices of Romania,[20] she also demonstrates her facility (and thus to a certain extent acceptance of) performing writing practices of her new country—a transnational handwriting, since she engages with both orientations in the exchange. She shows she knows how things are done in France (turns 72, 77) and that she is able to reproduce letters in the accepted fashion, though she is also happy to share her knowledge of Romania. Emmanuelle endorses codified, standardized French expression, all the way down to the appearance of each letter—a francohegemonic/national handwriting. In this way, a French monolingual ideology is upheld, at least to a certain extent. The heritage, transnational, and hegemonic handwriting in this exchange coexist in the mosaic FLE space.

Smith (2019: 21, 67–8) asserts that, for immigrants, proving cultural legitimacy involves both linguistic and racial factors; here we see that it also depends on aesthetic qualities (and subsequent judgments) of their language production. Throughout this exchange, Emmanuelle emphasizes that foreign handwriting is illegible, that no one can

---

19   Interestingly, the infamous crossed *q* originally appeared in the verb *expliquer* (to explain) (turns 1–4).
20   Andrei, Bianca's Romanian classmate, confirmed her explanation in turn 66. Bianca is one of three Romanian FLE students, while Diego is one of two Brazilian students in the class.

understand it (turn 59). The Q Episode demonstrates that it is via the mastery of minutiae in handwritten forms in French that one is (visibly, on paper) deemed a legitimate participant in French society. Consider the following fieldnote, from a different class period, in which two of the more remedial students, Faizan (Pakistan) and Dritan (Albania), discuss handwriting with Emmanuelle:

> As Faizan is writing, Dritan turns to Emmanuelle and comments on his handwriting saying that his *r*s look like *l*s. Emmanuelle agrees and says she's going to show him how to write *r*s. She says his *r*s look like *n*s ("on dirait n" [you'd think it were an *n*]). She shows Faizan how he should write them and says, "pour qu'on arrive à te lire" [so that people can read you (i.e., your writing)]. (fieldnote, May 24, 2016, 9–10 a.m. class)

Faizan, newly arrived from Pakistan, is still in the very early stages of his French learning, and often encounters difficulties forming letters in the new script. In this exchange, his teacher and his peer, both proficient users of the Roman alphabet, comment on his inferior production of the letter *r*. One's legibility is thus legitimizing to the extent that via the presentation of "correctly" formed letters (those recognizable as the hegemonic handwritten shapes of the national language), one can become (however partially) validated as a participant in a francophone setting. The stakes of conforming to accepted literacy practices can be particularly high, for example in the legibility of official paperwork to be filled out by hand (Mendes, 2018b).

The Q Episode is a pearl whose "irritant," the letter *q*, is layered with factors including transnational mobility, social class, and language ideology which all become apparent thanks to this small detail. Handwriting and legibility, even in the writing of a single letter, are the points of contention around which distinct practices compete for recognition and legitimacy. Handwriting aesthetics constitute a gatekeeping mechanism of integration; foreign handwriting is subject to judgment, reformulation, or dismissal. This exchange is just a glimpse of the varied literacy practices present in the Sud FLE class, originating in different spaces and languages, and meeting on Corsica, in French—colliding in Diego's writing of the letter *q*.

§2.3.2 A Parent

This second pearl deals with language learning and standardized testing. One of the main goals of FLE education is to prepare students to take the DELF (Diplôme d'études en langue française, diploma of French language studies) exam. At Sud, students prepare to test out of level A1[21] during the month of May, and spend the majority of their time in FLE working toward achieving this benchmark. The exam is meant to ensure that students have a baseline of language skills to function in "normal" classes. Each school district has the authority to choose which DELF exams will be administered. Though exams for levels A2 and B1 do exist, the Académie de Corse administers only the A1 exam.[22] This local policy decision has wide-reaching implications which could reflect, on one hand, limited resources for FLE and, on the other, a lax approach to allophones' language development. In fact, certain research participants requested that I inquire as to the Académie's decision to only offer the A1 exam, reflecting a concern that while A1 proficiency may be enough for students to get by in normal classes, it may not suffice for students to succeed academically. What's more, the request that I inquire about this policy decision showed me that there is perhaps not a consensus as to how FLE education is administered in the district. Like the condensed pearl episodes, this single policy decision encapsulates struggle between the national, the regional, and the local (implementation of policy at each individual school), and illustrates the branching structures which inform the goings-on in the Sud FLE class. Students' preparation for the DELF exam, as we will see, is not at all as simple as imagined in sterile standardized assessments when real life enters the scene.

April 18, 2016, 11 a.m. class—The focal participants in this exchange are Andrei, a student from Romania who tends to mediate for other Romanian speakers, translating course content with or without permission, and Yvette, the other FLE teacher (also from Corsica). She often makes use of pronunciation patterns of *le français régional de Corse* (Corsican regional French; see Jaffe, 1999), which is especially

---

21 The Common European Framework of Reference (CEFR) language proficiency levels range from beginner (A1) to advanced (C2).
22 This was the case at the time of my fieldwork (CASNAV interview, 2016), and to the best of my knowledge there is no indication that this has changed.

salient in her pronunciation of some of the students' first names.[23] In this lesson, the students are working on a speaking activity in the style of a mock exam. For this activity, they work one-on-one with an evaluator. Yvette had previously explained the staging of the exercise to the class: the students are given an appointment time and a room number. They wait until the student before them has finished and left, then knock and enter the room. They politely say hello and answer any small-talk questions the evaluators ask, for example where they're from or how long they've been in France/Corsica. The evaluators will be FLE teachers from throughout the Académie de Corse; the students at Sud will not be evaluated by Yvette or Emmanuelle, their own FLE teachers. The class rehearses this mock exam and the language exercises that comprise the oral portion over several days, complete with exiting the room, knocking, and re-entering, working one-on-one with Yvette at the front of the room while the rest of the class looks on.

The first actual language exercise of the oral portion involves question formation. Yvette had explained previously that there will be slips of paper face down on the table that they must choose from. Each slip has a vocabulary word written on it with which the students must formulate a question to ask the evaluator. Yvette says that all of the vocabulary used will be rather straightforward words that they will have seen before in class. The students are expected to create clear, full questions, making use of the formal subject pronoun *vous*, since they are speaking to teachers.

The day of this exchange, the class was practicing this exercise as a group, that is, without one student at the front of the room. Yvette was giving the class basic vocabulary words, and the group was creating questions aloud that they could use for the exam. As the following excerpt begins, the class has just finished with the first word:

> They move on to the next word, which is "parent" (parent or relative). Yvette writes on the board: 2. Parent (she asks if they know what this means). The students begin chiming in, giving possible questions they could ask: "Est-ce que vous avez des

---

23 The most salient way this appears is in the apocope (dropping) of final vowels at the end of names, for example Bianca is pronounced as [bjɑ̃k] rather than [bjɑ̃.ka], akin to the stereotypical pronunciation of Corsican places names like Ajaccio as [a.jatʃ].

parents?" (Do you have parents?). This prompts a discussion of the fact that everyone has parents, but someone says, yes but some people's parents may have died. Yvette agrees and says *ça peut toucher* (that can be upsetting). So she says that that question is *à éviter* (to be avoided) because it is a question *qui touche et peut faire mal* (that can cause pain). (fieldnote, April 19, 2016, 11 a.m.–12 p.m. class)

Throughout the exercise, many of the questions the students create contain much the same formulation, for example: "Est-ce que vous avez …?" or "Est-ce que vous aimez …?" (Do you have …?, Do you like …?). This illustrates not only formulaic language use, but lexical chunking, that is, the use of phrases beyond the level of the individual word as units of language. This is evident here in that most of the questions contain not only the interrogative chunk "est-ce que" but additionally, since they know they will be using vous, "est-ce que vous," and more often than not "est-ce que vous avez" or "est-ce que vous aimez." In short, if the students can memorize the question chunk, the exercise becomes more of a rote fill-in-the blank activity than a communicative exchange.

In the class's discussion of the word *parent*, the students' comments revolving around family life and whether or not one has living parents are not necessarily within the realm of the language exercise, strictly speaking. Yvette's agreement with the students that the question is potentially hurtful confirms that the personal nature of the question is not socially acceptable, and they should thus avoid asking it. The class has moved from a formulaic question-formation exercise toward building their understandings of sociolinguistic and cultural-pragmatic competence about acceptable topics of discussion in French society generally. The exchange continues with further erratic conversation concerning parents:

Someone says that there are people with no parents. Yvette says, *Oui*, that *orphelin* (orphan) is the word for someone that doesn't have parents. [I realize that this is quite a sensitive topic and wonder if Yvette foresaw this in including this word in the activity, especially with the varied and difficult family situations of some of these students]. (fieldnote, April 19, 2016, 11 a.m.–12 p.m. class)

Yvette's frank definition of the word *orphelin* came originally as a surprise to me; recall that four of the students in the Sud FLE class live in the local *maisons d'enfants*, without adult family members with them in Corsica.[24] What originally began as a vocabulary and question-forming exercise has burst open, and the class moves increasingly into the sphere of the deeply personal. The solidarity among the students is evident—they are no strangers to shaky family circumstances—even as they take on the language exam task. The question as to the teacher's choice to include such a word in the activity can be interpreted as pragmatic: as part of everyday language, the students will need to know how to manipulate questions related to family and parents, so this choice is realistic rather than unsympathetic. She could not, however, have predicted exactly how the discussion of the word would have unfolded in class:

> Someone then suggests the sentence "Avez-vous déjà fait des voyages avec vos parents?" (Have you ever traveled with your parents?) [...] Someone else adds the question: "Est-ce que vos parents sont en France?" (Are you parents in France?). This is, again, another very interesting question that the students have come up with. It acknowledges/reinforces their own varied international, migrant experiences, and that these often have involved a separation from their families. (MY HEART!) (fieldnote, April 19, 2016, 11 a.m.–12 p.m. class)

The additional question offered as part of the exercise asking if one has ever traveled with their parents ("Avez-vous déjà fait des voyages avec vos parents?") seems rather innocent on the surface. It breaks with the "Est-ce que vous avez ..." and "Est-ce que vous aimez ..." formulations, and provides a well-constructed full question

---

24 Rovera (2013) describes how family dynamics can still play a role in the school life of MIE students: "Une première spécificité du travail éducatif avec des MIE est que celui-ci est réalisé en l'absence de la famille sur le territoire. Ainsi, l'accompagnement n'est pas focalisé sur la préservation des liens familiaux. Mais le travail sur la famille n'est pas exclu pour autant. [...] Un MIE peut, par exemple, avoir des difficultés à parler de sa famille" (A first feature of academic work with MIEs is that it takes place in the absence of the family on [French] territory. Thus, support is not focusing on preserving family connections. But the work on family is not excluded as such. [...] An MIE can, for example, have difficulties speaking about their family) (19).

in grammatically correct French. It does, however, gesture to questions of socioeconomic status and financial means to be able to travel. The issue of mobility is further echoed in the second question ("Est-ce que vos parents sont en France?") which adds nuance to the previous explanation of "orphan" as well as ideas about travel. Though four FLE classmates live in *maisons d'enfants*, at least two other students live with extended family on Corsica.[25] My personal aside at the end of this section ("MY HEART!") underscores the fact that, knowing the students and their situations, these kinds of conversations about families and personal duress are never easy to hear as they surface in class. No one in the classroom—students, teacher, or observer—is ever neutral or exempt from subjective emotion or personal circumstance, despite seemingly innocuous tasks at hand. Yvette moves on:

> Yvette calls on Andrei and says she hasn't heard him talk yet today in class. [I realize I rarely hear him speak aloud in these class discussions. (…)] Andrei asks a question: for the DELF exam oral, what should he ask about *parents*? [It seems like he doesn't know what is appropriate to ask, as far as socially acceptable expectations]. There is a discrepancy as to how Yvette interprets his question. She basically begins re-explaining the directions. She begins re-explaining this section of the oral exam [which they've already practiced] in which they'll have to pick five *tickets* (slips) with words on them and then *poser des questions* to the examiner using the words. She says that they are normally questions that they've seen before in class. [...] So, Andrei makes a question and says: "Est-ce que vous habitez avec vos parents?" (Do you live with your parents?) The students laugh, saying that the examiner they'll be with, as an adult, won't be living with their parents! (fieldnote, April 19, 2016, 11 a.m.–12 p.m. class)

The discrepancy between what Andrei seems to be trying to ask and what Yvette understands illustrates the foregrounding of the assessment framework within this exchange. That is, Yvette shifts

---

25 There was never an explanation of possible nuance with regard to the fact that *parent* can also mean relative; language production here is expected to be simple and to the point, without straying from the task. Regarding the difficulty of teaching the topic of "family" in foreign language classes, see also Kramsch and Zhang (2018: 67–8).

back from discussing what are or are not socially acceptable topics of discussion regarding parents, and instead begins to re-explain the directions for the activity. These directions have been reviewed several times in class, and the students have practiced this activity together on several occasions already. Here, Yvette foregrounds a central tenet of the French educational system: "respecter la consigne" (follow the directions). She expects Andrei to not stray from the outline of the activity and wants him to simply think of a question. Previously, Yvette admitted that certain questions should be avoided as being potentially offensive or hurtful. Such an admittance on her part is rare, as reflected by her preference here to stick to the book and follow directions. She does not reiterate her previous warning of careful avoidance of certain topics. Rather, by repeating, step-by-step, the outline of the activity, she authoritatively promotes a top-down approach to successfully completing the assessment. The students are expected to stay within the lines, so to speak. Creativity and nuance are not rewarded within the context of the exercise.

It is perhaps no surprise then that Andrei reverts to an ostensibly safe question: "Est-ce que vous habitez avec vos parents?", even though, as his peers tell him, this may be a bit silly to ask of an adult. In the end, however, Andrei has successfully completed the task. He has also, in his own way, attempted to attend to cultural norms by avoiding potentially offensive topics of conversation and opting for what he supposes is an innocent question. Although we can imagine that Andrei could guess that this question would be a sensitive one to bring up with some of his classmates, he follows Yvette's lead by creating a question involving life with parents which is supposedly unproblematic. His decision could thus be interpreted as both adhering to the assessment protocol at hand and adopting a rather normative perspective in which asking about family members is nothing remarkable.

From the very outset, the activity is framed as an encounter with the other. Recall that Yvette had explained that potential small talk from the evaluators could include questions of origin or the amount of time spent in France. Though this small talk seems fairly innocent, it is enough to explicitly situate the gatekeeping characteristic of the exchange by highlighting what is foreign and what is French. The oral assessment with the DELF evaluator is a task at which ENAs as foreigners must succeed in order to be admitted into mainstream French settings. And, one could interpret the beginning of the exchange, with a simple question (Where are you from? How long have you been in France?), as reminding the students that they do not yet belong. Outsiders, students literally waiting outside a room, vie for validated access to French society by way of satisfactory performance of standard language. As we have seen, the assessment scenario is hardly exempt from eventually intertwining with students' personal lives. This pearl reveals how minute details in course content inadvertently layer with complicated and unpredictable family circumstances and socioeconomic catalysts of mobility.

In this exchange, the actual linguistic construction of a question is not what students seem to spend the most time on. Indeed, the students' syntax and conjugations are all fine, and Yvette has not had to correct anyone. We see, then, that even within a seemingly straightforward assessment context wherein students' language production uniformly aligns with normative expectations (i.e., standard French grammar), students' apparently harmless responses to a simple exercise ("Est-ce que vos parents sont en France?") reflect their complex trajectories, personal lives, and concerns. Despite having supposedly moved into the sterile realm of a standardized exam, language is always personal and political.

§2.3.3 Eyelids

The final pearl I present illustrates the explicit linkage in France of the acquisition of standard language and Republican ideals of societal integration. Though a rather brief exchange, this final example encapsulates the drive behind much of the FLE experience in a concise, charged moment.

May 23, 2016, 10 a.m. class—In addition to the classmates we saw above (see §2.3.1), the other focal participant in this exchange is Rovena, who is from Albania; she sometimes speaks with Emmanuelle about her family in Albania, usually sits in the front row, and is praised for her advanced French. In this lesson, Emmanuelle is working with Bianca (Romania), Rovena (Albania), and Magda (Romania) on a reading. They come across the word *baiser*, and Emmanuelle clarifies that in the text, the verb means *faire des bisous* (kiss).[26] The following

---

26 Today, *baiser* usually refers to sexual intercourse and is considered vulgar. In everyday language, it has been replaced with *embrasser*, to mean to kiss.

fieldnote excerpt picks up as the class is clarifying the action of a character in the text, who has kissed another character's eyelids:

> Emmanuelle clarifies *bisous* (kisses) mentioning kissing the *paupières* (eyelids), since that is what it says in the text. They clarify *paupières*. Emmanuelle is motioning to her eyelids and saying it's like where you put eyeshadow. Bianca then says, Oh yeah, and goes to tell the word to Magda in Romanian and then seems to have a revelation—she tells Emmanuelle she is forgetting things in her native language. This sparks a conversation among the girls and Emmanuelle. Emmanuelle says, *T'as oublié ta langue maternelle?* (You've forgotten your mother tongue?). (fieldnote, May 23, 2016, 10–11a.m. class)

Originally, the class pauses from their reading to clarify a new vocabulary word, *paupières*. Bianca, the youngest of the Sud FLE group, often functions as a language intermediary when her Romanian-speaking peers do not understand something in class. However, her attempt to translate the word to Magda is revelatory—she cannot do it. Even Emmanuelle seems taken aback, and asks her if she is forgetting her native language. The discussion continues as Rovena chimes in:

> Rovena says that sometimes when she's speaking in Albanian she adds French words without meaning to. Emmanuelle says that *ça doit être bizarre* (that must be bizarre), but she is happy about it and says that this means that *l'intégration ça marche bien* (the integration is working well) and later *tant mieux pour vous, l'intégration fonctionnne* (so much the better for you, the integration is working). [...] Bianca boasts that she has been here *même pas un an* (not even a year). (fieldnote, May 23, 2016, 10–11 a.m. class)

Here, we see the voices of ENAs from different countries who report experiencing similar incipient dominance in French. The three students involved in this exchange are from two different home countries and language backgrounds. Importantly, all three of the focal students in this exchange are female. They are achieving such advanced

---

However, the word's appearance in a text is less surprising, as an example of refined, outdated, or elevated vocabulary. In any case, Emmanuelle does not offer an explicit explanation of this nuance, preferring simply to provide a synonymous phrase, "faire des bisous" (to give kisses).

fluency that it is detrimental to their first language recall (at least for Bianca and Rovena, it seems). Of all the students in the Sud FLE class, those with greatest facility in French are mostly girls and those with the least French or who are most remedial are mostly boys. These international and gendered characteristics of this pearl contribute to how we view the encounter—it is complex and layered.

Earlier in their discussion, Emmanuelle asks Bianca if she's forgotten her first language, and is rather surprised ("T'as oublié ta langue maternelle? [...] ça doit être bizarre"). Emmanuelle recognizes and imagines the strangeness of the experience of losing one's mother tongue. This is a rather rare moment in which the students' experience is permitted to outshine the importance of institutional, national interests of French dominance. Recall how students' international handwriting in Diego's Q Episode was quickly subordinated to French practices as illustrated by the dictionary and Emmanuelle's own handwriting. Here, Emmanuelle considers the students' position, if only for a moment. And it is fleeting—soon thereafter, her surprise and intrigue at the girls' disappearing first languages turns to approval. Emmanuelle's valorization of the students' progress in French is illustrated by her repeated and enthusiastic praise: "l'intégration ça marche bien" and "tant mieux pour vous." Emmanuelle openly displays her investment in the girls' linguistic achievements, proudly stating that their French facility has led to an integration whose workings, reflected here in the present tense ("l'intégration fonctionne"), are apparently not over yet. Emmanuelle's acknowledgment of the girls' grappling with coexisting languages has transformed into an effacement of their knowledge as it is superseded by her claim that this is success. Her pride in their integration extends to the students' own feelings about their French learning, reflected by Bianca's contentment as to the brief amount of time she's been in France/Corsica ("même pas un an"), and her ability to learn so quickly, despite the fact that she is apparently gradually losing her Romanian.

Though Emmanuelle has not provided an explanation as to what she understands integration to mean, one could read an implication that it somehow involves replacement. As the students pursue intensive French learning, they may neglect their other languages (the beginnings of subtractive bilingualism; Wong Fillmore, 2000). In Bianca's case, any further growth into her native language may prove nonexistent. Bianca is, after all, the youngest in the class, and as such it would make sense that she be among those to learn French the quickest and most fully.[27] This has the potential to be a quite salient issue in the French middle school, as the age range of students encompasses four years of early to mid-adolescence. So, not only do ENAs represent remarkable transnational experiences, cultural hybridity, family circumstances, and struggles within the postnational economy, they are faced with a task of forgetting.

The weaving together of the ideas of integration and vision (or what protects/impedes it, namely eyelids, *paupières*) makes for an intriguing reading of this pearl. With figurative eyelids closed, one's previous cultural and linguistic experiences are kept locked away and left to atrophy. The ideal of integration is the great hoodwink of French Republicanism—a forceful blindfolding, a covering of the eyes—which, rather than helping refine one's vision, leaves one deprived of a critical faculty with which to interpret the world: one's native-language-and-culture baggage.

§2.4 Globalizing Surges

In this chapter, I have interpreted interactional data from my case study of the Sud FLE class. My reading has engaged with an extended metaphor, pearls, to attempt to operationalize a complex sociolinguistic approach and to understand the data in a multilayered way. The layers identified include the themes of mobility, family, gender, and language learning among many others as they relate to the students' transnational trajectories. The case of ENAs presents an opportunity to explore how globalization affects immigrant youth. These students' transnational experiences and family situations among other things shed light on the various mobilities and liminal multilingual repertoires they bring with them as they learn French under the influence of French Republican ideologies of integration in the insular context of Corsica. In "The Q Episode," the teaching of handwriting revealed notions of appropriate display of language knowledge related to one's transnational experiences. In "A Parent," I showed how seemingly innocuous vocabulary and assessment scenarios are never immune to

---

27 The Critical Period Hypothesis (e.g., Abello-Contesse, 2009): that younger learners are more easily able to attain fluency than those beyond puberty.

deeply personal connections students may make with course content. Lastly, in "Eyelids," we saw how language attrition can undergird discourses of integration. The case study of this class illustrates a specific dimension of peripheral multilingualism (Pietikäinen et al., 2017), namely the immigrant periphery within a European minority language community. Within the metaphorical framework presented, each of these factors—sociolinguistic context, increased mobility, neoliberal economics, institutionalized multilingualism in schools, family dynamics, national language ideologies—is a layer of nacre which contributes to the formation of pearls.

Indeterminacy and instability, as reflected in the pearls, are central premises of complex approaches to social inquiry, and engaging with metaphor is one part of expanding the breadth of this kind of work (Blommaert, 2012, 2014). The stories of newly arrived immigrants and their linguistic and cultural experiences in their new host societies reveal that there is much work yet to be done, for example in critical literacies (Pennycook, 1999; Fairclough, 1989, 1992), critical language policy (Tollefson, 2006), and multilingualism and social justice (Piller, 2016). The analysis of speech coupled with qualitative linguistic-ethnographic fieldwork data contributes to the investigation and interpretation of social life more generally—language, culture, politics, economy—and links everyday, on-the-ground interactions to globalization.

The idea of globalizing surges offers a fruitful and nuanced way of thinking about globalization phenomena as outside an individual's personal control (Ramanthan, 2013a; Mendes 2018b). Our global present moment (Blommaert, 2010)—characterized by increased mobility, multilingualism, new forms of technology, and a neoliberal economy—is messy. Surges in the natural world, such as storms, tidal waves, or volcanic eruptions, are outside human control, wild, unruly forces. Akin to Phipps's (2013: 98) unmoored multilingualism, in which vulnerable populations experience radical unpredictability, globalizing surges help us think about the "lack of agency and control" (Ludwig, 2016: 36) of groups like newly arrived immigrant youth. Globalizing surges in the FLE classroom emerge amongst "collages of histories, policies, borders, and crossings that do not add up to tidy snapshots" (Ramanathan, 2013a: 9–10).

For example, what mobility means in the case of these adolescents is not at all straightforward and cannot be taken for granted. Particularly in the case of the MIE students, these children's situations complicate our understandings of transnational mobility, as they have arrived "in France" in strange and often unclear ways. MIEs are often especially at the mercy of institutional systems within their new host country, which may involve the need for further movement, as we have seen in the case of children being sent to *maisons d'enfants* in regions of France where there is available space. Further factors such as the labor market, the intersection of immigration and curricular policies, and even religion come to light within these children's experiences of FLE (Mendes, 2018b). Though these adolescents are of course insightful and agentive in various ways, their mobilities illustrate that how one experiences globalization is outside of one's control. The imagined sterile quality of educational endeavors like standardized tests, which prefer to ignore personal experiences and emotions, is a farce. Encountering the personal and the global in messy ways is inevitable in any teaching or learning endeavor.

It is not only the personal circumstances of the student interacting with globalizing surges that contribute to the eventual formation of what I am calling pearls. There is also the rigid presence of the institutional context, which we can imagine here as the oyster itself, constraining and dictating how the pearl, born of an irritant, is built up layer by layer, ultimately determining its shape and hue. Yet, while the institutional framework is indeed confining and unyielding in certain ways which limit creativity and flexibility, an oyster's shell is also what protects the treasure it holds. For ENAs at Sud, Yvette and Emmanuelle are among the adults with whom they spend the most time; they represent the most powerful sources of French linguistic and cultural capital in the students' lives. They are guides, counselors, and protectors.

A pessimistic interpretation of FLE education could consider it a steely vestige of French cultural and linguistic imperialism, even within "French" spaces. As Kramsch and Zhang (2018) affirm, "the national French language mediates access to and integration into French society and the international community through intellectual rigor, critical reading of texts, precise and coherent writing (and not just language for special purposes), appreciation of beauty, felicitous pronunciation, and morally acceptable norms of behavior such as discipline and respect of institutional authority" (6). This integration through learning French is reflected in the Sud FLE class in the push to imitate perfect handwriting and even to replace one's mother tongue. On the other hand, an optimistic interpretation of Yvette's and Emmanuelle's pedagogical choices—adherence to French monolingual ideologies, strict obedience to the rules of standardized testing, and insistence on linguistic integration—could find a pragmatic function therein. The teachers attempt to instill in these newly arrived adolescents behaviors and ideologies with which they must learn to function if they are to participate and thrive in French society. In other words, it is both thanks to and in spite of teachers' rigidity, this productive tension, that one can see a kind of care and concern.

If the institutional context is the oyster, then the French national ideology of integration is the water itself in which the pearls are grown. As in pearl aquaculture, French speakers are meticulously groomed and uniformly cultivated. As we have seen, learning to integrate in this way can even involve a self-effacing measure of forgetting one's first language. Indeed, the trend of the term *français langue d'intégration* (French as a language of integration) replacing *français langue étrangère* (French as a foreign language), foregrounding the acquisition of French as a means to social integration and citizenship, attests that this drive to integrate linguistically is alive and well (Feyfant, 2012). The ebb and flow of the tides from which the pearls emerge are the globalizing surges of the extended metaphor. We are seemingly at the mercy of the crashing, monstrous waves of hypermobility and transnational trajectories, cultural and linguistic hybridity, unpredictability and nonlinearity, demands of the postnational economy, and the difficulty of facing these at times alone. The pearls offer a metaphorical heuristic for analyzing concrete instances of interaction with regard to globalization phenomena, illustrating that though FLE is ostensibly centered on French acquisition, personal stories and globalizing forces are squarely present in everyday classroom interactions.

This chapter has offered a linguistic-ethnographic snapshot of a Corsican middle school FLE class. This study has offered an exploration of various curricular policy factors and illustrated that globalizing surges and language learning interact with the deeply personal as attested by charged moments in class. Additionally, this chapter has drawn from metaphor to interpret these instances and unpack their multiple layers which come into play. While the Sud FLE class underscores the idea of social integration by way of learning French, the following chapter pivots to explore language learning and linguistic integration *vis-à-vis* the maintenance and revitalization of Corsican.

Chapter 3

ABCs

Introduction

It is mid-morning on a Thursday in early June. The Sud FLE classroom, located on the third floor, receives plenty of sunshine onto its east-facing windows, and it has been quite warm during class in recent weeks. Especially on days like today with just a few students, quiet time in the heat can lead to everyone feeling sluggish. Aside from Emmanuelle and I, there are currently only four students this hour: Lavinia (Romania), Bianca (Romania), Rovena (Albania), and Faizan (Pakistan). The girls are busy on an activity based on the vocabulary for the different ways of cooking meat (French, *la cuisson*), while Faizan works independently on the computer at the front of the room (Mendes, 2022). He is the most neophyte francophone of the class, and Emmanuelle has given him some listening comprehension activities to work on. There is a lull in the class, and I have stood up from my regular seat toward the back of the room to stretch. The classroom is not elaborately decorated, aside from a world map on one wall next to a cork board which was usually completely empty. Today, however, there is a full-page newspaper clipping newly tacked to it. I walk over to take a closer look.

 The article includes a photo of some teachers I recognize from Sud viewing a presentation of some sort and one or two of the boys from the FLE class. Emmanuelle walks over to me and says that she has not yet had a chance to read it, but explains that it covers the publication of a photography project the class undertook the previous semester, as it so happened on the alphabet and the Corsican language. I was fascinated to learn that this topic, the local language being learned by foreigners, was receiving some attention, though I was a bit surprised. When I'd asked students about their knowledge of Corsican over the previous months, this was usually met with nervous giggling; they'd offer a slang word or name a local food. The publication of the FLE class's alphabet photo book was, nonetheless, cause for celebration, as the school was clearly quite proud of the students' work, the article hung as a reminder of their job well done.

Continuing from the previous chapter's emphasis on the question of students' experiences of language and globalization in class, this chapter turns to print culture to explore how linguistic multiplicity is staged. The chapter begins to bridge the insular classroom and the wider public space by investigating alphabet books that combine language with illustrations of local things and places in order to show how multilingual dynamics (or their representations) differ between classrooms and other contexts. The main difference is that while French is obviously foregrounded in the FLE classroom, these books signal a foregrounding of Corsican, while (in part) engaging the very same student body. Here, I will compare and contrast two Corsican alphabet books (French *abécédaires*, Corsican *abicidì*). I will analyze the staging of language therein to explore discourse on language-and-place on contemporary Corsica. Analyzing these texts allows for the opportunity to question how such representations are influenced by institutional and political factors, and how these representations might reflect wider social trends.

The two texts I present, though quite different, both reflect and contribute to sociolinguistic placemaking—transforming physical space into meaningful place via language (Johnstone, 2011)—which inevitably also involves local culture, politics, and community. This chapter explores questions such as, To what end are different languages, vocabularies, and concepts deployed in the representation of language-and-place dynamics? How should we interpret them? According to the books, how are allophones expected to participate linguistically as members of the local community? I will briefly introduce the importance of alphabet books as regards language ideologies, including an explanation as to how we might read them via a linguistic landscape (LL) approach (Daly, 2019). The chapter concludes with a discussion of the differing representations of Corsican and the politics of language maintenance and revitalization.

§3.1 *Abécédaires*

Alphabet books are one locus at which to investigate language ideologies. As such, they are particularly useful artifacts[1] for the study of minoritized languages and non-standardized codes and gesture to important issues for cases of language maintenance, revitalization, and reclamation such as script and lexical choice, ordering (in the case of bi-/multilingual texts), and intergenerational transmission. As language ideological and pedagogical tools, they carry implications for the study of multilingualism more generally.

Tracing the history of ABC texts from the Middle Ages to the present, Litaudon (2014) analyzes how discourses therein reflect wider social trends such as class struggle, the development of industrialization, distinct religious and secular pedagogical approaches, and the relationship between art and language in teaching/learning. Alphabet books in France were historically used as one tool among many with which to render the population literate in French and eradicate *patois*. Indeed, alphabet books have been used for various economic and political projects such as standardizing communicative practices within a single national language, enticing rural populations with promises of technological progress, and advocating for multicultural/multiethnic coexistence, not to mention much more violent examples of overt war propaganda (Litaudon, 2014: ch. 8). Each of these is clearly not without its own history of struggle and conflict. Though today ABC books may often escape close scrutiny, they are anything but disinterested and reflect ideological projects at play throughout the history of children's literature.

Here I focus on representations of language and place in alphabet texts. Studying language and place draws from work in human geography and the broader humanities to investigate "how places can be socially constructed through language" (Johnstone, 2011: 203). Work on language and place

> explores the dialectical relationship between physical space and meaningful place: spaces become human places partly through talk, and the meanings of places shape how people talk. 'Discourse' in this sense refers to talk, writing, and other practices

---

1 What Litaudon (2014) refers to as "l'objet-livre" (319–20).

involving language, as well as to the ideology that is produced and reinforced through talk. In other words, it is through ways of talking that arise from and evoke particular linked sets of ideas that people come to share or attempt to impose ideas about what places mean and how to behave in them. (211)

With a similar emphasis on place, work on LLs attempts to study the "symbolic construction of the public space" (Ben-Rafael et al., 2006). The alphabet books I analyze are artifacts representative of the discursive complexity involved in trying to both crystalize and teach a multifaceted linguistic ecology and its relationship to place.

For the purposes of my analysis, I draw on approaches to the study of LLs, focusing on the semiotic construction of space via language, materials, colors, symbols, and so forth (Scollon & Scollon, 2003; Blommaert, 2013). Previous work (Aronin & Ó Laoire, 2012) has termed the LL of educational spaces the "schoolscape"; signage and texts within the schoolscape represent language ideologies at work in pedagogical tools such as textbooks (Aronin & Ó Laoire, 2012; Mendes, 2020). Daly (2019) analyzes the LL of multilingual picturebooks, positing that "each picturebook can be considered a small LL in its own right" (281). Daly explores the construction of dominance, differential status, and competition for space between various languages, showing that "multilingual picturebooks mostly reproduce existing power structures" (298). She found that dominance was illustrated by text order, size, and font, which reflected relative status and institutional support. Meanwhile, linguistic diversity, including orthographic diversity with the inclusion of different scripts, was largely symbolic rather than informational. Nonetheless, one important conclusion Daly draws is that picturebooks can aid in readers' development of print literacy, including the development of an awareness of relative status—and thus an explicit knowledge of power relations—among languages as reflected in their representations together. In this way multilingual picturebooks can play important roles in language maintenance and revitalization efforts, rendering hegemonic power structures explicit and thus prone to interrogation and potential change. My reading of the two Corsican alphabet books draws on Daly's LL approach to reading multilingual picturebooks, with close attention to semiotics and power dynamics at play in the texts.

§3.2 *Abbiccì dì*

Frédérique Bertrand's (2015) *Abbiccì dì* is the product of a collaboration between the author-illustrator, the Una Volta cultural center in Bastia, and the bilingual teacher's association A Scioglilingua. The title is a bit of a play on words. *Abbiccì dì* is a spelling variant that doubles the first two consonants (as opposed to *abicidì*).[2] Additionally, by having *dì* stand alone, it becomes the verb "to say," and thus reflects the idea of saying the ABCs. The text begins with an introduction in Corsican (without a French gloss) by Bastia's then-mayor Gilles Simeoni (see Introduction). He explains that the project began as a game of 22 cubes decorated with letters and images. The game was then "put to the test" and used at a local bilingual school over the course of a year before then being turned into a hardcover publication for purchase (2).

The book version presents the images as if one had flattened out a cube, six square images meant to fold into a 3D box. The text is a synoptic alphabet: it presents a variety of shapes of each letter (block/cursive, upper/lower case). Each centerfold features the six smaller squares on the left-hand side: one uppercase letter, one lowercase letter, one uppercase letter formed as a collage rather than normal print, the chosen representative (acrophonic) word written in block capitals in a similar collage style, the same word written in lowercase cursive, and finally an illustration of the focal word. The layout of the six squares changes with each letter, though they all share some borders as a reminder that originally these were the edges of actual physical cubes. The right-hand page of the centerfold features the entry's illustration with no words or letters.

The acrophonic words presented (those beginning with the letter they illustrate) vary widely; some are nouns (*manu*, hand), others are adjectives (*grande*, large/big) or verbs (*saltà*, to jump). Some are words one might readily expect of a contemporary alphabet book, such as *elefante* (elephant) or *luna* (moon). Others are rather surprising, like the opening entry *azezu* (angry).[3] The text also includes entries for the Corsican trigraphs *chj* [tj] (*chjucu*, small) and *ghj* [dj] (*ghjucà*, to

---

2   Corsican is not standardized in the normative sense; it is quite common to see spelling variants of the same word, sometimes even within the same text.
3   If we take all the words as representative of Corsica, this entry could perhaps be interpreted as a play on the stereotype of Corsicans as violent or angry.

play), considered letters unto themselves rather than three separate letters combined. The inclusion of dedicated space for these special letters demonstrates investment in specifically Corsican alphabetic conventions, and the inclusion of both print and cursive lettering brings further diversity to the text's visual presentation of graphic forms. The interplay of language and place in Bertrand's text is a simplified one that draws from isolated words chosen as representative of the island. For example, *pesciu* (fish) and *zinzì* (sea urchin) highlight marine life also featured in Corsican cuisine. Others, like *uva* (grape) and *castagna* (chestnut), underscore flora associated with local agriculture and traditional foodways. With an emphasis on this kind of nature-related vocabulary, it is thus unsurprising that *isula* (island) figures as the *i* entry, encapsulating the insular experience of Corsica. Nature, territory, and culture are presented alongside one another to illustrate Corsica.

Two other aspects reveal an additional layer of detail in the text. The *D* entry presents *diavule* (devil) as its featured word, a not-so-subtle gesture to various belief systems regarding evil, and, in my reading, somewhat surprising for a children's alphabet book. The spooky illustration centers on a fiendish red character with a frighteningly simple face, eyes, and horns. The other detail I'll call attention to appears in a brief note in the glossary where there is a clarification regarding the letter *H*: "U santacroce corsu conta 23 lettare trà e quale l'H. Nisuna parolla cummencia cun H, issa lettera ùn apparisce dunque micca in stu Abbiccì Dì. / L'alphabet corse compte 23 lettres, dont le H. Aucun nom commun ne commençant par H, cette lettre n'apparaît pas dans cet Abbiccì Dì" (The Corsican alphabet contains 23 letters, including *H*. Since no common noun begins with *H*, this letter does not appear in this Abbiccì Dì) (47). This passage, in Corsican, uses the word *santacroce* for "alphabet." French and Corsican distinguish between the alphabet (Fr. *alphabet*, C. *alfabetu*) and alphabet books (Fr. *abécédaire*, C. *abbiccì*). Alternative Corsican terms—*santacroce* (santa+croce, holy cross) or *salteriu* (psalter)—can mean either alphabet or alphabet book, and their etymologies reflect the religious tradition of these kinds of texts. *Croix de par Dieu* (Cross of God, Corsican: *santacroce*) can refer to the image of the cross at the beginning of early alphabet texts, a wooden cross-shaped table on which alphabets appeared historically, and an alphabet text as a whole (Litaudon, 2014: 375). The hint at a Corsican synonym (*santacroce* instead of *abbiccì*) is buried in the glossary

Image 3.1 *Ghjucà* (to play).
Credit: Frédérique Bertrand.

68   *Countervocalities*

Image 3.2 *Zinzì* (sea urchin).
Credit: Frédérique Bertrand.

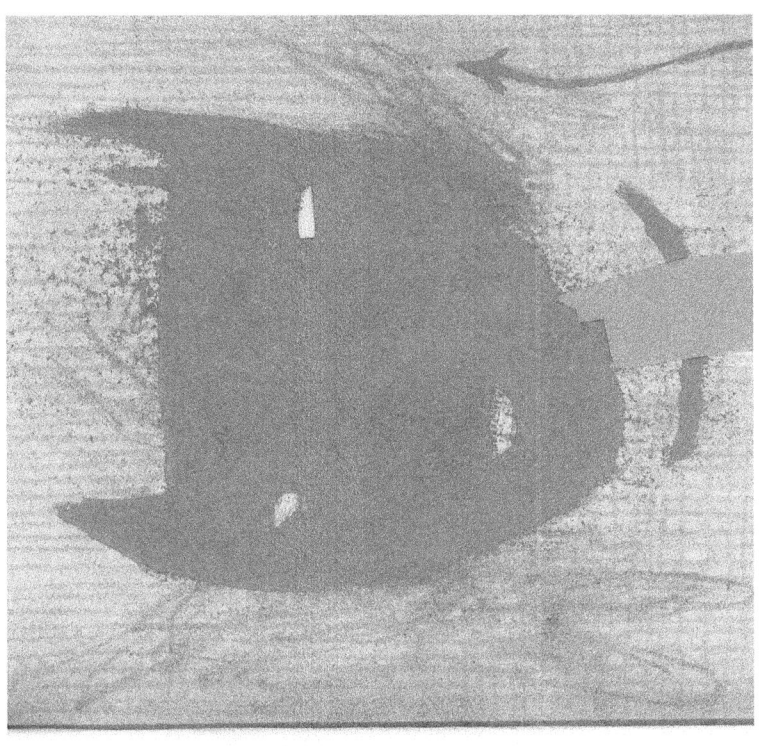

Image 3.3 *Diavule* (devil).
Credit: Frédérique Bertrand.

of Bertrand's text for those who know to look for it. These two details, *diavule* and *santacroce*, can be interpreted as small though clear connections between the history of the Corsican language and religious heritage on the island as connected with the teaching of reading and writing historically. Literacy in Corsican, in all its many varieties, is multilayered, akin to Blommaert's (2004) layered simultaneity, and can often seem labyrinthine.

The text's introduction by Simeoni briefly explains the collaboration between the author-illustrator and the cultural and teaching nonprofits. It goes on to state:

> Oghje hè per noi una primura maiò di pudè permette à tutt'ognunu d'accede à sta creazione. Stu ghjocu torna libru chì palesa l'impegnu doppiu di Una Volta: quella in leia à tempu cù l'illustrazione cuntempuranea è cù l'amparera di a lingua corsa. (2)

> (Today it is our foremost concern to be able to permit anyone to access this creation. This game becomes a book that reveals the twofold task of *Una Volta* linked at the same time to contemporary illustration and to the learning of the Corsican language)

This introduction by the head of local government represents institutional support of the arts project—and of the propagation of the teaching and learning of Corsican more generally.[4] Simeoni takes care to underscore that making the game into a book can reach a wider audience (*à tutt'ognunu*, for anyone), not just children in a bilingual school. Indeed, readers could be of any language background.

The glossary at the end of the text presents the clarification on the letter *H* (mentioned above) in both Corsican and French as well as a complete list of the Corsican words and their French translations. Interestingly, then, we see that formal (political) messages, public statements like the introduction, are rendered monolingually in Corsican while secondary details, like the metalinguistic commentary in the glossary, appear bilingually in both Corsican and French. While the majority of the text is a visual weaving of illustrations with isolated Roman letters and Corsican vocabulary, the language choice creates a somewhat uneven form of address. That is, there is a notable

---

4 A wide range of political parties are in favor of promoting the Corsican language (see Introduction, above; Fazi, 2020).

difference between the monolingual introduction and main text versus the bilingual glossary: the body of the text is for the teaching of Corsican alone. Nonetheless, readers may have varying ease of access to portions of the text that appear solely in Corsican, depending on their knowledge of the language. In any case, the mayor's symbolic gesture to introduce the text monolingually in Corsican frames what follows with confidence and enthusiasm for public projects involving the language.

Bertrand's *Abbiccì dì* represents the creative transformation of a children's block game into a pedagogical text. The picturebook is a colorful and lighthearted endorsement of the learning of Corsican and vibrantly illustrates introductory vocabulary. Its publication is a feat of collaboration between several Corsican institutions (schools, cultural centers, government) in Corsican to promote Corsican—an artistic tool-keepsake for language activists, families, and learners alike.

§3.3 I Spy

I now turn to a Corsican ABC book that opens onto other languages, primarily French, the *Abicidì fotogràficu corsu-francese* (Corsican-French Photographic ABC Book, henceforth the ACF) produced by the Centre méditérranéen de la photographie (Mediterranean Photography Center, CMP) in 2015–16. My goal is to investigate the staging of language and the local cityscape, following Daly's (2019) approach to studying the LL of multilingual picturebooks, to better understand the ideologies promoted therein.

In Fall 2015, the CMP undertook a project to create a bilingual ABC book which would combine the learning of Corsican and French with the fostering of an appreciation for Bastia's *patrimoine*. The CMP's approach explicitly engaged foreigners: the FLE class of newly arrived immigrant students from Chapter 2. The project aimed to teach Corsican and French language, a connection to the local *patrimoine*, and photography methods. In the words of the CMP director Marcellu Fortini, the goal was to "apprendre à lire et à regarder le monde en découvrant son lieu de vie … à travers la langue corse et la langue française" (teach to read and see the world by discovering the place where one lives … through Corsican and French) (personal communication, May 2017). The project represents a symbolic bridge between

Image 3.4 "A—Museu di Bastia—Palazzu di I Guvernatori Musée de Bastia—Palais des Gouverneurs" (tree, air, friendship).
Photo credit: Marcel Fortini, Centre méditerranéen de la photographie.

corsophones and allophones, or at least between Corsican alphabet books and bi-/multilingual ones.

Two important formal differences between Bertrand's *Abbiccì dì* and the ACF are their shape and medium. Bertrand's text is a square print book, which Litaudon (2014) explains has historically signaled a text for young children (194–5). The ACF, by contrast, is a vertical letter-sized internet publication, which orients its readership as both older and able to navigate digital texts. The first entry of the ACF is a photograph of a beige building against a clouded sky. The photo frames the building's clock tower. There are ornamental spirals on either side of the tower, and the top of the building provides a horizontal line dividing it from the sky. The top of the tower rises to a peak in the center of the page. The words *arburu/arbre*, *aghja/aire*, and *amicizia/amitié* are printed above the tower in the gray sky of the top of the page. Readers may at first be stumped as to the pairing of the words "tree," "air," and "friendship" with this building, as their combination is not self-evident.

Fortini explains that the process of making the ACF involved several steps. The students got to know the classic layout and formula of an *abécédaire* by analyzing examples in class and at the school library. The class took fieldtrips throughout town and students photographed objects in the local environment which resembled the forms of letters—for example, the triangular point of the *palais des gouverneurs*' (governors' palace) clock, in Image 3.4, was meant to resemble an *A*. Their photography venture was a game of I Spy. Fortini explained that the project, in teaching French and Corsican, aimed to "considérer la photographie comme une pédagogie du regard" (consider photography as a pedagogy of the gaze) (personal communication, May 2017). To accompany the photos, the class chose three words that began with the particular letter, an object, a place, and a moral value in Corsican and French. Given the students' limited knowledge of French and Corsican, it is reasonable to assume that, although it was a collective project, they would have had help coming up with words like *chjarezza* (clarity of mind) or *martellu* (hammer), and that the adults involved facilitated the selection of vocabulary to feature. The ACF is quite unlike other alphabet books that present introductory, everyday words (cat, house, sun, etc.); rather, it is a presentation of a specific set of vocabulary, ideas, and images chosen to best represent Corsica in objects, places, and values.

In navigating new sociocultural and linguistic environments, photographing shapes of letters in the local space demanded that the students be creative and consider new perspectives, literally (getting to know their new surroundings) and figuratively (in searching for the forms of the scripts they were learning). One can imagine the task of finding letters in the local cityscape could be difficult for those students still mastering the Roman alphabet. What's more, the meaning of the words could be difficult for readers to decipher, as the accompanying images—normally a core part of the pedagogical method of alphabet books (Litaudon, 2014: 242)—correspond only to the form of the first letter of the word: "Tout repose sur une confrontation formelle de l'objet et de la lettre, que l'enfant va devoir observer pour en relever les analogies" (Everything rests on a formal confrontation of the object and the letter, that the child must observe in order to pick up on the analogies) (113–14). Twentieth-century ABC books developed a tendency to present words and images that were unrelated to one another, aside from their first letter: "Toute la difficulté du jeu en effet naît de l'assemblage de ces mots" (The whole difficulty of the game is in effect born from the assemblage of these words) (118). In this way, these alphabet books are semiotic assemblages "that interpellate us into forms of socialization" (Pennycook, 2018: 121; Mendes 2020), in this case endorsing the Corsican *patrimoine* in its varied material and social facets, even if the words and images presented are at first seemingly unrelated.

The ACF includes introductory remarks, a paragraph each in French and Corsican from Emmanuelle de Gentili, then Première adjointe à la Ville en charge de la politique de la Ville, du renouvellement urbain et de la vie des quartiers, des affaires européennes et internationales (First City Deputy in Charge of City Policy, Urban Renewal and Neighborhood Life, and European and International Affairs) and Fortini, the Director of the CMP. Each page afterward is then a photograph of a place in the city's built environment (walls, streets, buildings, etc.) with the form of a letter as the central focus (e.g., the loose *A* shape of the *palais*). Accompanying the image are the three acrophonic words. Unlike the introductions, which appear in French first, the letter entries are presented with Corsican first and French second. The following are examples (the locations specified are taken from the text's index):

- C -   quartieru di Sant'Antone
        Quartier Saint-Antoine [Saint-Antoine neighborhood]
          Carrega – chaise [chair]
          Citadella – citadelle [citadel]
          Curaghju – courage [courage]
- CHJ – carrughju di u Collu – Rue du Colle
          Carrughju Dirittu – Rue droite [Right Street]
          CHJarisgia – cerise [cherry]
          CHJostru – cloître [cloister]
          CHJarezza – clarté (d'esprit) [clarity of spirit]
- L –   mediateca di u centru culturale Alb'oru
        Médiathèque du centru culturel Alb'oru [Alb'oru
        Cultural Center Library]
          Libru – livre [book]
          Liceu – lycée [high school]
          Laicità – laïcité [secularism]

In its presentation of bilingual vocabulary, the ACF is economic in only including words and concepts that are rather similar in both form and content across the two languages (e.g., *zelu* vs. *zèle*, zeal), an important factor to consider when presenting translated or multilingual ABC texts (Litaudon, 2014: 227). In doing so, the ACF, like Bertrand's text, utilizes the Corsican alphabet as its guiding framework, foregrounding the preference for Corsican over other languages. Corsican, unlike French, does not have *J*, *K*, *W*, *X*, or *Y*.[5] The inclusion of these letters would not allow for equivalent Corsican words in their entries. In other words, the inclusion of a word beginning with *J* would mean having to present French first in that entry, since the Corsican equivalents use other letters (e.g., French *jardin* gives Corsican *giardinu/ghjardinu*, garden).

One specific example of this is again the letter *H*, as we saw above in Bertrand's *Abbiccì dì*. *H* was introduced in *Intricciate e cambiarine*, the authoritative orthography of Corsican published in 1971 by Pascal Marchetti and Dominique Antoine Geronimi. *H* is used as a

---

5   *H* and *J* do, however, appear within the trigraphs *chj* and *ghj*. We can interpret the exclusion of these letters in the ACF, at least to a certain extent, as a sloughing off of all foreign linguistic (orthographic) elements—not only those imported via French influence, but any outside, non-Corsican source.

Image 3.5 "L—Mediateca di u Centru Culturale Alb'oru Médiathèque Centre Culturel Alb'oru" (book, high school, secularism). Photo credit: Marcel Fortini, Centre méditerranéen de la photographie.

convention in very few words, such as the plural of *amicu*, *amichi* [a.'mi.gi][6] and to distinguish à – a – hà (respectively "to"/"at," the singular feminine definite article, and the third person singular of *avè*, "to have," i.e., "has") and è – e – hè (respectively "and," the plural feminine definite article, and the third person singular of *esse*, "to be," i.e., "is"). Some sources exclude *H* as a letter unto itself in the Corsican alphabet since it is only used as a diacritic (Culioli et al., 2010; Gaggioli, 2012). Some purists refer to the *H* when used in Corsican as *l'acca bastarda*, "the bastard *H*."[7] Presumably for practical reasons, then, *H* is not included in the presentation of letters in the ACF, since the only two words that begin with *H* in Corsican are *hà* ("has") and *hè* ("is").[8] Rather than cede the priority of Corsican to French in this way, the ACF excludes these letters altogether, foregrounding Corsican alphabet/writing conventions.[9] The text does not give equal treatment to both languages; the bilingualism presented prioritizes Corsican.

The vocabulary included in the ACF's entries obviously offers much to explore with regard to language ideology. As we saw in the *Abbiccì dì*, alphabet texts often include underlying religious themes. While in Bertrand's *Abbiccì dì* the religious themes are slightly more overt (the reference to the devil and the use of *santacroce*), religious undertones in the ACF are even more subtle: the very first acrophonous word listed is *arburu/arbre* (tree). Litaudon asserts that often in contemporary alphabet books, "La prégnance du fond biblique … reste visible en palimpseste" (the weight of biblical content … remains visible in palimpsest) (227).[10] The tree (or apple) is a religious image that has lost its strictly religious symbolism as the tree of knowledge, the forbidden, or unknown, and has come to signal the pursuit of secular reason (Litaudon, 2014: 259–62).

---

6   N.B. the difference from the Italian plural *amici* [a.'mi.tʃi]
7   Recall that *h* is not considered a distinct/separate part of the Corsican trigraphs *chj* and *ghj* since these should be read as letters unto themselves rather than "*c + h + j*" or "*g + h + j*," respectively.
8   See Jaffe (1996, 1999) for a discussion of language ideology as related to Corsican orthographic conventions.
9   The exclusion of these letters does create cohesion, since in this way all of the entries for each letter begin with the same letter in both languages. The exception would be the trigraphs, which do not exist in French.
10   Regarding palimpsests in the Corsican linguistic landscape, see Chapter 5 §5.2.4.

In attempting to define Corsica as a unique culture entity,[11] ideas of language, culture, territory, and the built and natural environments are often conflated in conceptions of the Corsican *patrimoine* which draws from multiple sources (Mendes, 2020), and the ACF is no exception. The central focus of the presentation of *patrimoine* is that of the built environment (beyond mere roads, fountains, and lampposts: the *palais des gouverneurs*, the citadel, etc., all particular to the city) but which also incorporates the island's natural environment with the text's inclusion of nature-related vocabulary—*arburu* (tree), *petru* (stone). Like the *Abbiccì dì*, the ACF appeals to the island territory itself: the only shared word[12] between the two texts is *isula/île* (island). Indeed, as Litaudon (2014) notes, "l'élément fondateur de la nation, c'est le territoire" (the founding element of the nation is territory) (290). In addition, in the ACF, words for everyday objects are presented alongside social values like *dignità* (dignity), *tullerenza* (tolerance), and *ghjustizia* (justice)—an explicit declaration: in this place we endorse these morals. The ACF's pedagogical task becomes one of teaching its readership—newcomers to the island (the FLE students, also the text's authors)—Corsican language and place as well as expected behaviors. These categories, culture and nature (place) along with morals, overlap in the text: "Stories of place therefore become stories of morality" (Benwell & Stokoe, 2006: 218). This layering can be understood as an essentializing move that fosters particular behaviors (linguistic, spatial, moral) within the confines of the island territory.

While paying special attention to foregrounding Corsican space and language, the ACF simultaneously upholds French Republicanism with the inclusion of words like *laicità* (secularism) and *fraternità* (brotherhood). As Litaudon (2014: 10, 289) asserts in her analysis of Australian alphabet books, ABC texts are particularly prone to reflect a desire to define the unique character of a nation or community while continuing to orient to former colonial powers, "des apprentissages au service du pouvoir" (learning at the service of power) (268).

---

11 See, for example, Litaudon (2014: 289), in which she explores Australian alphabet books' attempt to define the nation with regard to territory, ethnicity, language, and history.

12 Though they are not exactly the same, Bertrand has *ghjucà* (to play) and the ACF *ghjocu/jeu* (game), gesturing to the ludic potential of learning through language and image.

Image 3.6 "U—Scale di Santa Chjara Rue Sainte-Claire de Bastia" (urn, university, utopia). Photo credit: Marcel Fortini, Centre méditerranéen de la photographie.

In imagining the city socioculturally, the ACF juxtaposes elements like the *palais des gouverneurs* with concepts like *natura* and *laicità*; the cultural, the natural, and the political are presented on equal footing. The *palais des gouverneurs* (the clocktower *A*) is iconic in Corsican history and represents a type of local authority that has withstood the test of time. It is a stronghold of Corsican culture and today houses the city's museum. The inclusion of *laicità/laïcité*, a notoriously French national value of secularism, undergirds the theme of integration as a driving force of the ACF. Indeed, "the display of the minority language does not necessarily overthrow the prevailing language ideology" (Pietikäinen & Kelly-Holmes, 2013: 224). That is, the foregrounding of the Corsican regional language and culture does not efface the biting undercurrent of French secular, integrationist influence. In this regard, the ACF presents a Corsican-French binary, an example of "the dual model of national identity, namely cultural as opposed to civic" (Blackwood & Tufi, 2015: 106). Cultural discourses can simultaneously orient to various authoritative ideologies. The natural environment of the island itself (*natura*) is caught in the middle of the struggle between the *patrimoine* of Corsican culture (the *palais*) and the politics of the French State (*laicità*). The ACF appropriately selects *utopia/utopie* (utopia) among its *U* entries; striking a perfect balance between Corsican and French socially, politically, and linguistically certainly seems quixotic.

The ACF represents a staged, fixed, and idealized notion of what constitutes the local *patrimoine* and how foreigners should approach it. As Fortini explains, the ACF is a tool that will "Inviter les nouveaux arrivants à apprendre le corse et le français ... mis à disposition des futurs arrivants étrangers" (invite newcomers to learn Corsican and French ... [and will be] made available to newcomers in the future) (personal communication, May 2017). It will serve as "un lien social d'insertion représentant un levier d'éveil à l'esprit critique et de dialogue entre les générations et les nationalités différentes" (a social connection of integration representing a call to critical spirit and dialogue between different generations and nationalities.) The ACF thus aims to teach newly arrived immigrants the local language and culture to then allow for its authors and users to serve as examples for future immigrants to the island. What is absent is a presentation of other languages. Gentili goes on to acknowledge the political importance of the ACF, stating:

> S'infatta chì a pulìtica de a Cità hè una pulìtica di inserimentu, di spartera è di scambii, di rispettu di sè stessu è nanzituttu di l'altru, a Cità di Bastia vole sustene i prugetti chì fàcenu da roba cumuna è framìschjanu e storie, i valori, e culture, l'idee è l'emuzioni. (Centre Méditerranéen de la Photographie, 2016)
>
> (Given that the politics of the City is a politics of inclusion, of sharing, and of exchanges, of respect for oneself and of others above all, the City of Bastia supports projects that share and mix stories, values, cultures, ideas, and emotions)

It is, then, the local city government, one of the project's supporters, that underscores the political nature of the Corsican version of inclusion put forth in the text. The ACF is anything but free from the institutions that shape it; it is not a disinterested linguistic record. On the contrary, it idealizes the multilingual make-up of the city to foreground Corsican.

§3.4 Mirrors

The FLE classroom context (Chapter 2) is laden with trajectories, discourses, and policies pushing and pulling social actors in multiple directions; these ABC books reflect less francohegemonic sociolinguistic orientations on the island with the appearance of more Corsican. The ABC texts are an example in which language pedagogy and kinds of signs intersect. The texts can be seen as mirrors, imperfect reflections of one another proffering rich examples of staged Corsican.

Litaudon (2014) develops a comprehensive typology of alphabet books broken down into four major categories, Lesson, Game, Activity, and Spectacle. She asserts that texts can and often do fall under more than one grouping: "Cette polyvalence est un critère souvent révélateur de l'ingéniosité d'un ouvrage, de sa richesse et de son intérêt pédagogique" (This criterion of polyvalence is often revelatory of the ingenuity of a work, of its richness, and its pedagogical interest) (367). Both texts under analysis here indeed pertain to multiple categories. Bertrand's *Abbiccì dì* is certainly a Lesson in its most basic function, but also a Game, having derived from a children's block set, and a Spectacle, since it highlights the artistry of the author-illustrator and was displayed in local exhibits. The ACF, similarly, is a Lesson that teaches multiple languages and vocabulary, an Activity in which students participated in collective authorship and artistry, and a Spectacle that underscores a photographic aesthetic.

ABC books are usually intended for early childhood education and represent a basic pedagogical tool for the development of literacy (broadly speaking), vocabulary, and morals (Litaudon, 2014). However, the linguistic choices made and vocabulary employed in these books (especially by the ACF) underscore that a reading of such a text is anything but neutral. Indeed, as Cotnam-Kappel (2014) asserts of reading language in public space on Corsica, "it is fundamental to reiterate that 'politics of representation becomes increasingly important—whose representations are these, who gains what from them, what social relations do they draw people into, what are their ideological effects, and what alternative representations are there' (Fairclough, 1999: 75)" (63). The ACF encourages the public's reading in a certain direction, to manipulate the public image of Corsican and to shape public opinion as to the place and role of language more generally: the text includes prominent landmarks of the local cityscape like the *palais des gouverneurs* as well as widespread ideals of French national identity like *fraternité*. These "semiotics of participation and belonging" (Blackwood & Tufi, 2015: 120) steer newcomers' learning of Corsican into a francohegemonic national narrative of citizenship. This endeavor to control the reception of the text and the reputation and ideological alignments of the corsophone community as represented in alphabet books is one that promulgates Corsican as the most valued minority language and cultural heritage of the island, within a wider French national frame.

While Daly (2019) argues that picturebooks reflect existing power dynamics, these ABC books show that they can also illustrate idealized, imagined, or desired sociolinguistic realities (Pietikäinen et al., 2017: 44). That is, the folding into the community or the ability to adopt Corsican on the part of newly arrived adolescents and the possibility for these efforts to serve as exemplary for other newcomers. If, as Daly argues, the LL of multilingual picturebooks is important in maintenance and revitalization of minority languages, like Corsican, she also concedes that they can "suppor[t] a certain language hierarchy. Some audiences are given more power than others" (296). While involving newly arrived immigrants, the ACF does not accord space to other minority languages or scripts—foregrounding instead the idea that these newcomers can or should take up local codes, Corsican and French. This is one paradox of language maintenance and revitalization: the endorsement of one language or variety can be (is) at the expense of others.

Leonard's (2011) notion of language reclamation is useful here. A nuanced take on maintenance and revitalization, reclamation orientations acknowledge contemporary realities of speakers and their practices, for example hybrid English-Miami use in digital communication (151–2). This allows for necessary flexibility and less stigmatization in attempts to foster a speech community in the minority language. The ACF should certainly be understood as a step toward language reclamation in that the project acknowledges the island's diverse cultural make-up as it involves newcomers' participation. In doing so, however, it foregrounds Corsican while linguistic diversity (the presence of other languages) is minimized (Groff, 2017: 143) and nearly erased (Irvine & Gal, 2000). Indeed, the only mention of other languages in the text is indirect—the end of the book lists the student-authors' nationalities, allowing readers to thus imagine the languages they might speak. This erasure points to what Jaffe (1999) calls the resistance of reversal, in which a minority language community endorses top-down models of language use. This orientation derives from a reaction to what the community experienced with the imposition of colonizing or imperial languages, for example Corsicans' experience of the imposition of French. These ABC texts in a way reflect this kind of reversal while foregrounding Corsican.

In a more recent study, Jaffe (2019) explores the "poeticizing of the economy" of the small Corsican village of Pigna. The artists' haven includes large amounts of Corsican in its signage and musical soundscaping which allows for an "intimate commercial relationship" in the sharing of the minority language and culture with consumers. This "tightly orchestrated" "staging of language" reveals "a redefinition of the role of language-as-practice in the collective imagination of how language is implicated in heritage [… and] in the making of place" (24–5). Corsican heritage is rendered attractive and accessible to tourist consumers largely via displays of the minority language. This underscores the question of when and how a minoritized heritage can or should be made available to outsiders: should it be taught to new residents? Should it be for sale?

The ACF is another example of carefully staging the Corsican language for a non-Corsican audience. Its "representational program" (Jaffe, 2019: 18) recruits newly arrived immigrants to paint a picture of Bastia, a staging of language in a placemaking project that imagines what things, concepts, and ideas to showcase as well as who should use what languages and how. While Jaffe's focus is tourism, the case of the ACF shows that the "creative local control over the way linguistic and cultural forms are mediated and staged" also applies to the migrant economy (2019: 13). That is, these same representational processes are recruited in interfacing with other kinds of outsiders, not just tourists but newly arrived immigrants as well; they offer Corsican for the endorsement of tourist consumers and new foreign residents of the island alike.

Despite the fascinating viewing these two ABC books offer, they are certainly not representative of widespread language shift; they speak from and to a relatively narrow audience of Corsophiles, language activists, locals, politicians, and educators as well as learners of Corsican. The two texts are also drastically distinct in their composition, for example in their material manifestation, one physical and one digital. And yet they offer insight into similar processes at work across media in the construction of Corsican alphabet books. Each is representative, in unique ways, of social actors creatively producing in a minoritized language. The profusion of a particular language in marked spaces or in print culture does not, however, indicate sociolinguistic vitality of the speech community. On the contrary, the presence of a thriving community of speakers of a given language may not be at all visible in publicly marked space (e.g., immigrant languages rendered invisible) (see Chapter 5).

In the *Abbiccì dì* and the ACF we can read "a LL of globalization experienced as exclusion" (Blackwood & Tufi, 2015: 115). Indeed, a restrictive incorporation of speakers of other languages is constructed, allowing for only particular kinds of multilingualism in the texts. For example, the inclusion of *laicità/laïcité* and the very limited visibility given to allophone identities reflect a carefully staged Corsican *bi-plurilinguisme* (Chapter 1). Recall (Chapter 2) that the languages of the class of newly arrived immigrant students who undertook the ACF project included Albanian, Arabic, Italian, Portuguese, Romanian, and Ukrainian, and their second/additional languages included Hungarian and English. The CMP gave lengthy explanations as to the inclusion of newly arrived foreigners in the work of constructing the bilingual imagery of the city in the ACF. Despite the local city policy to "aghjevuli l'inserimentu per via di a cunniscenza di e culture di e sfarente pupulazione, è aghjevuli dinù l'adopru di a lingua corsa" (favor integration by way of knowledge of different populations' cultures, and to also facilitate use of the Corsican language) (Centre Méditerranéen de la Photographie, 2016: 2), the remainder of the participants' language repertoires beyond Corsican and French, in which the students have a range of competencies, are absent. The foregrounding of Corsican in the texts appears as a kind of veneer with the power to render other languages mute, revealing a "relative invisibilité des langues d'immigration en context public ... et donc une forme de repli vis-à-vis d'attitudes portant à la mixité sociale" (relative invisibility of immigrant languages in public contexts ... and thus a form of withdrawal *vis-à-vis* attitudes surrounding diversity) (Ottavi, 2013: 145). Corsican is ideologically prioritized *vis-à-vis* French (and other languages) in the linguistic hierarchy presented.

Historically, alphabet books were often given as special gifts with a "fonction votive" (votive function) promising language as a means by which children would progress in their learning and in society

(Litaudon, 2014: 79–80). The votive functions of the ABC texts under analysis here are similar. While with Bertrand's text, Simeoni hopes the city can share the learning of Corsican in the local community, the ACF's hopeful function is that foreigners learn and use Corsican (and French) vocabulary as they become further acquainted with their host society. If legitimizing existing social order, constructing morals, and defending national identity are trademarks of ABC books throughout the nineteenth and twentieth centuries (Litaudon, 2014: 268), the ACF maintains these with the specific task of attempting to bring foreigners into the Corsican speech community.

But, despite the ACF's "fonction votive" to fold the foreign into the local by propagating the learning of Corsican (and French) by allophones, the text does so in a way that renders these newcomers' involvement in the project nearly invisible. Although the text is presented as a bilingual Corsican-French book, we can understand it as multilingual by virtue of the allophone students' participation and rich and varied linguistic trajectories. And yet, it's not quite that easy. Gramling (2016) asserts that "resolving that surface monolingualism conceals truly existing multilingualism is itself a political claim that obscures, in this case, the means by which speakers 'reconfigure the materiality of public space, and produce, or reproduce, the public character of that material environment' (Butler, 2011)" (80). That is, we must recognize the creative agency of these students in language learning endeavors in their new host society and how they choose to contribute to shaping contemporary multilingual Corsica.

At the same time, it is unclear how exactly, outside this school project, newly arrived immigrant students (can or should) use Corsican. A news article reporting on the publication of the ACF rightly observed that the newly arrived immigrant students involved in the project "doivent travailler davantage que les autres pour à la fois suivre leur scolarité, apprendre le français et le corse" (must work harder than the other [students] to both pursue their studies, [and] learn French and Corsican) (Carlotti, 2016). The obscured discrepancy is that at school the students really only focus on French, while the ACF presents an idealized pursuit of Corsican by foreigners (i.e. the idea that it is good that newcomers learn it). A holistic observation drawn from my fieldwork in the Sud FLE class (Chapter 2) was the obvious priority of learning French above other languages. FLE education's goal is achieving the benchmark of passing the DELF exam in order to mainstream allophone students into normal classes. So, the publicly professed hope in the ACF that students learn both French and Corsican is rather incongruent with what goes on at school.[13] Students in the Sud FLE class professed to have little to no knowledge of Corsican language/culture, with the exception of one or two hackneyed vocabulary words like *figatellu*, a Corsican sausage, or *fratè* (dude). I observed very little in this regard, aside from the students' apparently nearly nonexistent experiences of the Corsican language/culture, or at least their inability (or refusal) to render these explicit. It is perhaps ironic, then, that the ACF project engages these students to be model newcomer-foreign-learners-of-Corsican when they have relatively minimal opportunities for learning, practicing, or using the language.

Despite the best efforts of teachers and language activists to proffer the learning of Corsican, there are clear discrepancies between these desires and how these are able to be played out in school and in wider day-to-day life. Other institutionalized minority language situations have seen such discrepancies play out, as in the case of Schulte's (2018: 601–2) work on Romanian speakers in Valencia, Spain. For example, he observes that though there is a widespread awareness among this group that Romanian and Valencian share more formal similarities than Romanian and Spanish, the majority choose to learn and use Spanish. This, despite co-official status of Spanish and Valencian in the region and pervasive mixing of Valencian and Spanish in spoken discourse by both locals and foreigners. Policy and social efforts to render minoritized languages adoptable by immigrant allophones are no guarantee of their eventual use.

Litaudon (2014) asserts that ABC texts affirm children's ability to discover and make the world their own ("s'approprier," appropriate) (361). This notion of appropriation appears in both the *Abbiccì dì* and the ACF. While then-mayor Simeoni frames the learning of Corsican in the *Abbiccì dì* as "open" ("apertu") and foregrounds the idea of "access" ("accede") (Bertrand, 2015: 2), the ACF is more explicit. In a newspaper interview, CMP director Fortini explains that the project

---

13 Only two of the newly arrived immigrant students in the Sud FLE class at the time of my fieldwork were enrolled in Corsican language classes. If newly arrived students take an additional language beyond French, the majority choose English. To pursue yet another new language, presumably from scratch, is a serious commitment.

"consiste à apprendre le français et le corse, tout en découvrant sa ville. Les jeunes ont appris à voir, à lire, à écrire, à s'approprier quelque part ce territoire sur lequel ils vivent désormais" (consists of teaching French and Corsican while discovering one's city. The children learned to see, to read, to write, and in a way to appropriate this territory on which they now live) (Carlotti, 2016). Once again, both geographic and cultural elements (the island territory and the local language) are conflated into an idea of the Corsican *patrimoine* that can be appropriated by newcomers. This is striking given that, much like other minoritized languages, it is usually understood that Corsican is an insider code, a language of the private, family sphere, and not one keen to be shared with non-Corsicans. Thus, the ideas of openness, access, and appropriation, in my reading, function as a kind of permission for all kinds of learners to take up some use of Corsican, if minimal (Mendes, 2020). By offering the appropriation of Corsican and French, the ACF illustrates one example in which the local government and activists of the minority language revitalization cause attempt to render Corsican an unmarked, public language. In order to do so, minority languages that might seem "excessively obvious" in their regional context face the task of illuminating the permeating invisibility of hegemonic State languages (Woolard, 2016: 66).

What does it mean for newly arrived immigrants to have tools like these ABC texts at their disposal? Fortini asserts that the ACF "met en avant la volonté d'un mieux vivre ensemble" (foregrounds the will to better live together) (personal communication, May 2017). The shared ways of knowing reflected in these books have the potential to facilitate newcomers' growing awareness of their host society, providing symbolic and cultural capital and allowing for new, creative ways of social participation and access to information (Daly, 2019; Piller, 2016). As in Jaffe and Oliva's (2013) analysis of the use of Corsican in tourism on the island, we see how "the choice of languages and their functions *presupposes* and/or *stages* imagined linguistic communities, audiences, and linguistic interactions," much like the choice to foreground Corsican-French *bi-plurilinguisme* in the ACF (101; original emphasis).[14] French-Corsican *bi-plurilinguisme*, as implicitly endorsed in the text, "establishes criteria of better and

---

14   See also Pavlenko and Norton (2007) on "imagined communities."

worse citizenship" (Jaffe, 2020: 79). The Corsican "polynomic spirit" (Comiti, 2011) touts Corsican as "a tool for social cohesion" (Quenot, 2020: 154) and celebrates (French-Corsican) linguistic and cultural diversity. This particular social cohesion is undergirded by a drive to integrate and suggests "an idealized image of Corsicans as minoritized 'hosts'" as the island becomes home to speakers of various languages (Jaffe, personal communication, May 2018).

Litaudon (2014) argues that ABC books

> mettent en question le fossé longtemps maintenu entre artiste et illustrateur, entre public adulte et public enfantin. Sans doute, bien au-delà des clivages traditionnels, l'abécédaire contemporain interroge-t-il de façon essentielle les enjeux du langage et de sa transmission, entre dire, voir et savoir, entre littérature, art et culture. (195)

> (call into question the long-held division between artist and illustrator, between adult and children publics. Beyond a doubt, well beyond traditional cleavages, the contemporary ABC book essentially interrogates the stakes of language and its transmission, between speaking, seeing, and knowing, between literature, art, and culture)

We can add to this list the blurred distinction between author and reader/learner as the students have become participating author-photographers. Importantly, with the shifting hierarchies of dominant, minoritized, and heritage/immigrant languages in the texts, we see a fostering of translanguaging that theoretically considers a holistic repertoire of the languages present in the community (corsophones, francophones, allophones). Further, the ACF is illustrative of what Canagarajah (2018: 43) has called "translingual practice as spatial repertoires" in which "the boundary between text and context [is] permeable." Indeed, "people use [spatial repertoires] to accomplish their communicative activities," and the ACF clearly shows this in the use of the local city spaces and shapes to illustrate discourses of Corsican culture.

Much like the wider linguistic landscape, alphabet books are reflective of the sociopolitical circumstances in which they are produced: "L'abécédaire, au fondement du savoir, transmet avec lui les principes idéologiques de son pays et de son temps" (The ABC book, at the foundation of knowledge, transmits with it ideological principles of its country and of its time) (Litaudon, 2014: 19). The teaching and learning of languages, paired with the discourses of language-and-place, combine to produce these rich language artifacts. In the case of newly arrived immigrant youth on Corsica, these texts are one example of having to cope with dynamics related to globalization outside our personal control, globalizing surges. This makes it difficult to answer what Litaudon identifies as a central question that ABC texts help us ask: "Que pouvons-nous dire du monde?" (What can we say of the world?) (264). Hard to tell, when we often do not have control over how our own story is told, the story of our languages and our voice.

This chapter has offered a reading of two Corsican alphabet books to explore representations of print culture in the minority language and multilingual sociopolitical dynamics therein. The ABC books draw from built and natural environments as well as particular national values in their construction of place. These places are comprised of inhabited, transhistoric, and local Corsican *patrimoines* (Mendes, 2020). Though not at all the same, the texts are "firmly anchored in physical spaces that narrate localized stories and relational processes within given sociocultural sites" (Blackwood & Tufi, 2015: 205). Bertrand's *Abbiccì dì* offers a playful children's text and vocabulary in Corsican. The ACF is a staging of bilingualism, promoting an integrationist perspective by way of coming to know the Corsican language, culture, and place. Both are endorsed by the local government in its broadcasting of the Corsican language, as it offers the territory and language for newcomers to adopt. And yet, Litaudon (2014) probes: "L'éducation acquise ne serait-elle, au fond, qu'un habillage, un vernis?" (Might acquired learning be, deep down, a costume, a veneer?) (320). These ABC books reflect a complex sociolinguistic situation for locals and newcomers, one that is represented with a particularly Corsican flair. The texts offer an artifactual record of contemporary Corsican language teaching and learning efforts. In the next chapter, I turn to accounts of language teaching on the island from the perspective of multilingual teachers.

Chapter 4

Stories

Introduction

I returned home exhausted after riding the bus back to my apartment in the *vieux port*, an additional half hour tacked onto my evening after finishing Corsican class. I had had long days running between schools, meetings, interviews, and night classes and felt tired. This particular evening, I attended a more advanced class at the suggestion of my teacher. In doing so, I had needed to reintroduce myself to the group who were curious to know about the newcomer in their class. I had practiced this brief introduction to myself over and over, in French and Corsican, but it seemed to never come out right in the moment when I was nervous. "I'm studying multilingualism among middle school students." I got blank stares. When Lucien, our teacher, began excitedly speaking of language dynamics and explaining that I had previously spent a year in Corsica, classmates seemed less closed. I felt it was Lucien's warmth toward me and apparent enthusiasm for my interests that facilitated my time in class. When a classmate asked me what languages I meant by "multilinguisme," Lucien jumped in saying, "anglais, italien, corse, bien sûr" (English, Italian, Corsican, of course), and then turning to me, "Ici, c'est plutôt le bilinguisme" (Here, it's more bilingualism). Throughout my work, situations like these have proven to be moments in which it is difficult to not feel shut down all while trying to maintain a curiosity about how we (participants and I) were talking past one another about (and sometimes in) different languages. Here I further explore these slippages.

This chapter presents my reading of interviews conducted with educators on Corsica. These teachers are colleagues and acquaintances who teach (or taught) various languages in and around Bastia. In analyzing the data, I draw from Menard-Warwick's (2014) comparative study of teacher identity wherein interviews are read as narratives that participants co-construct with the researcher, presenting identities, ideologies, and pedagogies bound to teachers' subjective experiences of language teaching and globalization. My goal is to examine participants' understandings of multilingualism and globalization—what they are, what they are for, and how they manifest on Corsica. What are the language and globalization dynamics on the island as experienced and defined by these language teaching professionals? These accounts illustrate subjective experiences of "homogenizing and heterogenizing discourses" on the island (Jaffe, 2020: 80).

First, I discuss challenges I encountered explaining the topics of my work and situating myself among language educator-activist dynamics on Corsica. I draw from Bakhtin's (1981, 1986) theories of language and dialogue as well as work on multilingual teachers (Kramsch & Zhang, 2018) in order to frame the data. I then begin a reading of the interviews, weaving together participants' stories and my analysis throughout (Menard-Warwick, 2014). I give particular attention to participants' experiences with language and globalization phenomena on the island in order to tease apart divergent perspectives thereof. I conclude with a discussion of place, time, and embodiment as they relate to multilingualism and globalization on Corsica.

§4.1 Language Stories

Blackwood's (2008) study of Corsica identifies the (French) State, language activists, and islanders as the principle social actors involved in language policy dynamics on the island; these groups often overlap as identities and social positions inform various practices and policies. I will nuance this slightly and say that throughout my work I have needed to situate myself in the teacher-activist-islander complex of social actors in language education on Corsica. While teachers on the island certainly navigate French State policies and institutional contexts, here I focus on the subjective experiences of language teachers, their transnational trajectories: their life histories, language and cultural identities, professional pursuits, and pedagogical practices. By activism, here, I refer to both those actively involved in the Corsican "cause," namely language and cultural reclamation of Corsican, as well as the active engagement of language educators in promoting and investing in the languages they teach. Teaching, activism, and residency on the island—practices and places—affect one another. Thus, my role as a former educator in the Corsican school district, investment in Corsican language learning, and presence on Corsica (at the time of my fieldwork and previously) helped put me in conversation with those I interviewed as we share(d) personal, professional, and material interests and experiences, however partially.

The narratives (Kramsch & Zhang, 2018) that follow were recounted in semi-structured sociolinguistic interviews themed on issues of language, culture, and globalization on Corsica. These interviews should be understood as situated accounts of subjective experience, influenced by my presence and contributions as well as my and my interlocutors' positionings of one another; these data are necessarily co-constructed by interviewer and interviewees in dialogue (Menard-Warwick, 2014: 23; Kramsch & Zhang, 2018: 149). Together as interlocutors, interviewer and interviewees reproduce existing language ideologies and social relations "in and through the interview itself" as a site of collaborative meaning-making (Talmy, 2011: 40). My discussions with participants treated topics such as education, relationships, transnational mobility, employment and professional pursuits, cultural encounters, and current events. These narratives, fragmented and presented by the researcher (Menard-Warwick, 2014: 60, 91; Talmy, 2011: 31), are discursive instantiations of ideologies, beliefs, and material and symbolic practices. By discourse, we can "refer to concrete ways of 'conceptualizing the world in words' (Bakhtin, 1981: 292)" and their attendant, sometimes unspoken, ideologies and "material causes and consequences" (Menard-Warwick, 2014: 60). Gee (1990) broadly conceptualizes Discourse as "*saying-(writing)-doing-being-valuing-believing combinations.* [...] Discourses are ways of being in the world, or forms of life which integrate words, acts, values, beliefs, attitudes, social identities" (142; original emphasis). As they recount their experiences, participants often draw from the speech of other interlocutors in a kind of rehearsal of previous discourses. As Menard-Warwick (2005: 534) explains, "competing perspectives are constructed through dialogic voicing (Bakhtin, 1981) that draws upon varied societal discourses (Fairclough, 1992, 1999)." This voicing of others in our own utterances is reflective of Bakhtin's (1986: 76) idea of an ongoing "chain of speech communion" in which we all participate. The educators I dialogue with here tell stories drawing from a range of spacetimes to weave an account of linguistic and cultural experience, reflective of the ongoing task of attempting to establish a satisfactory multilingual subject position (Kramsch & Zhang, 2018: 221).

Participants' discussions of linguistic diversity on the island reflect what can be interpreted as heteroglossia, "an ongoing struggle between dialects, registers, and genres, in which standardized national languages (such as 'American English') compete for space, and no one language variety can view its own place as secure" (Menard-Warwick, 2014: 37). As Bakhtin puts it, "Languages throw light on each other: one language can, after all, see itself only in the light of another language" (Bakhtin, 1981: 12). Heteroglossia in these data is rather obvious given the fact that participants speak in and of diverse languages, dialects, and accents. While we can certainly see an ongoing struggle between language varieties on the island, I am more keenly interested in divergent notions of *combinations* of different languages that coexist and are more or less salient as evidenced by participants' stories, a kind of packaged jockeying (e.g., when I say "multilingual" and Lucien counters with "bilingual," above). What are the competing conceptualizations of linguistic multiplicity according to these language professionals? How are language hierarchies rearranged in their experience? These competing perspectives illustrate a multiplicity of voices, interviewer and interviewees included, variously contributing to wider "homogenizing and heterogenizing discourses" (Jaffe, 2020: 80) and their interrelated ideologies. As Gee (1990) explains, Discourses are "changing and often are not fully consistent with each other; there is often conflict and tension between the values, beliefs, attitudes, interactional styles, uses of language and ways of being in the world which two or more Discourses represent" (145). The tensions between conflicting discourses have elsewhere been called discursive faultlines, "competing ways of referring to and evaluating particular topics" (Menard-Warwick, 2014: 2; Kramsch, 1993). These discrepant accounts are the countervocalities I have sought to explore throughout the chapters, rendered all the more poignant here in participants' own words. In thinking about the ways that social, political, and economic forces relate to multilingual dynamics, participants often discuss how they see themselves *vis-à-vis* what I have been calling globalizing surges. Issues of global capitalism, as one facet of these surges, thus arise in the interviews and represent an integral part of participants' experiences with language and culture on the island.

Below, I present my discursive analysis of the interviews. The focal participants are educators working in various language-related capacities in schools throughout the greater Bastia region. Following Kramsch and Zhang (2018), I understand these teachers as "multilingual instructors" since they "know and use more than one language in their daily lives and live or have lived in more than one culture" (31). They come from Corsica, Italy, Morocco, Sweden, and Valencia (Spain) and range in age from mid-twenties to late fifties. I present them below in order of the amount of time they have spent on Corsica, from shortest to longest. Aside from one full-time, permanent teacher, the participants represent various positions that language teachers hold in the region, including language teaching assistant, long-term substitute, adult school instructor, and a teacher working between multiple schools and age groups. By drawing on narratives from an array of nationalities, ages, language backgrounds, professional positions, and length of time on Corsica, I illustrate the diversity represented within the language education network on the island. By way of their transnational mobilities, cultural knowledge, and linguistic expertise, these educators inform and enact particular understandings of multilingualism and globalization in the local Corsican context. Importantly, interviewees display a relative awareness of different stakes in their discussions of their language-related experiences on the island. For example, there are tensions between a foregrounding of economic and political concerns—securing employment versus supporting particular political causes—which further illustrate ideologies caught up in shifting language hierarchies. Rather than interviewing only "natives" or "locals," engaging with perspectives of those on the island temporarily or shorter-term underscores how language teaching as a market is caught up with mobility and the neoliberal economy on Corsica. In what follows, I present one participant at a time in an attempt to give as robust an account as possible of each voice represented.

§4.2.1 "Une langue assez ... rigolotte"

Giorgia[1] (Italy) is a middle school Italian language assistant.[2] She is from a "petit village" (small village) in Tuscany, a town she describes as smaller than Bastia, and holds an undergraduate degree in English and a Master's degree in French. Her mother studied French at university, and Giorgia participated in a semester abroad in Paris. She has found it easy to communicate with Corsicans, who she explains easily identify her as Italian by her accent. Upon conclusion of her time as a language assistant, she plans to work as an English-teaching au pair for a family in Mallorca.

Having completed her studies, Giorgia explains that the only work experience she had had prior to becoming a language assistant was waitressing, nothing at all to do with her university studies: "c'est pas évident que uh tu vas trouver un boulot juste parce que tu as un licence ou un Master, donc il faut s'adapter à n'importe quoi" (it's not easy to find a job just because you have a university degree or Master's, so you have to adapt to anything). She hadn't sought out the language teaching assistantship, and only saw it advertised by chance, which she describes as "vraiment au hasard" (really random). Neither did Giorgia specifically request Corsica in her application, leaving the region to which she would be assigned open to all possibilities. Cities in continental France share public resources with Corsica, in this case the available positions for language assistants.[3] Even having the choice to rank preferred regions in her application underscores Giorgia's relatively privileged position regarding her international mobility compared to that afforded some others (Chapter 2; Mendes, 2018b). Transnational trajectories are not entirely within one's control, but rather shaped by various institutions, human and material resources, the job market, and, as Giorgia says, chance.

Having observed similarities between Corsican and Italian throughout her time on the island, Giorgia compares the relationship between

---

1 All names are pseudonyms.
2 Language assistants typically spend around nine months on Corsica, about the duration of the school year. Giorgia was nearing the end of her time on the island.
3 This is similar to the *maisons d'enfants* to which unaccompanied minors are sent and for which Corsica serves as a kind of overflow for the continent (Chapter 2).

Corsican and French as similar to that between dialects and Italian (Tuscan) in Italy, languages of the family versus languages of the public sphere, in a classic description of a diglossic divide. Though she laments that she doesn't really have a dialect to speak of given that the variety she speaks is basically Tuscan, she describes each region in Italy as having its own language: "pour chaque ré-région il y a un dialecte, et ce sont vraiment des langues […] Ce sont vraiment des langues étrangères. Complètement à part" (for every re-region there is a dialect, and these really are languages […] These are really foreign languages, completely different). The linguistic plurality Giorgia identifies is generational and regional: dialects are varieties spoken by older generations and are used in their respective regions. Smith (2019: 64) has shown that regional sociolinguistic variation in Italy influences newly arrived migrants' conceptualizations of Italian. Similarly, we see here that a sensitivity to such dynamics can influence Italians' perceptions of linguistic diversity abroad. Compared to dialects in the Italian context, France's regional languages are undeniably less valorized than the national language, French. What surprises Giorgia in her appraisal of the Corsican situation is the institutional support the local language receives:

> Giorgia: ça a été une grande surprise de trouver de trouver cette langue corse […] qui était si important pour les gens qu'on allait l'étudier dans les écoles aussi, ça, ça m'a beaucoup étonnée, quand on, quand on étudie la langue uh à côté de l'anglais de l'italien, donc comme si c'était vraiment une langue du cadre euro-européen, et … bon j'ai, j'ai trouvé une langue assez … rigolotte mais en même temps qui est compréhensible parce qu'il est très proche de l'italien, donc uh, et ç-c'est une uh élément de uh, comment dire, de mm, qui te permet d'être proche aux Corses aussi.
>
> (Giorgia: it was a big surprise to find to find this Corsican language […] that it was so important for people that they study it in the schools as well, that, that really surprised me, when you, when you study the language uh next to English to Italian, so as if it were really a language of the European framework, and … well I, I discovered a rather … funny language but at the same time one that's intelligible because it is very close to Italian, so uh, and i-it's a uh element of uh, how to put it, of mm, that allows you to be close to Corsicans also)

To Giorgia, languages' coexistence in institutional settings is expected only among larger and more widely used "European" languages (like Italian and English in schools). Her qualification of Corsican as funny or amusing ("rigolotte") notwithstanding, Giorgia goes on to underscore how Italian-Corsican communication is facilitated by the languages' relative proximity, "les liens qu'il y a, géographiquement, culturellement" (the links that there are geographically, culturally) "qui te permet d'être proche aux Corses" (which allows you to be close to Corsicans). Geography and culture are closely aligned: languages are associated with the region they're from, and relative geographic (and thus cultural) proximity facilitates communication. She explains how locals in stores and around town often identify her as Italian by her accent and begin speaking to her in Italian or Corsican, stating that she often speaks more Italian or Corsican with locals than French. She says this is thanks to her being easily identified as Italian: "un Américain ou ... des gens espagnols ou un Anglais ne peut pas faire ça ... parce que déjà un Corse ne peut pas parler en corse et être compris par un Anglais ou un Américain" (an American or ... Spanish people or an English person can't do that ... because a Corsican cannot speak in Corsican and be understood by an English person or American). This intercultural communication is facilitated only between groups who understand one another as relatively "close."

The language teaching assistantship program in France accepts native speakers of various languages from around the world to work in French public schools as support for teachers and students, as Giorgia put it, as "un ambassadeur de ta langue et de ta culture" (an ambassador of your language and of your culture). Here, language and culture are embodied in the role of the language assistant. Giorgia describes the diverse make-up of the cohort of assistants she worked with in 2015–16, who ended up, in her view, naturally dividing into two sides: "le côté méditerranéen" (the Mediterranean side) made up of assistants from Italy and Spain and "le côté anglophone" (the anglophone side) made up of assistants from England, Scotland, and the US.

Curricular policies and enrollments inform which languages are offered in schools as well as the number of language assistantships available for various languages. French national and Corsican regional curricular policies at the secondary level have shown a bifurcation between the promotion of English and other European languages (especially German) on one hand and Mediterranean languages, particularly Western Romance, on the other (Mendes, 2021). The academic, professional, and language markets are divided geographically in what could be interpreted as a further instantiation of the Corsica-continent binary. What Giorgia describes is the Europe/anglophone-Mediterranean divide of these curricular policies brought to life in interpersonal dynamics among colleagues. Participants mentioned this divide among the students as well: the majority enroll in English as their first *langue vivante* (foreign language) and others choose Corsican, Italian, or others. I read the Mediterranean "rapprochement culturel" (cultural merger) that Giorgia mentions as an echo of her experience of easily communicating with Corsicans and "being close" to them thanks to the cultural and linguistic proximity of Italy and Corsica. The way she describes this division pairs speakers' languages and nationalities such that, *intra*textually (Menard-Warwick, 2014: 99), we see that language, culture, nationality, and geographic region often all are conflated when discussing language teaching and teachers' backgrounds.

Giorgia shared how in her teaching she explored things like Italian cuisine as well as topics like racism, as she brought songs and other aspects of her culture to share with her classes. She underscores that a language assistant "c'est d'une importance fondamentale" (is of fundamental importance) allowing students to hear "un vrai accent italien" (a real Italian accent). As she explains, even if teachers are well-traveled or have Italian heritage, "quand même ils sont pas Italiens" (they still are not Italian). If a language assistant works well, she asserts, it is "une chose très précieuse" (a very precious thing). Cultural explanations and pronunciation are understood as "real" because they come from a real Italian person, and not the teacher, something Giorgia finds completely natural. On one hand, this essentializing discourse can be understood as upholding impossible standards of perfect native speakers in classroom settings, which precludes most learners from establishing legitimacy in the target language. Even if language assistants can serve as a cultural resource, their presence may reinforce the notion of languages as bounded and separate entities that, even with professional practice, years of travel experience, and family ties, cannot be fully or truly accessed by "non-natives." This seems counter to Giorgia's previous insistence on fluid intercommunication between Italian and Corsican. In other words, though she insists one can speak across divides, there is still some sort of divide. On the other hand, upholding assistants' expertise as native speakers provides them some professional legitimacy (Kramsch & Zhang, 2018), even as they are often the newest, youngest, and least experienced colleagues in their schools.

In addition to the special language dynamic she saw on the island, Giorgia observed that locals were somewhat closed to outsiders. This is often explained via discourses of insularity when discussing cultural difference on the island, something Giorgia reiterated:

> Giorgia: le fait que c'est une île et renfermé ça-ça conditionne beaucoup je dis la la jalousie et l'attachement qu'ils ont à leur île et ça-ça mène aussi à être renfermé par rapport aux autres, aux autres et je pour les autres je dis les autres en général et les Français aussi.
>
> (Giorgia: the fact that it's an island and closed off that-that influences a lot I mean the the possessiveness and attachment that they have for their island and that-that leads also to being closed off in relation to others, to others and I by others I mean others in general and the French also)

This closed-off attitude is sometimes described as necessary for preserving the island (see below), and Giorgia concurs, finding a positive side to this detachment: "c'est une mentalité renfermée, donc uh ça je l'apprécie pas mais, oui, je j'apprécie certains côtés, ç-, j'apprécie le fait d'être lié comme ça à-à ses origines à-à sa langue ça je l'apprécie beaucoup" (it's a closed-off mentality, so uh that I don't really appreciate but, yes, I I appreciate certain sides, I, I appreciate the fact of being tied like that to to one's origins to to one's language that I appreciate very much). Thus, even for non-Corsicans, a certain closure can be good in order to maintain a connection to one's origins and language.

This connection with one's roots is part of what Giorgia sees as a grounded sense of familiarity with one's surroundings on Corsica. She juxtaposes this feeling of belonging with a feeling of being disoriented in large cities such as Paris or Lyon. Having studied in France for a semester during university, Giorgia recalls Paris as much more difficult to navigate than Bastia. The absence of a booming city allows for the possibility of establishing friendships, communicating more easily, and leaving one's mark: "xxx l'impression que j'ai laissé une trace là" (xxx the feeling I've left a mark here). Place—and the specific make-up of a place—influences one's affective meaning-making more broadly.

§4.2.2 "Ils ne vont pas te comprendre"

Miquela (Valencia, Spain) is a long-term substitute teacher for middle school Spanish and has been on Corsica for three years. She holds a degree in Human Resources and has also studied Anthropology, which fed her initial interests in languages. Her French learning progressed as she developed a relationship with a Corsican man, whose family helped her learn about the local culture, including the similarities between Valencian and Corsican. She is considering pursuing a CAPES (national teaching credential) to remain in France as a Spanish teacher.

Unhappy with working in human resources in Valencia, Miquela identified au pair work in France as one means by which she could travel and learn another language. In deciding where to go, she compared Corsica and Paris. Much like the islanders, for Miquela Corsica constitutes much of what Paris is not, in its faraway geography as well as in the lifestyle there (i.e., an island not a major capital city), attractive even to someone who has never traveled to Paris or Corsica. Miquela recounts the trip of a lifetime getting to the island:

> Miquela: c'était le voyage de ma vie, parce que je devais le faire moi seule en voiture, tu vois? Et c'est bien d'arriver jusqu'à Barcelone et tout ça, parce que j'ai fait toute la route de la Méditerranée. Mais après quand je suis arrivée en Catalogne, je devais croiser la frontière, je n'avais plus de repères, je ne parlais pas la langue, j'avais une petite carte comme ça, et voilà.
>
> (Miquela: it was the trip of a lifetime, because I had to do it alone by car, you see? And it was fine getting to Barcelona and all that because I did the whole coast road. But then when I arrived in Catalonia, I had to cross the border, I had no points of reference, I didn't speak the language, I had a little map like this, and that's it)

Even given the relative geographic proximity of Corsica to Spain, linguistic, physical, and logistical hurdles to reaching the island proved quite considerable and involved crossing international borders and the sea and therefore multiple modes of transportation (car, ferry). Reaching Corsica, literally and figuratively, requires significant effort.

Having arrived in Corsica with almost no French, Miquela underscores how her relationship with her Corsican boyfriend facilitated her understandings: "il y avait beaucoup de codes que je n'arrivais pas à comprendre, beaucoup beaucoup, même si c'est une culture méditerranéenne" (there were a lot of codes I couldn't understand, really a lot, even if it's a Mediterranean culture). Throughout her time on the island, particularly with her boyfriend and his relatives, Miquela observes that locals speak neither fully in French nor Corsican, but in a kind of hybrid, densely inflected by the island's history and politics:

> Miquela: c'est pas du français, ce n'est pas non plus le corse, parce qu'ils n'utilisent pas trop. Par exemple mon ex-copain il parlait mi-corse, mi-français parfois. Donc c'était très intéressant parce que là tu vois beaucoup les influences de l'histoire, comme l'Italie a influencé la langue corse, et comment les Corses ils essaient de parler en français, mais aussi en s'appuyant dans sa nation, tu sais, corse, avec ces petites expressions, ça m'a beaucoup marquée, et là j'ai vu que, je ne sais pas, que c'était, que j'avais fait un bon choix, c'était très cool de voir.

> (Miquela: It's not French, and it's not Corsican either, because they don't use [it] a lot. For example, my ex-boyfriend spoke half Corsican, half French sometimes. So it was interesting because there you see clearly the influence of the history, like Italy influenced the Corsican language, and how Corsicans try to speak French, but by also relying on their nation, you know, Corsican with its little expressions, I was really struck by it, and there I saw that, I don't know, that it was, that I had made a good choice, it was really cool to see)

Miquela equates the Corsican language with the Corsican "nation," an important conflation in the language-culture-nation composite as they are envisioned as the Corsican *patrimoine* in the wider popular imagination (Mendes, 2020: 160). Her boyfriend helped her to get to know the island and its culture by telling spooky stories from the mountains and introducing her to traditional dishes such as *pulenda* (chestnut flour polenta) and *figatellu* (boar sausage). Beyond learning about local lore and cuisine, Miquela's relationship with her boyfriend's family was an investment in cross-linguistic communication which required patience and an active desire to understand the other: "parfois on arrivait pas trop à se comprendre, mais comme c'était des gens qui voulaient me comprendre on a toujours eu la façon" (sometimes we couldn't understand one another much, but since they were people who wanted to understand me we always found a way).

Over the course of her time on the island, Miquela gradually learned and improved her French. While she found some locals very willing to listen and patiently try to understand the speech of someone learning the language, she describes other mundane activities that were rendered difficult by "des gens qui … ne voulaient pas te comprendre" (people who … did not want to understand you):

> Miquela: Si tu vas comme pour acheter du pain, tu vas acheter du pain, et tu vas trouver la vendeuse qui va être très souriante, et quand tu vas lui parler en français avec ton accent espagnol: "ah madame, désolée, qu'est-ce-que vous dites?" et c'est une baguette, il n'y a que des baguettes, tu vois? Mais non, elle ne va pas te comprendre. Et après, je ne sais pas pourquoi, je crois qu'aussi autre chose, parce qu'ici j'ai rencontré plus d'étrangères que quand j'étais chez moi parce que je suis étrangère donc, de toutes les nationalités, et là tu vois aussi qu'on a tous un accent, mais on se comprend. Même si on dit n'importe quoi, et après, et on parle pas du tout la langue française. Et tandis que tu vas parler avec des Français,[4] tu vas faire l'effort de parler le mieux possible, ils ne vont pas te comprendre. Et ça, ça m'a fait beaucoup rigoler, mais c'est une expérience que je n'avais pas avant. C'était intéressant.

> (Miquela: If you go like to buy bread, you go to buy bread, and you find the seller who will be very smiley, and when you go to speak to her in French with your Spanish accent: "ah madame, sorry, what are you saying?" and it's a baguette, there are only baguettes, you see? But no, she will not understand you. And after, I don't know why, I think also something else, because here I've met more foreigners than when I was at home because I'm

---

4 N.B. the conflation of francophones as French people.

a foreigner so, all nationalities, and there you also see that we all have an accent, but we understand one another. Even if we say whatever, and then, and we are not at all speaking the French language. And whereas if you go to speak with French people, you will make the effort to speak as well as possible, they will not understand you. And that, that made me laugh a lot, but it's an experience that I didn't have before. It was interesting)

While communication breakdown can occur in the seemingly most simple of activities, communication among foreign friends in French as a common language seems to happen just fine, even if everyone has an accent and even if what they speak is "not at all" French. Miquela paints a picture of a community where French is used, but very differently by different groups. Corsicans "try to speak French," but end up using a mix of French and Corsican. When foreigners try to use French, their accents can be a significant obstacle, as interlocutors "dubiously clai[m] not to understand" (Smith, 2019: 74; Lippi-Green, 1997). In other words, there is no French that is not infused (Benor, 2019) by something else; there is no neat, neutral French. This contrasts starkly with the widely upheld francohegemonic ideology of needing to produce a perfect Standard (Chapter 2).

After a year working as an au pair, Miquela explains, "je voulais trouver un travail plus sérieux" (I wanted to find a more serious job). She had researched how to become a Spanish teacher and was in the process of applying for the licensure program when the opportunity to work as a long-term substitute suddenly presented itself; much more quickly than she'd anticipated, she was given the keys to her classroom and her student rosters. This sudden change of job can be read as an echo of Giorgia's assertion (above) that one "must be prepared for anything" as far as work, even if it is not related to one's studies or training, a flexible thinking-on-your-toes required by the unpredictable global job market—caught up with language.

Suddenly a brand-new Spanish teacher, in her classes Miquela saw a celebration of cultural diversity brought by students of different national and linguistic backgrounds:

Miquela: J'ai vu dans les cours qu'il y avait beaucoup, surtout pour les élèves que c'était leur première année d'espagnol, ils étaient très attirés de voir qu'il y avait des mots, pour les Magrébins par exemple, qui ressemblaient à l'espagnol, donc c'était

Alex: En arabe?

Miquela: Oui, en arabe, oui. C'était très cool et je voyais comme eux ils se sentaient plus touchés, du coup ils étaient plus intéressés à apprendre la langue, pour les Portugais ils comprenaient tout, tout ce que je disais ils le comprenaient. Donc je voyais beaucoup aussi cette multi-culturalité dans les cours, ça enrichissait beaucoup parce que ces élèves qui étaient d'autres nationalités qui comprenaient bien, ils poussaient les autres et ça les donnait envie aussi de connaître même la culture au Maghreb et la culture portugaise, et c'était cool. Ils proposaient leurs chansons pour les écouter ensemble dans les cours, on voyait les rythmes différents.

(Miquela: I saw in the classes that there was a lot, especially for the students that it was their first year of Spanish, they were really attracted to see that there were words, for the North Africans for example, that resembled Spanish, so it was

Alex: In Arabic?

Miquela: Yes, in Arabic, yes. It was really cool and I saw how they were touched, so they were more interested in learning the language, for the Portuguese they understood everything, everything I said they understood. So I also saw a lot of this multiculturality in the classes, that enriched it a lot because these students that were of other nationalities that understood well, they pushed the others and that made them also want to know the culture of the Maghreb and Portuguese culture, and it was cool. They brought their songs to listen to them together in the classes, we saw the different rhythms)

Similar to the notion of *bi-plurilinguisme* (Chapter 3) which foregrounds Corsican and French in a tight nexus of translingual practice and ideologically upholds them hierarchically in Corsican society, modern language curricula in the Corsican school district often foreground the Mediterranean in their promotion of language study (Mendes, 2021; Evers, 2018). These curricula are a kind of extension of the *bi-plurilinguisme* discourse that frames multilingual dynamics on the island as inclusive of other western Mediterranean Romance languages, underscoring for example Corsican's proximity to Italian and Spanish as codes and cultures of nearby areas. Often, though these curricula explicitly promote a sort of holistic Mediterranean linguistic diversity, languages of North Africa, notably Arabic, are usually not included (Mendes, 2021: 184). Miquela, however, saw these Mediterranean connections actively arise in her class as students discovered similarities between languages and shared parts of their cultures, via music for example. She even discovered similarities between Corsican and her native Valencian when Corsican teachers would ask her about certain words. Mediterranean multilingualism in the school setting can thus be inclusive of languages often excluded from the curriculum (Arabic) and even other Romance minority languages (Valencian).

Miquela saw a particular pride in Corsican identity among her adolescent students:

> Miquela: Et les élèves corses, j'ai vu beaucoup de nationalisme dans les cours, et genre les premiers jours, c'était une petite activité pour se présenter, (et j'étais): "je ne suis pas français, je suis corse!" tu vois des petites choses comme ça, que d'avance ils veulent te dire, ils veulent (t'en penser) que tu saches bien que tu traites pas avec un Français, tu vois? Et on voyait comment tous les élèves
>
> Alex: Déjà à 12 ans, à 10 ans.
>
> Miquela: Oui, ils prennent parti de leur identité, tu vois? Et ça c'était très intéressant pour moi.
>
> Alex: Donc ils se présentaient en espagnol en disant ça?
>
> Miquela: Oui, avec leur accent corse: "Yo me llamo" [imitates Corsican accent]. Tu sais l'accent corse, c'était très très cool de l'entendre.
>
> (Miquela: And the Corsican students, I saw a lot of nationalism in the classes, and like the first days, it was a little activity to introduce yourself, and (I was) "I am not French, I am Corsican" you see these little things like that, that right away they want to tell you, they want you (to think) to know well that you are not dealing with a French person, you see? And we saw how all the students
>
> Alex: Already at twelve years, ten years old.

Miquela: Yes, they decide upon their identity, you see? And that was very interesting for me.

Alex: So they introduced themselves in Spanish saying that?

Miquela: Yes, with their Corsican accent "Yo me llamo" [imitates Corsican accent]. You know the Corsican accent, it was very very cool to hear)

The foregrounding of Corsican identity is labeled as nationalist. Corsican identity shines through in students' speech in their pronunciation patterns, as they have overlain their Spanish with typical Corsican intonation,[5] something I recall hearing during my time teaching English on the island. Corsican identity is thus agentively infused (Benor, 2019) into speech in French and other languages.

Miquela admits that racial tensions often accompanied students' remarks in class, that connections to Corsican identity among adolescent students gave way to slurs and a physical division in her classroom between Corsicans on one side and students of foreign descent on the other. She sees this as due to a lack of broader cultural awareness, related to the changing nature of contemporary Corsican society today, for example locals' growing awareness of Portuguese populations on the island with the latter increasingly making up an important part of the workforce, especially in construction. As Miquela identifies recent trends in economic immigration on the island, she also discusses the role language teachers and assistants have to play in helping foster open-mindedness through cultural exchange: "c'est très bien je trouve pour une ouverture de leur esprit" (it's very good I find for opening their mind). The presence of immigrants in all three dimensions of the student-parent-teacher axis she describes (her students, their parents, and Miquela herself) is at the heart of both tensions and the forging of conviviality on the island.

---

5   Corsican intonation is characterized by heavy penultimate stress with a sharp de-emphasizing of final syllables, which sometimes disappear, especially in southern varieties (see Jaffe, 1999; Romano et al., 2011).

§4.2.3 "My weakness was my strength"

Elsa (Sweden) has lived in Bastia for five years and works teaching English for Tourism at a local adult school. She studied feminism and sustainable development at university in Sweden before going on to work for ten years at a yoga and wellness center based in India, traveling the world with her boyfriend teaching, including across Europe and the US. She has also taught English in villages in India. She says that on Corsica she is often mistaken for a German tourist because of her blond hair and blue eyes. She speaks Swedish, Norwegian, German, English, Tamil, Spanish, and French as well as some Danish and Swiss German.

Elsa came to language teaching unexpectedly, and her work depends on the season. This seasonal or temporary nature of various language teaching positions is a defining element of many instructors' experiences. Participants were driven to temporary teaching positions by chance like Giorgia, out of interest like Miquela, or out of necessity like Elsa. As a young adult returning from a stint in Ireland to her hometown in Sweden, Elsa was able to secure work as a substitute for a teacher on maternity leave thanks to her reputation as a good student at the middle school she had herself attended; she taught Swedish, German, and English. But this was not a calculated career move; she simply "needed money." Later, after ten years working in India, Elsa ended her relationship with her boyfriend and moved to Bastia, where she had friends she had met through her yoga work abroad, to pursue her childhood dream of learning French: "I thought it [French] was one of the most sensual, intellectual, academic, sexy languages in the world," she says. She explains that though she now speaks several languages thanks to her work and travels, growing up in Sweden there was widespread preference for learning German over French:

> Elsa: I wanted to learn French but everyone was telling to me that it is useless: "Why would you study French?" You know, "Study German."
>
> Alex: Why?
>
> Elsa: That was just the people I was with at that time. There are so many opportunities to work with German-speaking people in Sweden. We've got so much German tourists.
>
> Alex: So it's an economic reason to learn German?

> Elsa: Exactly. For my career, you know, whether I would be an engineer or a doctor that would be to study German. So coming here, learning French, I've got that possibility.

In a dialogic voicing, Elsa echoes popular support for the learning of German to bolster careers in tourism, engineering, and medicine. Indeed, German is seen as a leading language, alongside English, in European secondary curricula which promote its utility in students' future careers, for example in France's Réforme du collège 2016 (Middle School Reform 2016) (Mendes, 2021: 7).

After one year of studying French in a center for adult education in Bastia, Elsa was recruited to teach English for Tourism at the same center, "So I started working as an English teacher, not at all having any kind of these diplomas or anything." She explains needing to overcome her self-consciousness about her imperfect French:

> Elsa: So I was very nervous because my French was so poor, and I was like "Shit, I'm going to be laughed at," you know. "How am I supposed to teach English not being able to speak French?" And actually, my weakness was my strength. Because when having an imperfect teacher, all my students could relax and say: "Wow, this is another human being who's not the perfect model of what a language is supposed to be. She is able to communicate to us in French. We can understand her, and this is what she wants us to do in English. She wants us to learn, to be like her, to communicate, to travel, to work, to use this language as a tool of communication, not to have 100 out of 100. We are not here to pass a baccalaureate, or you know to have 20 out of 20 on the *bac*.[6] We are here to learn how to communicate."

Elsa is conscious that she is modeling the behaviors she wants her students to emulate, including the concomitant rather utilitarian stance that "language [is] a tool of communication" used for work and travel. Indeed, she is teaching a language for specific purposes course, English for Tourism, and her commentary reflects an awareness of the language's place in the web of global capitalism.

While Elsa in part foregrounds an economically driven teleological

---

6 *Le baccalauréat* or *bac* is the exam French students take to earn their high school diploma.

orientation to her students' language learning (Mendes, 2021), she also acknowledges that people see cultural value in learning a language and how it can play a role in self-discovery: "people are looking at English as a magic language which will open up doors that will be closed for them unless they learn how to decode the language." Elsa is aware of the access English provides to multiple spheres (employment, travel), and the very real function of language proficiency as a gatekeeper. But she is not wholly oriented to the economic value of learning English. In this way we see that economic/instrumental or cultural/symbolic notions ascribed to a language can be co-present (Evers, 2018: 469; Mendes 2021), even within a single speaker's subjective experience.

Elsa tells me her students are mostly from France, Corsica, and North Africa, but from other countries as well, for example Poland and Palestine. She explains that her student body is largely supported by the French *pôle emploi* agency which pays a stipend for those unemployed to pursue training, for example learning English for Tourism. She clarifies that students must attend class in order to receive their financial aid, which she sees as negatively influencing their motivation to learn. Elsa recounts how, despite this seeming lack of motivation, she has engaged her Corsican students by drawing from popular discourses on the worldly character of the father of the Corsican nation, Pasquale[7] Paoli:

> Elsa: I think that there is a way to motivate almost anyone. So whether they are Nationalists and you say "Your great ancestor Pascal Paoli, he was talking Greek and Latin and English and French and Corsican fluently, why shouldn't we be just as bright and cool as he is?" Whether you do it that way or whether it is for rich Corsicans who would like to travel to a non-French speaking country or colony or whether it's just people who love music, or video games, or who really need a new job.

Aside from its economic utility in providing training for job opportunities, learning English is not divorced from the cultural context of Corsica. It is for those looking for work and for other kinds of locals, "nationalists" and "rich" alike: "utility and pleasure [can] coexist" (Smith, 2019: 142).

---

7 In Corsican, Pasquale; in French, Pascal.

Seasonal employment is a key characteristic of the local economy, driven as it is by high levels of tourism in warmer months. Elsa's position, then, is an auxiliary to this workforce; her skills, however plural or partial, are commodified—she is employed thanks to her language skills—in order that her students might develop similar skills to then compete for work. Like her students, her work is seasonal: she works in the low tourist season (colder months) since the classes she teaches are not given during the high tourist season when her students are busily employed (warmer months). Elsa and her students' livelihoods are thus bound to State institutions (*pôle emploi*), transnational mobilities (their own and/or those of tourists), and the neoliberal economy (seasonal service work opportunities)—they are caught up in globalizing surges (Chapter 2; Mendes, 2018b).

In her teaching, Elsa experienced frustration regarding the widely held belief that French people are bad at learning languages. She blames this in part on the strict nature of teaching in France:

> Elsa: There's so much humiliation in the French school. How they are being insulted in front of others. How not only the teachers, but their friends are laughing at them if they are too good, and they are laughing at them if they are too bad. And there's really nothing in between "too bad" and "too good." So whenever you open your mouth, you're being laughed at. So there's no way that you can study English here and not be affected by it. It is traumatizing for everybody.

Elsa describes the severe reactions of teachers and classmates to students' performance in class, what I mention in the Introduction as the "evaluative monologue," which was so shocking to me for many of the same reasons. This commentary often seems unnecessarily harsh and discouraging, ridiculing, and indeed "traumatizing."[8] Elsa finds this "humiliation" to be one cause of the "myth" that French people are bad at learning languages. So, unlike French language teachers, Elsa consciously pivots from an endorsement of perfect language performance, as she says, turning her "weakness" into "strength." She found that her imperfect French and multilingual background, paired

---

8 It is worth noting that this interpretation is itself also driven by culturally informed biases and expectations of schooling.

with the theatrical and "clown" personality she brings to her classes, facilitated her teaching and students' learning.

After having taught English for some time, Elsa was recruited to also teach German for Tourism, as well and English and German in a school for at-risk youth.

> Elsa: And I was also asked to start teaching German, and I was really nervous about that because I've been living in this English world, and I was like I doubt that I'll be able to teach German. And actually I had incredible success because I teach German to French students in English. Because English and German are so close, and French and German not at all. So I'm used [to] seeing that as kind of a doorstep.

She explains that those learning German "all already have some kind of notion of English." That is, English skills are somewhat taken for granted and give way to the learning of other languages. In this way the "English world" she had been living in, which she had anticipated would hinder her work in other languages, was exactly what facilitated it.

Alongside the acknowledgment that her teaching involves various languages, Elsa describes how in her classes she tries to explicitly valorize the different languages present. She draws from different language varieties present in class (Algerian and Classical Arabic), underscores how languages feed into meaning-making across divides (students can understand Italian thanks to Corsican), and shares how she allows students to teach her words in their languages, thereby destabilizing hierarchies. In her explanation, she gestures to local beliefs about the Arabic language as "dirty," conscious that by demonstrating interest in it as the teacher she is challenging this denigrating perspective. By explicitly drawing from students' language backgrounds in her English class, she attempts to orient her students to her way of thinking: that knowledge of other languages is not a heavy baggage which should inspire "shame," but something that can be actively drawn from when learning another language and communicating.

We can interpret Elsa's teaching as a kind of translingual praxis (Canagarajah, 2013). She refuses to ideologically uphold standards of perfect language production by her students, and indeed models this herself. Instead, she fosters an orientation to language learning in which students can communicate in order "to travel, to work." The holistic repertoire she draws from in her teaching is attested by her and her students' multilingual backgrounds and orientations, as she states, "I teach German to French students in English."[9] What's more, she asserts that this work has allowed her to progress in her continued learning of French via English, in which she is already very proficient. Her learning and teaching across languages are multidirectional. "Communication" is not reserved for those who have some imagined "full" command of the target language. She adds, "I think that people think it's very fun that they've got a Swedish English teacher in Corsica, or a Swedish German teacher in Corsica." So not only does actively drawing from her mixed language background in her teaching and learning prove effective, it is also seemingly attractive and "fun" for students given the perhaps unexpected combination of origin, target language, and place. She continues, "So I think that when people meet me, that kind of gives them a lot of hope that all people have that capacity to learn different languages." Multilingual teachers have a unique capacity to inspire hope via translingual praxis.

Elsa sees Corsica in a wider Mediterranean context. Like Miquela, who made connections between Corsica and Valencia (above), Elsa understands Corsica not solely by way of its connections to France or Italy, but thinks even further afield to the Eastern Mediterranean:

> Elsa: Corsica is not like Cannes or like Nice. Corsica is French, but at the same time it's Corsica. So you've got that kind of Arab culture, it's very Mediterranean, it's very Arab, French, Spanish, it's very Greek, like people are short, people are the way, physically you can see that they are Corsican [...] there is like two thirds of it is the major reserve, and the Nationalists have been fighting a lot not to be invaded by this huge hotel industry. I think that it has a very heavy energy, has a very heavy lethargic, you know, if I stay here for longer than two months not leaving Corsica, I start to feel lethargic and a bit depressed. But I'm realizing now that sometimes that is preserving this island. Changes are happening so slowly here that instead of quickly

---

9   Here we can also observe that she does not distinguish between Corsican and French people, but conflates them as "French" based on the common language they share, much like in Miquela's use of *Français* above to refer to French speakers generally.

changing things and being efficient, you know in the German way how I've been raised, looking at being very goal-oriented, here things take ages to move, and that is also preserving it.

The untamed nature of large parts of the island that Elsa mentions, the regional park which accounts for approximately 40 percent of the island's total area, remains largely preserved, as others have mentioned to me, "thanks to the Nationalists" with no enormous chains invading, no Hilton, no McDonalds. Elsa draws from temporal notions of speed and change, contrasting her "goal-oriented," "German" way of thinking efficiently with the lethargy she feels on Corsica. She goes on:

> Elsa: I start to realize that I appreciate this kind of slow living. Like in Italy you've got the slow food movement, and I'm realizing in Corsica you've got these slow change movement, slow living movement, slow thinking, everything is like slowly, slowly happening. But I also think that is very respectful, like instead of rushing into another stupid solution, which creates new problems, like what's happening all over the world, they can go from one failure model to, instead of reproducing the same thing that would happen anywhere, they can slowly slide into the future. Because they are always behind time here, everything is so much way behind. But it's preserved by this kind of giant, slowly moving in space and time.

The slow rate of change Elsa observes is not a preservation that is nostalgic or backward-looking. Instead, she sees it as similar to the slow food movement in Italy, which promotes taking time rather than precipitating failure. Elsa paints a picture of the island as a "giant" "slowly sliding into the future," cultivating a "respectful" pace for the preservation of place. This is not an anti-global or closed Corsica, but one that tempers the neoliberal push for more and faster.

§4.2.4 "Elle est morte, elle est finie"

Hamid (Morocco) is an Arabic teacher working between several schools in the greater Bastia area. He worked for the Moroccan government teaching Arabic in other posts abroad before settling in Bastia, where he has been for over 30 years, having raised his family there and eventually becoming a French citizen. Hamid is nostalgic for times when international mobility was easier, as in his youth, when he could hop from place to place. He is disappointed in the current state of affairs with regard to the status of Arabic in the local school district and tensions between the French and Moroccan governments *vis-à-vis* language education and cultural exchange endeavors. School district colleagues have described Hamid to me as "quelqu'un de modéré" (someone moderate), that is they approve of the fact that he does not make affiliations with Islam central to his outward identity, implying that one's publicly affirmed religious (or at least Muslim) beliefs should be discreet.

Hamid recalls his youth in Morocco and how at his school they had teachers from all over the world (from Belgium, France, Hungary, Romania, and the US) thanks to the principal who was an American linguist. He credits his sense of open-mindedness to this exposure to foreigners: "on avait cette liberté d'appréhender le monde" (we had this freedom to understand the world). While visiting family members who lived in Paris in the 1970s and 1980s, Hamid had noticed the divide between the youngest Maghrebi generations, establishing themselves linguistically and culturally in France, and the parents who spoke broken French:

> Hamid: J'ai senti ce manque de suivi chez ces enfants. Leurs parents ils parlaient arabe avec un français à peu près, c'est pas du français mais c'est à peu près des rudiments de français. Donc les enfants ils étaient à l'école dans un monde, ils creusaient leur monde, les parents s'éloignaient par ce fait de creuser, et puis j'ai senti vraiment qu'il y a quelque chose à faire, il faut vraiment faire quelque chose.

> (Hamid: I felt this lack of follow-through in these children. Their parents, they spoke Arabic with a nearly-there French, it's not French but it's more or less the rudiments of French. So the children were at school in a world, they were widening their world, the parents were drawing away because of this act of expansion, and then I felt really that there was something to be done, one must really do something)

This lack of intergenerational transmission is what initially sparked in Hamid an interest to pursue what we might think of as heritage language education: "pour mettre en place la possibilité à ces enfants d'étudier la langue arabe et la culture marocaine dans l'esprit d'un retour" (in order to set up the possibility for these children to study the Arabic language and Moroccan culture in the spirit of a return). What Hamid describes here is a foundational concept in *l'enseignement des langues et cultures d'origine* (the teaching of languages and cultures of origin, or ELCO) in France. In her work on linguistic authority and minority languages, Woolard (2016) explains that traditional notions of authenticity are grounded in discourses of origins. By inviting foreign, "authentic" native-speaking instructors to teach immigrant and heritage-speaker students, the French curriculum indeed establishes an orientation to origins, as explicitly indicated in the title of the initiative. This is an essentializing move common in heritage language industries that "eras[es] the dynamic nature of language and identity formation as a social and cultural practice, [and] constructs a more simplistic view of language as a repository of tradition and cultural knowledge" (Das, 2016: 6). Smith (2019: 101–2) contends that discourses of "origine," employed by those who hold power and privilege, signal an in-group/out-group dichotomy which understands racialized individuals' presence in France as problematic, effectively rendering them culturally and linguistically illegitimate. As Hamid explained to me, teachers were invited from abroad to teach their languages and cultures in France to children whose families had moved there, with the goal of inspiring "a return."

Created between 1973 and 1986, ELCO programs were based on agreements between France and eight partner countries: Algeria, Morocco, Tunisia, Turkey, Portugal, Italy, Spain, Serbia, and Croatia. In 2016, then-Minister of Education Najat Vallaud-Belkacem abruptly announced the end of ELCO programs for their lack of pedagogical quality and their way of closing off students from others in school: "ils ne véhiculent pas un 'enseignement linguistique de qualité' et enferment les élèves dans une 'logique entre soi'" (they do not convey a "quality linguistic teaching" and confine students in a "logic of self-segregation") (Collas, 2016). Long criticized by those of the right, ELCO instruction, particularly the teaching of Arabic, has been suspected as a kind of "Trojan Horse" operating in French schools to sway students to follow Islam. The teaching of language and culture alongside religious content violates the French national value of *laïcité* (secularism), the division of Church and State that dictates a complete absence of religion in public schools. Having been trained in their respective countries of origin, some argue that ELCO teachers have functioned as "électrons libres" (free agents), flying under the radar outside the limits of national standards imposed on other teachers. That is, their teaching was "[u]n enseignement très national,[10] en somme, dispensé par un ressortissant d'un pays pour former de bons citoyens de ce pays" (a very national teaching, in short, provided by an expat of a country to shape good citizens of that country). ELCO teaching was not French enough.

In order to "sortir par le haut du dossier embarrassant des ELCO" (come out on top of the embarrassing ELCO issue), Vallaud-Belkacem planned to transform these classes such that they would be open to all students and taught like any other foreign language in the national curriculum. Two important caveats followed. First, the instructors would then be subject to pedagogical inspection like any other teacher in France, and second, special bilingual class sections envisioned would be open to students based on their academic performance. As such, access to this learning is reserved for already high-achieving students in a neoliberal shift that views students as clients. Thus, the teaching and learning of languages like Arabic are somewhat sterilized in this move from their being taught as heritage languages (infused with content driven by host-country knowledge and offered to students of immigrant families) to their teaching as foreign languages (constrained by the national curriculum and offered to select students based on their scholarly achievement). Heritage language classes are bleached, hung to dry, and reserved for the highest bidders.

Hamid tells me that after six years teaching middle school in Morocco, he participated in the "grand concours pour enseigner à l'étranger" (big competitive exam in order to teach abroad). Of the almost 400 applicants that year, Hamid was among the 11 who were selected. As he puts it, "c'était un hasard, c'était un hasard" (it was chance, it was chance). He worked for one year in Amsterdam before being sent to France, and had now been in Corsica for over 30 years. At the time of our interview (summer 2016), France was preparing to end the ELCO programs (Collas, 2016; Vallaud-Belkacen, 2016). Looking back on his career, Hamid sees all the work he and other

---

10 "National" referring not to France, but to the partner countries.

ELCO teachers have done as wasted due to the fact that, in the end, the teachers on the ground and governments funding the programs had different objectives. He compares this situation to trying to build a railroad:

> Nous on a fait les rails, eux ils ont envoyé les trains, mais ils ont enlevé les rails. Ce n'était pas le même objectif. [...] Le but de l'État à cette époque-là, et de ces deux états, c'était de retourner, mais il n'y a pas de retour. Nous on a travaillé pour qu'ils s'intègrent ici, et s'intégrer ici et sans perdre leur culture.
>
> (We made the rails, they sent the trains, but they removed the rails. It was not the same objective. It was not the same interests. [...] The goal of the [French] State at that time, and of these two countries, was returning, but there is no return. We worked so that they [the students] would integrate here, and integrate here and without losing their culture)

As Hamid spoke to me of his life on the island and all he has built ("tout ce que j'ai construit"), he gestured to the house in which we sat, which he literally built himself, motioning with his hands to show the work he has done, further underscoring that there is no going back, no erasing the place that is now his home. The goals of ELCO instruction, and the relationship between Morocco and France, have shifted over the course of the last three decades. A backward gaze or movement is no longer possible—or desirable.[11]

During our conversation in Hamid's living room, his daughter Hadiya brought us coffee and cookies. Hamid told me to help myself, but that he would not be joining me as they were fasting for Ramadan.[12] Hadiya returned to the living room to show me two small kittens and we played with them a bit. On our way to Hamid's house, we had picked her up from school. In her first year of middle school, Hamid tells me Hadiya is taking English and Corsican. We continued chatting:

---

11 See also Smith (2019: 108) on Senegalese migrants' experiences abroad wherein several participants describe a widely upheld idea of eventually returning to Senegal, "But they never go back."
12 An interplay between language, religion, and the local economy, specifically with regard to the period of Ramadan, appeared in other encounters with multilingualism on the island during this work, see Mendes (2018b: 205–8).

She says that next year, she will take Italian and Latin. I am surprised and I ask her why, she says she likes them. Four languages—I say it's great that she likes languages, just like her dad, and that they also speak other languages at home, I look at [Hamid], I say you speak Arabic at home, right? He shrugs. I don't want to press the issue. Maybe he doesn't want to share this with me? Maybe they don't and he's embarrassed? (fieldnote, June 6, 2016)

If I had already been impressed by Hadiya's several languages (French, Arabic [my assumption], English, and Corsican), I was even more happily surprised that she planned to pursue two more. I realize now that my question about them speaking Arabic at home was indelicate. Though Hamid lived and taught, in his words, in a spirit of openness, perhaps it had been hard for him to foster intergenerational transmission of Arabic in his own family (Géa, 2005, 2006, 2016). Perhaps I was misinterpreting his dodging of the Arabic question, and their family instead spoke Tamazight. Hamid's ambiguity regarding speaking Arabic with his daughter could be taken as further evidence of his distancing himself from the goals of ELCO teaching. I let the issue drop; the story of languages spoken in their home was left untold, a narrative erasure (Kramsch & Zhang, 2018: ch. 5). To me, this absence is sufficient evidence of the enormously powerful ideologies these different languages exude and the wider struggle to create a semblance of their peaceful coexistence.

Hamid juxtaposes the idea of return with integration. His conceptualization of integration is different from other orientations that we've seen so far. Recall Emmanuelle, the Sud FLE teacher, for whom the idea of integration was illustrated by students forgetting their first languages which were replaced by French in a textbook example of subtractive bilingualism (Chapter 2). For Hamid, the notion of integration is an equilibrium between participating in French society while actively valorizing one's own culture. By way of illustration, he mentions how each year he has ten or so students take the *baccalauréat* optional modern language exam in Arabic, something he is quite proud of, given that he has followed their learning throughout the years: "c'était vraiment une fierté de les voir, de me sentir les suivre dès leur petit âge" (it was really a source of pride to see them, to feel I had followed them from a young age). In this way, he sees that valorizing one's language "of origin" is indeed possible in a French context. The teaching of Arabic on Corsica is, to Hamid, indeed prioritized, and the language belongs to a wider ensemble, not apart from it:

> Alex: Est-ce que vous trouvez qu'il y a une forte priorité mise sur l'enseignement de l'arabe ici en Corse?
>
> Hamid: Priorité? Il y est priorité. Et quand je dis arabe, il n'y a pas seulement arabe, il y a berbère, parce qu'il y a une forte population ici. C'est comme si je vais dire à un Français, français, mais il y a corse aussi.

(Alex: Do you find that there is a priority placed on the teaching of Arabic here in Corsica?

Hamid: Priority? It is priority. And when I say Arabic, there is not only Arabic, there is Berber [Tamazight], because there is a large population here. It's like if I'm going to say to a French person, French, by there is Corsican also)

Hamid describes how he considers Arabic to be prioritized alongside Tamazight in a parallel he draws between French and Corsican as state and minoritized languages, respectively. That is, French as imposed by the State can be seen as similar to the way that Arabic is imposed in Morocco. As colleagues have mentioned to me, many Imazighen (Tamazight-speakers) on Corsica reject the idea of Arabic language education for their children as discrepant with their linguistic identity as speakers of Tamazight. Arabic thus occupies a precarious position in the Corsican public school.

A colleague working in the school district told me a story of an Arabic language teacher who had been working in Corsican schools for some time. One day, he gloated to Corsican language instructors that he spoke "la deuxième langue de la Corse" ("the second[-most spoken] language on Corsica"), inciting fury among them. To his shocked interlocutors, he was suggesting that there are more speakers of Arabic[13] on Corsica than there are speakers of Corsican. The anger of his colleagues reflects an ideological assumption that heritage language education on Corsica should prioritize Corsican

---

13 His comment could have very well also referred to Tamazigt, not Arabic.

first, and other languages second. Or at least that discourses about language reclamation on the island—what is rendered as the account of this language teaching—should keep Corsican at the center of the narrative. This story has stuck with me. It illustrates the affective load borne by the work of language reclamation, the ideological language orientations to Corsican and Arabic as competing minoritized/heritage languages on the island, and the power of anecdote in shaping narratives that circulate about particular languages.

Arabic and Corsican, in the sphere of language education on the island, have more in common than one might initially suspect. They can both be considered heritage languages (Das, 2016: ch. 1), languages of the home, a means by which students might connect with their families' cultural backgrounds, and languages that students may have some proficiency in already. Speakers of these languages struggle against francohegemony in the sociocultural contexts in which they are used. Arabic-language education attempts to prove itself relevant to students in the teaching of skills like orthography and other cultural codes, as Hamid mentions. This can be interpreted as similar to the way Corsican is marketed as a language that will open students' horizons to other Western Romance languages and Mediterranean cultures (Mendes, 2021). The learning of Corsican and Arabic is touted as useful for broader cultural understandings. The human and material resources dedicated to the teaching of Arabic and Corsican on the island are certainly less than those devoted to others, like English. These languages (or those working to teach them, rather) jockey for a place in the French public curriculum but simultaneously they must lightly tread cultural-ideological divides in order to maintain enrollments and secure a continued place in schools.

Like the multilingualism at the school of his youth, Hamid encountered extraordinary linguistic diversity in some schools during his early years teaching on Corsica. Based on requests from parents for their children to take Arabic classes, enrollment grew to require ten to 12 Arabic ELCO instructors in the school district. As he puts it, they succeeded. In this golden heyday of Hamid's teaching in the 1990s, linguistic diversity among students seems to have helped secure Arabic's place in local schools and an ongoing multilingual exchange. Hamid sees his work teaching Arabic on Corsica throughout the years facilitated by this linguistic diversity on the island, despite the overwhelmingly dominant place of French:

Hamid: j'ai trouvé cette situation de langue aussi, corse, qui est une langue vraiment qui est écrasée par le français, comme, d'ailleurs, tout [...] on cherche les points communs, et on cherche la richesse où elle est, et elle est bien sûr dans cette différence. [...] La langue corse c'est une richesse très importante pour le français [...] il y a de l'histoire, il y a du vécu, et ça c'est très important pour comprendre le présent. [...] j'ai vécu dans cette ambiance, malheureusement qui s'est brusquement arrêtée, et ça on en peut plus, c'est la politique des états.

(Hamid: I found this language situation also, Corsican, which is really a language that is crushed by French, like everything for that matter [...] you look for common points, and you look for richness where it is, and it is of course in this difference. [...] The Corsican language is a very important resource for French [...] there is history, there is lived experience, and that is very important to understand the present. [...] I have lived in this atmosphere, which unfortunately suddenly stopped, and we can't do anything more about that, it's the countries' politics)

The multilingual coexistence Hamid imagines is inclusive of Corsican, Arabic, and Tamazight, but hierarchically dominated by the oppressive presence of French. He laments that, due to political decisions, ELCO teaching abruptly ended: "cet enseignement, ça y est, elle est morte, elle est finie" (this teaching, that's it, it's dead, it's done). For this reason, he plans to retire soon.

Hamid discusses the spirit of discovery he tries to foster in his teaching, one which he embeds in the Mediterranean context. The encounter with other cultures is exemplified for Hamid in what he calls the "métissage" (intermixture) that he sees in the Mediterranean between Latin, Arabic, and Tamazight. Although he mentions Romance languages in passing, unlike other interviewees, he never explicitly mentions Italian and instead foregrounds the place of Arabic and Tamazight, the North African component of Mediterranean "brassage" (intermingling). Hamid asserts that this cultural "discovery" is multidimensional and includes customs, cuisine, and dress, beyond just language. The assemblage of an overarching Mediterranean *patrimoine* (cultural heritage or legacy) that Hamid describes is an inclusive array of nationalities, materials, and practices (Pennycook, 2018: 48; Mendes, 2020). With this approach, Hamid finds a way to bring distinct communities together, to put them in dialogue as it were, despite the rampant mistrust he sees today. He pivots to touch on current economic conditions such as unemployment which contribute to an atmosphere of suspicion. In Hamid's brief mention of current events, one can read a gesture to increased racial tensions in France following the November 2015 Bataclan attacks in Paris. Shortly after our conversation, France also witnessed the Bastille Day attack in Nice in July 2016 and the burkini scandal that began just north of Bastia and erupted that August (Chapter 1). Despite these tensions, Hamid finds that intercultural dialogue persists, driven by people like him, language teachers who can bring communities together: "il y a une richesse, il suffit d'ouvrir les yeux" (there is a richness, you just have to open your eyes).

§4.2.5 "Il n'y a pas de petites langues"

Diana (Corsica) is a middle school Corsican teacher at the Collège du Centre in Bastia, and has been teaching for nearly 20 years. She hails from the Balagne region in the northwest of the island, holds a CAPES in Corsican, and she and her husband are raising their son in the language. Like many Corsican language teachers, Diana is also very active in cultural projects, for example the teaching and performing of the traditional Corsican song form *paghjella*. I see her as a bold feminist voice within Corsican cultural circles.

Diana's passion for language was inspired by her grandmother, who helped raise her and whom she credits for her advanced fluency in Corsican. She is acutely aware that advanced proficiency is relatively rare among her age group. The youngest of her siblings, Diana's grandmother was responsible for looking after the family's sheep, so she never attended school or developed a working command of French, the sole language of education at the time. Diana was driven to show her grandmother that Corsican, too, could be a language of learning:

> Diana: Justement en réponse au fait de son complexe, parce qu'elle ne parlait que corse, et le fait de parler que corse ça l'a coupée, si tu veux, de l'autre communication. Et moi j'ai voulu lui montrer qu'on pouvait être professeur de corse aussi. Et à l'époque, j'ai passé le CAPES à Paris, dans le Marais, et je suis

revenue avec mon CAPES, et ça a été la première à qui j'ai dit *Avà, sò prufissora di corsu*. Et c'était beau parce que j'étais fière. Et c'était aussi un peu pour réhabiliter au sens psychologique du terme, tout ce qu'elle n'avait pas pu faire, voilà. [...] quand je suis arrivée de Paris, et que j'ai dit à ma grand-mère, elle croyait que c'était une blague. Elle a rigolé tu vois? Pour te dire, pour te dire que c'était vraiment quelque chose qui était ancrée en elle. [...] Elle a eu du mal à comprendre.

(Diana: Actually in response to the fact of her hang-up, because she only spoke Corsican, and the fact of only speaking Corsican cut her off, if you will, from other communication. And me I wanted to show her that you could be a teacher of Corsican as well. And when I took the CAPES [exam] in Paris, in the Marais, and I came back with my CAPES, she was the first one to whom I said *Avà, sò prufissora di corsu* [Now I am a Corsican teacher]. And it was lovely because I was proud. And it was also a bit in order to redeem, in the psychological sense of the term, everything she wasn't able to do, there you have it. [...] when I arrived from Paris, and I said that to my grandmother, she thought it was a joke. She laughed you see? To show you, to show you that it was something that was anchored in her. [...] She had a hard time understanding)

Teaching Corsican, for Diana, addresses a sociohistorical need she situates *vis-à-vis* the past and the future: to rectify older generations' hardships by actively participating in the further institutionalization of Corsican and "pour leur laisser vraiment un heritage" for generations to come (to really leave them a heritage).

Diana recognizes the mixed backgrounds among her student body, who do not all speak Corsican: "ils ne sont pas tous corsophones, sinon on vivrait dans un monde parfait" (they are not all corsophones, otherwise we would live in a perfect world). Diana's school, Collège du Centre, was the first public school on the island to offer Chinese classes, making it, at the time, one of only two schools in the world to offer Chinese alongside Corsican (the other being the local private Catholic school). I ask her about this unique combination of languages in the school's curriculum, to which she replies:

Diana: Alors moi si tu veux l'enseignement du chinois, je n'y vois aucun inconvénient, bien au contraire, parce que je suis quelqu'un qui pense que plus il y a de propositions pour l'enfant, mieux ça vaut. Chacun a le droit de faire ses choix, en son âme et conscience, et l'enseignement des deux langues coexiste sans souci. Mais je me pose la question sur aller rechercher cette langue lointaine. Moi je pense qu'on aurait aussi intérêt à jouer la carte de la proximité en fonction des communautés qui sont présentes aussi. Je veux parler de la communauté portugaise par exemple, la communauté musulmane, voilà. Parce que le corse c'est une langue d'intégration aussi, et ça il faut le dire, voilà. Parce que la Corse elle a toujours fabriqué des Corses, ça c'est sûr, et on intègre aussi par la langue, c'est comme ça que ça se fait. Voilà, l'enseignement du chinois ça peut apporter énormément à un enfant, il n'y a pas de problème, ce n'est pas la question que je me pose, mais je me dis qu'il y a une ouverture sur la Méditerranée qui est logique et qui n'est pas toujours prise en compte.

(Diana: Well if you want Chinese to be taught, I see nothing wrong with that, quite the contrary, because I'm someone who believes that the more options there are for the child, the better. Everyone has the right to make their own decisions, in their soul and conscience, and the teaching of the two languages coexists without problem. But I wonder about going in search of this faraway language [Chinese]. I think that we would also be wise to play the proximity card to suit the communities present [on the island] as well. I'm talking about the Portuguese community for example, the Muslim community, yeah. Because Corsican is a language of integration too, and you must recognize that, there you have it. Because Corsica it has always made Corsicans, that's for sure, and you also integrate through language, that's how it's done. Yeah, the teaching of Chinese can bring a great deal to a child, there is no problem with that, that is not the question I'm asking, but I'm saying that there is an opening onto the Mediterranean that is logical and that is not always taken into account)

The institutional coexistence of Corsican and Chinese at the school is described by Diana in terms of a binary she constructs between Chinese as faraway ("lointaine") and languages of the island, such as Corsican, Portuguese, and those of "the Muslim community," as close ("la carte de la proximité"). What Diana briefly describes only scratches the surface of ideological investments that accompany students' and parents' choices of which language classes to enroll in at school. Colleagues told me how English was the predominant choice, Corsican was chosen by traditional local families, Latin and Greek by well-to-do families, and Chinese by students interested in manga, even though these comics come from Japan, not China. Diana underscores that, aside from its merits alongside other languages as an academic subject, Corsican has a powerful potential to facilitate social integration and "make Corsicans." Indeed, social integration and civic participation are among the main tenets that drive Diana's teaching and promotion of the language, as attested by a recent fieldtrip she took with her students.

Thanks to close friendships with some locally elected officials, Diana was able to put together a visit for her *quatrième* class (US: eighth grade) to visit the Corsican Assembly in Ajaccio. In addition to tours of historic sites such as the family home of Napoleon Bonaparte, her class was able to formally address the Assembly and ask questions they had prepared, in Corsican and French, related to current events:

> Diana: c'est un projet aussi sur l'éducation à la citoyenneté. Et il se trouve que la nouvelle majorité est, tu le sais une majorité nationaliste qui est extrêmement favorable et qui se bat depuis des années pour la langue et la culture. Et donc on a été reçu, je te le dis encore de façon très très sympa. Les élèves dès qu'ils sont arrivés on leur a dit dès qu'ils sont arrivés: "Mais ici, vous êtes chez vous, c'est votre maison, c'est un endroit où tout se décide, mais vous avez la place pour parler, on vous écoute," on a été écoutés et entendus je pense sur toutes les questions qui ont été posées, et les questions ont été posées dans les deux langues, avec les réponses dans les deux langues, chose qui ne s'est jamais peut-être passée. [...] Ce qui a été important aussi si tu veux pour les élèves, au-delà de l'accueil chaleureux, c'est de voir que la langue finalement elle est là pour parler du quotidien, elle est là pour, on peut parler de poésie, mais on peut parler aussi de choses importantes et officielles puisqu'on se retrouve dans un cadre particulier au sein de la Collectivité Territoriale, où se prennent les grandes décisions politiques de l'île. Donc ça a donné aussi pour eux un autre regard sur la langue, tu vois? Il était installé au niveau de l'institution, au même niveau que le français, on pouvait se servir des deux.

(Diana: it [teaching Corsican] is also a project for the teaching of citizenship. And it happens that the new majority is, you know a nationalist majority that is extremely favorable and which has fought for years for the [Corsican] language and culture. And we were received and, I'll say it again, very very nicely. The students, as soon as they arrived, were told as soon as they arrived, "But here, you are in your home, this is your home, this is a place where everything is decided, but you have space to speak, we are listening to you." We were listened to and heard I think on every question that was asked, and the questions were asked in the two languages with responses in the two languages, something that has perhaps never happened. [...] What was important also if you will for the students, beyond the warm welcome, is to see that the language at the end of the day it is there to speak of the day-to-day, it is there to, we can speak about poetry, but we can also speak about important and official things since we are meeting in the particular context within the Territorial Collectivity, where the big political decisions of the island are made. So that also gave them another view on language, you see? It was placed at the level of the institution, at the same level as French, you could use both)

Diana explicitly links the teaching and learning of Corsican to the learning of citizenship. The fact that both French and Corsican were used in the assembly hearing is symbolically important for the ideological leveling it provided in attempting to eliminate hierarchies between the languages, and pragmatically important for modeling that civic participation, access to political discourse, and an everyday practice of linguistic diversity (at least that between French and Corsican) can happen in tandem even in government institutions. Beyond any *de jure* statute of official bilingualism or institutionalization of Corsican, Diana insists that this use of Corsican was important for students to witness, to prove to them what is possible: "Si on parle corse nous, et si tous les jours on lutte, on parle corse à nos enfants, on essaie de parler dans la rue, etc., on n'a pas besoin que la décision vienne d'ailleurs" (If us we speak Corsican, and if every day we fight, we speak Corsican to our children, we try to speak [it] in the street, etc., we don't need the decision to come from elsewhere). Diana frames the learning and lived use of Corsican, a minoritized language, as a daily ("quotidien") practice and iterative ("tous les jours") decision rather than an obligation to fulfill or a rule to follow.[14] This choice to use Corsican can overflow into one's participation in civic discourse.

Diana understands her teaching as interdisciplinary; she draws from theater, song, and art in her work. A rather well-known local musician, she and her husband teach and perform *paghjella*, a traditional three-voice song form added to the list of UNESCO's intangible cultural heritage in 2009 thanks in no small part to the work of people like Diana who have helped keep it alive. Diana incorporates *paghjella* into her middle school Corsican classes and her students perform at local cultural events such as the Festa di a lingua ([Corsican] Language Festival). Her teaching also draws from other academic disciplines. For example, at the time of our conversation she was planning a project with colleagues from English and History-Geography on local historical figure Pasquale Paoli, considered the father of the Corsican nation. By tracing his life's work from his village on Corsica to his exile in London, the teachers will illustrate Paoli's influence beyond the island itself which extends even as far as the US. Their coursework will culminate in a trip to London to see the monuments they'll study.

While the effort to formalize such interdisciplinary work came with the Middle School Reform of 2016,[15] Diana insists that this kind of work has always been a part of her approach to teaching Corsican with a focus beyond language proper: "La démographie aussi tu vois, l'histoire, et la langue, ça, tu ne peux pas le dissocier. Et on se doit de partir en Méditerranée romane, donc voilà" (Demographics, too, you see, history, and language since you cannot dissociate it. And we owe it to ourselves travel to the Roman(ce) Mediterranean, so there you have it). These interdisciplinary projects abroad involve teaching language, history, geography, art, and culture, among other things. With her colleagues and students, she has carried out such fieldtrips to Sardinia, Malta, and Barcelona: "[À Barcelone] on a fait la comparaison corse/catalan, bon tu vois on a travaillé sur des mots, sur des phrases, donc il n'y a pas de soucis, on l'a toujours fait" ([In Barcelona] we compared Corsican and Catalan, so you see we worked on words, on phrases,

---

14 I cannot help but hear in Diana's words echoes of Freire's (2005: 79) poignant affirmation that liberation is a praxis.
15 See Mendes (2021) on the *équipe pédagogique interdisciplinaire* (interdisciplinary pedagogical team).

so it's no problem, we've always done it). Diana is at ease teaching in the interdisciplinary, comparative way she describes, and further is compelled to work this way driven by a sense of duty ("on se doit," we owe it to ourselves). Her teaching is affirming of Corsican's place within larger geopolitical and cultural ensembles.

The geographic scope of Diana's teaching is based primarily on Corsica's "logical" connection to the Mediterranean, especially with other island communities (Sardinia, Malta) and those of Romance minority languages (Catalonia). Her scope is also, however, inclusive of major parts of the anglophone world, England and the US, demonstrating the wide-reaching "traces," as she puts it, of Corsican heritage further abroad.[16] Place is thus an important way to ground language practices, despite or perhaps driven by globalizing surges. For Diana, the teaching and learning of one's heritage language is a powerful way to approach the rest of the world, where one can easily feel lost:

> Diana: tu vois moi je suis peut-être naïve, mais dans la mondialisation on se perd, moi je me dis qu'on a tellement besoin de se rapprocher de ses racines pour justement lutter contre ça, lutter attention c'est pas forcément, il n'y a pas forcément que du négatif, mais la mondialisation ça fait peur quand même, tu vois, t'as l'impression de te noyer dans, dans une masse complètement inconnue. Et plus tu te rapproches de tes racines et plus tu sais qui tu es, plus tu peux affronter tout le reste. Moi ça me fait pas peur.

> (Diana: you see, me, I am perhaps naïve, but within globalization you lose yourself, I say that you need so badly to draw closer to your roots precisely to fight against that, fight mind you that it's not necessarily, it's not necessarily only negative, but globalization is still scary, you see, you have the impression of drowning in, in a completely unknown expanse. And the more you draw closer to your roots and the more you know who you are, the more you can confront everything else. Me, that doesn't scare me)

---

16 I mentioned that I had seen a town in Colorado, my home state, named Paoli as well as a Paoli Lane off of Interstate 80 in northern California, where I was going to school. Diana enthusiastically accepted this as further proof of her points, venturing to add that she had heard that President Obama was apparently a big fan of a local ice creamery. Corsica's presence reverberates in the US.

Related to Giorgia's point (above) of feeling lost in a giant city like Paris, Diana paints globalization as an unknown expanse in which one loses oneself. While Giorgia seeks learning and professionalization, Diana seeks civic participation and political engagement; they are both nonetheless importantly implicated in their relation to place. For Diana, connecting with one's roots, one's heritage language and culture, and one's place (literal and figurative) in the world is thus not an act of closing oneself off, but precisely the way in which one can confront it, reassured and without fear. Intellectual and physical ventures abroad with students and colleagues are made with this affective anchoring to Corsica(n).

The rooted connection to Corsican heritage is, for Diana, maintained in the rural family homes to which locals retreat for weekends and holidays. As Diana tells me, while the family may not use Corsican to a large extent in their day-to-day life in the city, the village setting provides a valuable, predominantly corsophone environment for young learners. Unfortunately, this ability to immerse oneself regularly in a space steeped in Corsican is not necessarily available to everyone:

> Diana: tu as quelques personnes qui vivent en ville et qui tous les week-ends s'en vont au village, et là l'enfant si tu veux il a quand même quelque chose à quoi se raccrocher en termes de tradition et de langue. Mais tu ne peux pas comparer [la ville et le village], c'est trop différent. […]
>
> Alex: Et par exemple les élèves qui ne sont pas corses, qui étudient le corse, comment ils doivent partir au village?
>
> Diana: Et mais voilà, mais ceux-là non. Ceux-là si tu veux ils ne bénéficient pas et à ce moment-là l'enseignement du corse c'est comme l'enseignement d'une langue étrangère. C'est-à-dire que ces enfants-là ils doivent trouver leur compte dans les trois heures qu'on leur propose [à l'école]. Et après si tu veux, sauter sur l'occasion s'il y a un évènement culturel, d'aller et de faire la démarche. Mais ces enfants-là ils ont du mérite parce que leur connaissance elle se base sur les trois heures d'enseignement qu'ils ont dans la semaine.
>
> (Diana: you have some people who live in town and who go to the village every weekend, and there the child if you will still has something to latch onto in terms of tradition and language. But

you cannot compare [the city and the village], it's too different. […]

Alex: And for example the students who are not Corsican, who study Corsican, how would they leave [town] for the village?

Diana: And but yeah, but those ones no. Those ones, if you will, don't benefit and at that point the teaching of Corsican is like the teaching of a foreign language. That is to say that those children must find their way in the three hours we offer them [at school]. And after, if you will, jump on the occasion if there is a cultural event, to go and make a move. But those children deserve praise because their knowledge is based on the three hours of teaching they have during the week)

Not all children growing up on Corsica have the "village" experience. Even those who are Corsican may live in circumstances that make visits to the village difficult or emotionally taxing, such as long drives, houses falling into disrepair, separated families. Non-Corsican children perhaps forge a village situation, such as the North African student described in the Preface who would travel on the weekends to visit relatives in Ghisonaccia a couple of hours south of Bastia. It is also the case that second homes on Corsica are often purchased by continentals for vacation or retirement, driving real estate prices into ranges inaccessible for Corsicans themselves. As Diana puts it, "On aura plus d'argent pour acheter notre patrimoine" (We will have no longer have the money to buy our heritage). Another participant asserts that even if children do go to a village, there still need to be people there to actively speak with them in Corsican for this kind of idealized language transmission to work. All this to say that locals' relationships to "the village," while undeniably important and central to Corsican identity and lived experience, are complex and cannot be taken for granted.

Diana concedes that non-Corsican learners of Corsican are indeed at a disadvantage without access to a family village and must base their experience with the language on three weekly hours of class time. Without access to certain spaces, even as it is widely promoted as a language of integration, culture, and civic participation, Corsican risks being rendered foreign and inaccessible to some learners in this way. Fortunately, as Diana says, city municipalities put on several cultural exhibits and presentations each year, on theater, music, and language, which are open to the public and encourage participation. In this way Corsican is front and center, readily available: "tu vois tu peux toucher du doigt" (you see you can touch it). Diana encourages getting one's hands dirty, as it were, actively participating in living language and culture, whether in the city or in the village. She draws from her own life at the same time as she foregrounds seeing and doing things for oneself: students' opportunities to sing at local festivals, carry out traditions in the village, visit Paoli's bust at Westminster in London, and dialogue with government officials. Her teaching is oriented to experiential learning and enacting language and culture.

In speaking of her pedagogical goals, Diana, like Elsa (above), underscores the idea of communication and speaking in the target language. While Elsa emphasizes that any communication in the target language—by herself or students, and even seemingly imperfect or incorrect communication—is valid, Diana understands this task as one that additionally must work to break down stigma associated with speaking Corsican. In her quotidian tasks of helping her students find pleasure in speaking the language, Diana is the living link bridging the historical gap (Kramsch & Zhang, 2018) between the pain and erasure those of her grandmother's generation lived at the hands of French and the reclamation (Leonard, 2011) of Corsican she fosters in her students. But, she laments, French retains a stronghold: "c'est vrai que ce n'est pas evident, parce que la pression de la langue française elle est toujours trop forte" (it's true that it's not easy, because the pressure of the French language is still too strong). She shares the following anecdote to illustrate how Corsican is still often looked down upon with ridicule:

> Diana: Et il y a une dame un jour, une Continentale, que j'ai rencontrée dans un dîner d'affaire avec mon mari, qui était prof de sport, elle me dit: "Vous êtes quoi?" j'ai dit "Prof." "De quoi?" "De corse." "Ah, que de ça?" elle m'a dit. [...] Tu as encore des gens qui te disent, "Finalement, à quoi ça sert?" [...] il y a toujours un peu un résidu de complexe, un résidu de se dire que finalement c'est quelque chose de petit, alors qu'il n'y a pas de petites langues. Elles sont toutes grandes, et elles sont toutes respectables.
>
> (Diana: And there was this lady one day, a continental [French woman], who I met at a work dinner with my husband, who was a PE teacher, she says to me: "What do you do?" I said "I'm a

teacher." "Of what?" "Of Corsican." "Ah, only of that?" she says to me. [...] You still have people who say to you, "In the end, what is that good for?" [...] there is still a bit of a residue of a hang-up, a residue of saying to oneself that at the end of the day it's something small, when there are no small languages. They are all big, and they are all respectable)

The telegraphic rejoinders in the exchange illustrate the painful jabs of her interlocutor as she ridicules Diana's profession as a Corsican teacher. Though she says she was able to convince several people at the dinner of the merits of learning Corsican, Diana insists that this debasement of the language still exists and is often quite brazen. She maintains nonetheless that all languages are worthy of our attention and care.

§4.3 Mediation

As attested in their stories, the participants described three broad multilingual scopes which resonate on Corsica, indicative of how languages are positioned *vis-à-vis* one another in differently imagined hierarchies:

- *Bi-plurilinguisme* (chapters 1 and 3): an active promotion and foregrounding of Corsican alongside French
- A broad and inclusive Mediterranean: connections with Italy, North Africa, Portugal, Valencia, and Greece as well as Roman(ce) regions and the Muslim community
- Touchstones with the wider world: Germany, England and the US, China, Scandinavia, India

These groupings, however, do not allow for a sufficiently nuanced understanding of the dynamics between components (language repertoires, cultures, peoples, and spaces/places) within each conceptualization of multilingual coexistence. To return to one of my central questions, How is "multilingualism" understood on the island in participants' subjective experience? The interview data present a vast range of emic notions of and attitudes toward multilingual dynamics on Corsica: feeling overpowered by French, French as a middle ground, Corsican and French as rivals or as a complementary pair, Italian as a

Romance relative to Corsican (along with Catalan, Maltese, Sardinian, Valencian), Corsican as a way to find belonging, the thriving of English in the service industry, Arabic as dirty, Arabic and/or Tamazight and/or Portuguese as valuable players on the field, German and Italian as languages of tourism, German as something to be studied in order to get a good job, Chinese as something faraway to be viewed skeptically, and so on. In more extreme cases, other interviewees saw Corsican as an explicitly exclusionary force and an obstacle to inclusion and understanding. It is not that participants simply enumerated these points, but that throughout the data these ideas appear—or do not—alongside one another in various and seemingly infinite *combinations.*

A related, illustrative example comes from Smith's (2019: 57, 111) study of the Senegalese diaspora in New York City, which is simultaneously imagined as, on the one hand, a community that prioritizes Senegal's national languages and valorizes language learning (e.g., English, Italian) but, on the other, privileges Wolof in practice—and not a Wolof too heavily colored by English, but rather one that fosters connections with French. As Gal and Irvine (2019) describe language use in the Senegalese diaspora, "The salient units of comparison shift along with speakers' change in social positioning" (57). These countervocalities—these competing homogenizing and heterogenizing discourses, constantly rearranging language hierarchies, and constellations of various language ideologies and attitudes—illustrate the material and symbolic aspects of language dynamics constituting and mediating our multilingual neoliberal realities.

How, then, is "globalization" understood on Corsica, as related to multilingual dynamics? Participants' stories represent emic understandings of "globalization" as signaled by: a feeling of drowning or being lost; not being able to leave one's mark; random or limited mobility; infrastructural and economic development; temporary or seasonal work; institutional factors (formal training, unemployment benefits); the desire (or need) to learn English, German, or Chinese; an urge to prioritize one's heritage. These phenomena can be seen as driven by global forces outside one's control, but not causally, as their playing out does indeed constitute what is understood as globalization in a broad sense. These activities, feelings, and priorities are shaped by and shape the idea of globalization in a dialectic of globalizing surges (Chapter 2). These educators' participation in the global language teaching market reflects their value "across national contexts" (Menard-Warwick, 2014: 10). By way of their intercultural capital, they are able to communicate "across time/space divides and social geographies" (Luke, 2004: 1429). Mediation is a common thread throughout: the FLE curriculum mediating newly arrived immigrant students' encounters with the French language (Chapter 2), picturebooks mediating various discourses of language reclamation (Chapter 3), and the public space as a mediator of various language ideologies (Chapter 5). Here, these teachers mediate between foreign and local in place and time, body and language.

Throughout their stories, participants rendered explicit associations between language and place beyond the connection between the Corsican language and the island. For example, the learning and teaching of English on Corsica is related to distinct places and activities. On Corsica, students of English face a fork in the road when orienting to the language as one which will benefit their career, in a kind of class divide. There exists a bifurcation between the learning of English in order to remain on the island for work in the seasonal tourist industry, as Elsa mentions, and the learning of English in order to pursue higher education and work in technology and the sciences in continental France or abroad.[17] English on Corsica is for the service industry; English in France is for specialized work. Different languages are valorized in unique ways and are located at different points within distinctly imagined hierarchies.

Similar to Evers's (2018) work exploring who counts as a Mediterranean citizen, the scope of what is included as part of the Mediterranean shifts in each interviewee's account. Hamid foregrounds North Africa, discussing Morocco and Imazighen. He is the only interviewee to not explicitly mention Italy. Elsa is the only participant to refer to the Eastern Mediterranean and Greece in her conceptualizing of the Mediterranean space. Diana centers on Romance minority regions in her discussion, mentioning Catalonia, Sardinia, and Malta. Much like shifting language hierarchies of countervocalities, there is no single agreed-upon notion as to what constitutes the geopolitical and cultural place that is the Mediterranean, as the idea is transformed in each participant's subjective experience.

Deterritorialization and local anchoring can be viewed as two faces of globalizing surges (Rozenholc, 2014: 3). These stories illustrate both

---

17 This latter point was recounted by other interviewees not included among the focal participants here.

"local and global existence" (Kramsch & Zhang, 2018: 28), reflective of how the language teaching endeavor is one that involves subjective and transhistorical practice. Throughout the narratives, participants addressed their relation to various places (home culture, transnational experiences, their place on the island) and timeframes (how the past has influenced the present, their projected futures) (125). Multilingual instructors mediate between distinct spacetimes (Blommaert, 2010) as they find themselves "in a state of linguistic, geographic, and historical mobility" (Kramsch & Zhang, 2018: 222). They draw from their personal experiences and trajectories as they deploy various communicative resources in a local place, the linking of spatial repertoires of translingualism (Canagarajah, 2018; Pennycook & Otsuji, 2015: 83). Participants bring their linguistic and cultural baggage to their learning of linguistic and cultural orientations on the island, as in Miquela's discovery of the similarities between Valencian and Corsican in her encounters with her boyfriend's family and colleagues. As Elsa and Diana recount, the Corsican language connects one to faraway places (England, the US), forges connections within the closer Mediterranean region, and grounds one to the island in a geographic and affective anchoring. These teachers enact the foreign in their work while drawing from local experience, embodying a postlocal simultaneity (Lombardi, 2014: 49) wherein we can see that "the here is no longer here but there too" (Kramsch & Zhang, 2018: 214).

As they physically inhabit and move between various places, embodiment is a central facet of these teachers' work with language and culture as it relates "a certain subjective experience" (Bourdieu, 1977: 87 in Block, 2014: 58). As Kramsch and Zhang (2018: 180–1) have argued, "both learning and teaching a new language are eminently embodied experiences." Bucholtz and Hall (2016: 185) explain the body as "the deictic center, around which social relationships and cultural space are brought into interactional play." Participants draw from firsthand experience, in turns both visceral and emotional, in the telling of their language stories. This embodiment manifests in their accounts of witnessing (Giorgia: "je l'ai vu, avec mes yeux" [I saw it with my eyes]), constructing (Hamid: "tout ce que j'ai construit" [everything that I've built]), emoting (Elsa: "I start to feel lethargic and depressed"), and taking part (Diana: "tu peux le toucher du doigt" [you can touch it"]). These teachers "embod[y] the transnational multilingual subject" in a variety of activities and communicative practices as they agentively use different ensembles of languages and orient to diverse language hierarchies (Smith, 2019: 158).

While much work on translanguaging has privileged a focus on space over time, Kramsch (2018: 110) asserts the need to not lose sight of temporality and historicity as they inform our multilingual communicative practices. Language, she explains, "preserves our uniquely human capacity to embrace both the thrills of space and the vulnerabilities of time" (114). Here, we see that language teachers' mediating role extends to time as well. Diana's story of her confrontation with the woman who challenged the importance of her work as a Corsican teacher is an illuminating example; this incident from her past informs her passion for teaching in the present and the hoped-for future she imagines for the further reclamation of Corsican. Perceptions of change similarly contribute to this temporal dimension, as in Elsa's description of the island as a "giant, slowly moving through space and time" as she describes Corsica's economic development as much slower than what she has seen in German settings. We see an overlaying or collapsing of discursive spacetimes (Blommaert's layered simultaneity) wherein the local remains resilient (Lombardi's postlocal).

The multiple spatial, corporal, linguistic, and temporal dimensions with which these teachers make sense of the world signal translingual praxis. By praxis I refer to an iterative, ongoing application of knowledge or informed, committed action. Participants describe communicating across language boundaries (Giorgia with Italian and Corsican), foreigners speaking imperfect French together (Miquela and her friends), and teaching and learning actively using multiple languages (Elsa with English, German, and French). Translanguaging extends beyond linguistic repertoires to consider various kinds of semiotic resources. In their professional practice, these teachers demonstrate what Li Wei (2018) has called a translanguaging instinct that allows multilinguals to strategically navigate "differences, discrepancies, inconsistencies, and ambiguities" (19). It is with diverse semiotic resources and orientations that participants relay their experiences of the multilingual dynamics on the island. These teachers embody "the post-modern condition of the foreign language instructor who is at once an educator, a multilingual subject, and a decentered sensibility in [a] global microcosm" (Kramsch & Zhang, 2018: 153). As multilingual instructors constantly attempt to find a "satisfactory subject position" (221) navigating between (and beyond) various perspectives, codes, and spacetimes, so must the multilingual researcher attempt to mediate, often clumsily juggling paradoxes and contradictions, trying to find an "interideological" footing (127; see also Linares, 2019a and 2019b on the practice of multilingual research). While the competing perspectives on multilingual dynamics and globalization phenomena presented throughout this chapter are not necessarily reconcilable, it is possible for multilingual teachers and researchers to sit with and embrace such messiness—and forge forward.

Continuing with the productive alternation between interactive and artifactual data, the following chapter pivots from analyzing language use as related to school settings to consider language in the public space. Studying the linguistic landscape (signage, graffiti, inscriptions) allows for a further consideration of how translanguaging happens on Corsica by drawing on different spatial and semiotic resources in meaning making. By turning to analyze language in a setting not specifically related to language teaching and learning (the classroom [Chapter 2], language learning texts [Chapter 3], teachers [this chapter]), one can consider how multilingual dynamics play out in other public spaces and how these might offer similar or complementary perspectives regarding urban multilingualism on the island.

Chapter 5

For(z)a

Introduction

The Collège du Centre, in the heart of *vieux* Bastia, abuts the Église Saint-Charles Borromée which lets onto rue Droite, sloping steadily south. I worked there as an English assistant in 2012–13 and subsequently carried out parts of this research there as well. Returning for fieldwork in 2016, I rented an apartment on rue Chanoine Letteron (not realizing it was the same rue Droite)—conveniently located downtown near the port, bus stops, and the school. My first realization that rue Droite was not necessarily considered a normal place came when a friend picked me up from the airport and was driving me to the address I indicated. We passed rue Chanoine Letteron three times—each time she'd say *Where should I turn? It can't be here, this is rue Droite.* Finally, she called the landlord to verify the directions: *So it's on rue Droite?!* She was shocked, along with other colleagues, that I had rented an apartment there. *You should've told us, we would've found you something …*

I had not known the street's particular reputation, notorious for being a North African immigrant hub and supposedly the center of the drug trade in the city, what some colleagues called *la racaille de rue Droite* (the riffraff of rue Droite). In fact, rue Droite figured prominently in the media that summer: nighttime police raids resulted in the arrests of three young men and the seizure of large amounts of marijuana, cocaine, and cash (Nannipieri, 2016). But the colorful six-to-eight-story buildings that lined the narrow street seemed more or less in the same state as those on other streets in the neighborhood, with a few broken windows and vacant spaces on the ground floor. And the apartment itself was lovely, with a view onto the sea that showed the outline of Elba in the early morning. It did seem that most residents were immigrants of some sort: my landlord was continental French and the neighbors across the hall were Moroccan. In fact, the latter were friends of relatives of Ali, a student from the Sud FLE class who I would sometimes see when he visited them. Ali was extraordinarily studious and wanted to become a police officer; other students mocked him, laughing and saying he would become a terrorist. He was always enthusiastic about practicing his French with me when we would see each other on rue Droite. The street became an important point of reference for me, a side of Corsica I had not seen, much less inhabited, an urban immigrant space beyond the central periphery (Chapter 1).

This chapter presents a reading of the linguistic landscape (LL) of rue Droite to analyze the multiplicity of languages and messages attested on the street. While the previous chapter explored space and mobility as understood by interviewees, here place is constituted by an actual physical delimited setting. The presence (and absence) of different languages in rue Droite's LL helps us question widely circulated ideologies on Corsica regarding language, place, and belonging. My reading of the LL of rue Droite, focusing on a handful of focal signs, illustrates competing language-ideological orientations on one street. I ground my analysis in the reading of signs as situated artifacts and draw from a translanguaging approach to the LL that attempts to read the neighborhood holistically (Gorter & Cenoz, 2015). In the sections that follow, I briefly introduce work on Corsican LLs before offering my reading of rue Droite, a survey of signs therein with my interpretations woven throughout. I finish with a discussion of how this case contributes to our thinking about peripheral multilingualism within the broader francosphere, both constitutive of and affected by multilingual and transnational trends, especially with regard to notions of belonging.

§5.1 Corsican Linguistic Landscapes

The LL—the "symbolic construction of public space" (Ben Rafael et al., 2006)—helps construct many kinds of sociopolitical alignments and disparities. LL studies (e.g., Gorter, 2006; Shohamy et al., 2010) have analyzed the capacity of signage to construct social trends and power dynamics. As Blommaert (2013) asserts, the LL can "detect and interpret social change and transformation"; it is made up of "material forces subject to and reflective of conditions of production and patterns of distribution, [that are] constructive of social reality [...] Communication in the public space, consequently, is communication in a field of power" (2–3, 38–40).

Corsica, like the Mediterranean as a whole, is no stranger to linguistic and cultural plurality, and today the island experiences a high rate of immigration and tourist traffic (INSEE, 2015, 2017; Département des statistiques, des études et de la documentation, 2016). Though the rural is largely considered a stronghold of minority language practices (Jaffe, 1999; Pietikäinen et al., 2017), the urban is not usually considered a space in which the Corsican language is easily engaged—by allophone outsiders, or by anyone (see Diana's discussion of the village in Chapter 4). An ideological separation is maintained between Corsican and other languages on the island and is reified in the rural-urban divide. The expectation is that since francophones and outsiders are less present in the rural interior of the island, that Corsican is spoken more there with less interference, despite the fact that the cities are where schools, businesses, and (potential) users of the language mainly live. One of my goals is to trouble the idea that Corsican cannot flourish in city spaces, though it is perhaps quieter relative to other languages, especially French. My focus on the delimited space of a single street aligns with calls for attention to specific neighborhoods to analyze their special dynamics nested within larger urban areas (Shohamy, 2015; Gorter & Cenoz, 2015).

The Corsican language has a strong presence in the island's LL. Cotnam-Kappel (2014) explains that Corsican-language graffiti is omnipresent: "Corsica is an island covered in graffiti. These painted messages devastate/decorate the walls of cities, towns, schools and homes" (48). Other recent work on the LL of French and Italian coastal cities (Blackwood & Tufi, 2015) has analyzed the coexistence of regional languages of the Mediterranean (Catalan, Sardinian) and national standards (French, Italian) as well as immigrant/mobile languages (Chinese, English). Though Corsican is widely visible throughout Corsica's LL, somewhat reflective of ongoing revitalization efforts, we must keep in mind that visibility is not necessarily indicative of sociolinguistic vitality (Blackwood, 2015; Barni & Bagna, 2015). That is, seeing a lot of Corsican does not equate to the existence of a speech community (furthermore: who counts as a speaker?). Nonetheless,

Blackwood and Tufi (2015: 210) have shown that Corsican is much more widely attested in the LL of the island than other regional languages of the Mediterranean like Sardinian. Political representation by way of visibility is one important characteristic widely understood as linked to Corsican in public space (Cotnam-Kappel, 2014: 63).

Living on rue Droite helped me to realize that approaching an object of study that is a space one physically inhabits is different from studying other kinds of objects or spaces (e.g., a classroom). Further, since rue Droite is widely considered somehow dangerous, I was exposed on a regular basis to a space that was avoided by many locals. Living on rue Droite yielded information that friends and colleagues were unaware of, for example multilingual evangelizing efforts. Additionally, though rue Droite is already widely imagined as an immigrant space, my own identity informs my positionality *vis-à-vis* the space as an object of study (Tufi, 2017: 79). That is, since rue Droite is already understood as a space occupied by a marginal other, my personal background both aligned with and differed significantly from those living there. I was easily identified by neighbors as neither Corsican nor French, and was more often than not taken for a tourist and, as attested by the surprise of friends and colleagues, not someone who should be on rue Droite. These differences highlight a central question that I ponder here: which languages belong where, and according to whom? This question gestures to the issue of belonging more generally—ideas of where certain people do or do not belong, and how they are linguistically imagined, represented, or effaced in particular spaces. This focus ties back to the explorations throughout the chapters of linguistic multiplicity as variously conceived in different experiences and contexts.

§5.2 Reading rue Droite

My reading of rue Droite draws from the approach of previous LL work that analyzes public space with a linguistic-ethnographic foundation that takes multilingual coexistence as its point of departure (Gorter & Cenoz, 2015: 64; Shohamy et al., 2010; Abdelhay et al., 2016). This type of approach allows for the interpretation of emplaced language in light of larger power dynamics and social trends (Scollon & Scollon, 2003; Blommaert, 2013). What's more, aligning this work with translanguaging encourages us to move beyond enumerating languages as if they were neatly separable. My central question is: how does the LL of rue Droite, its "multilingual units" (Gorter & Cenoz, 2015), help construct local language attitudes and ideologies? Here I will showcase a sampling of salient examples from the LL of rue Droite, moving from either end of the street toward the center.

§5.2.1 The Bus Stop

At the northwest end of rue Droite, there is a bus stop[1] at the large traffic circle across from the local middle school. The bus stop is located at the northernmost culmination of the upward-sloping street, and serves as a main point of reference and traffic in the neighborhood. It is a glass-and-metal structure equipped with signage detailing the layout of Bastia's larger area and showing which bus lines run where. I have waited for the bus at this stop on many, many occasions.

One morning, there were newly written graffiti, in black and blue permanent marker, covering the glass and metal panels (Images 5.1 and 5.2). Written in French and Corsican were the phrases "Arabi fora" (Corsican: Arabs out),[2] "A droga fora" (Corsican: Drugs out), "Français de merde" (French: Shitty French), and "Rentre chez toi arabe" (French: Go home Arab).[3] These were accompanied by a simple line drawing of a coffin next to a suitcase with *ou* (French: or) in between, presumably signifying a choice between leaving the island (as symbolized by the suitcase) or death (the coffin). This is most likely an allusion to the slogan "la valise ou le cercueil" (suitcase or coffin) used during the period of conflict following the signing of the Evian Accords in March 1962, referring to the choice given to *pieds-noirs* (those of French origin) after its independence to leave Algeria or face threatening consequences. Here, the expression has been appropriated and redirected toward those of Maghrebi origin in Corsica. Interestingly, a large number of French civil servants in the

---

1 For an intriguing analysis of messages on bus stop benches, see Gal and Irvine (2019: ch. 7).
2 Translations are mine, unless otherwise noted.
3 Corsicans are more often than not French-dominant, and Corsican monolingualism is obsolete (or very nearly). That is, Corsicans may express themselves in Corsican, French, or both.

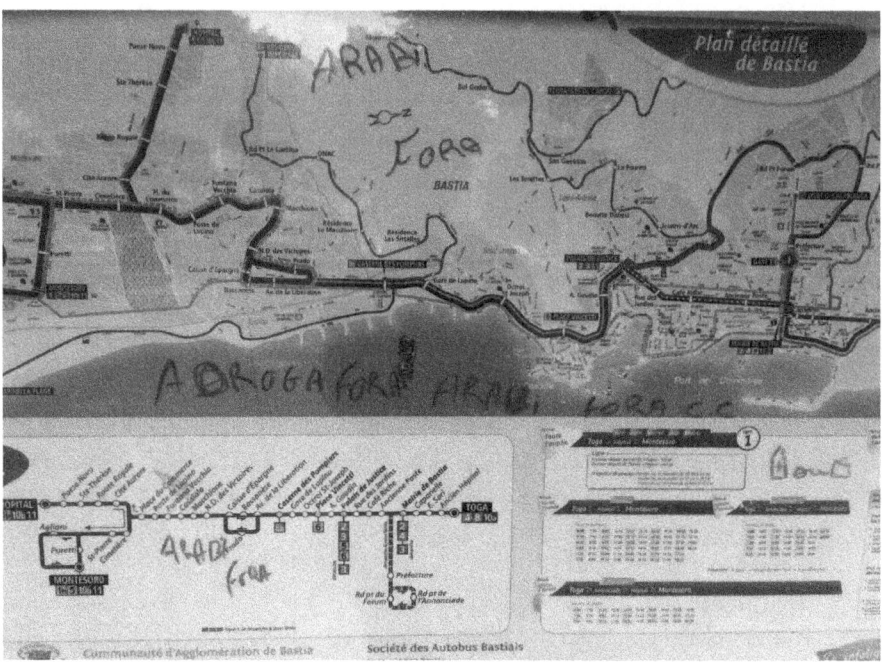

Image 5.1 Bus stop sign, "Arabi fora" (Arabs out). Note the small drawing of the suitcase and coffin toward the bottom right.
Photo credit: Author.

colonies were of Corsican descent: a colonized people carrying out the work of the colonizing State (Chapter 1; Mestersheim, 2002; Heller & McElhinny 2017: 102). Note that here the image reflects an inversion of the original phrase in which the coffin appears first and the suitcase second.

Such messages, particularly *arabi fora*, are unfortunately not uncommon on Corsica, and present a kind of conventional message as platitudes.[4] Cotnam-Kappel (2014) explains that on Corsica those "of all linguistic backgrounds are confronted by graffiti on a daily basis. Those who do not speak the Corsican language inevitably pick

---

4   "[L]a langue corse est systématiquement utilisée dans des tags racistes envers [la communauté maghrébine]" (The Corsican language is systematically used in racist tags against [the Maghrebi community]) (Ottavi, 2013: 153). Pietikäinen et al. (2017) state that "These graffiti are quite serious, as is the very real racism and violence directed against Arabs" (185).

Image 5.2 Bus stop bench. "Arabi fora rentre chez toi Arabe" (Arabs out go home Arab). Photo credit: Author.

up bits and pieces of the Corsican vocabulary due to these messages. [...] The words are written across the island and become a part of the island's vocabulary, inextricably linked to the Corsican culture" (64–5). In this way, "The messages that graffiti convey regarding Corsican culture and language form a hidden curriculum or public pedagogy that necessarily influences the inhabitants of Corsica" (67). *Arabi fora* is readily identifiable to islanders, even to those who do not speak Corsican. The expression appeared in the 1970s concurrently alongside the expression *Francesi fora* (French out), and the two coexist in graffiti throughout the island today (Martinet, 2015). *Fora* is also used in other political graffiti, for example *fascisti fora* (fascists out). As Abdouni (2016) asserts regarding the expression *arabi fora*, "Casser le Maghrébin (l'Arabe) était devenue une façon sacrée de se montrer un Corse pur et dur" (quashing the Maghrebi [the Arab] had become a sacred way of showing oneself a Corsican through and through).

Both Corsican and French political discourses often correlate North

African immigrant groups with drug trafficking. In the Corsican context, this resulted in the appearance of the slogan *A droga fora* (drugs out) in the 1980s and 1990s: "Ce slogan devint pour beaucoup synonyme d'un autre: '*Arabi fora*'" (For many, this slogan became a synonym of another: *Arabi fora*) (Fourquet, 2017: 139). Following hostility between adolescents of Corsican and Moroccan origin in March 2004, rue Droite was the scene of a nighttime bombing, the beginning of a series of attacks that targeted local Moroccan-owned areas and businesses (140). Fourquet observes "l'idéologie du '*Fora*' vis[e] à rejeter et à expulser tout corps étranger non assimilable" (the ideology of *Fora* aims to reject and expel any foreign body that is not assimilable); further, "ces actions engagées sont légitimées par ailleurs" (these politically committed actions are legitimated elsewhere), by those of the French far right (143, 141–2). So, while these sentiments are not necessarily unique to any one place within the wider French Metropole, it is not inconsequential that on Corsica they are expressed in Corsican, *arabi fora/a droga fora*.

In their work analyzing the use of Corsican in the island's tourist industry, Jaffe and Oliva (2013) interpret public use of the language as "foreground[ing] the symbolic and political aspect of displaying linguistic heritage" and "ideologically [conventional] in their function of using Corsican to symbolize Corsican identity" (103). The identity presented in the case of the graffiti at the bus stop defines a Corsican position as one opposed to outsiders, be they continental French (*Français*) or other foreigners (*Arabe/i*) (Jaffe, 1999). Indeed, Blackwood and Tufi (2015) explain that "Discourses of exclusion from the mainland […] have become sedimented in constructions of alterity" (105). In this example, the placement of the graffiti in such a high-traffic area is, perhaps, not as surprising as its proximity to the local school. It was removed within a few days.

§5.2.2 "The True Faith"

Another day, on the southernmost end of the street where rue Droite meets Place Prelà, a man and a woman stood next to a display of religious literature (Image 5.3). The display was made up of a printed sign and three shelves to hold pamphlets. The sign on the display was printed in Arabic and also included the church's website. The pamphlets were

Image 5.3 Display of Jehovah's Witness pamphlets in Arabic and French. Photo credit: Author.

two different Jehovah's Witness publications; four sets were stacked on the display, and all were printed in Arabic, with the exception of one in French. The first pamphlet features a woman sitting alone on a doorstep, crying with her head in her hands with a framed picture of a couple next to her on the ground; one can assume that she is grieving. The Arabic texts read, "When death takes away your loved one," "You are welcome to take a free flyer. Ask for one in your language,"[5] "JW.org Jehovah's Witnesses' official website," and "Control Tower[6] announces Jehovah's Witnesses."[7] The second pamphlet, in French, reads "La vraie foi: le chemin qui mène au bonheur" (The true faith: the path leading to happiness). The image features a nuclear family, the father sitting with a book open in his lap while the mother, brother, and sister stand around him smiling.

The multilingual dimension of this evangelical literature is not trivial. Piller (2016) argues that multilingual signage, while inclusive on the surface, actually highlights certain groups as nonconforming and therefore as the target of societal criticism and exclusion:

> Proponents of linguistic justice often make the facile assumption that multilingual signs by their very nature are more inclusive than monolingual ones. However, it all depends on the context. It is true that a sign such as [a] Chinese-English "no smoking" sign includes Chinese readers as potential recipients of the message. However, at the same time, the sign excludes Chinese readers from polite society by singling them out as likely transgressors. (56)

The pamphlets on rue Droite identify Arabic speakers as doubly nonconforming members of the local community, religiously and linguistically. The fact that evangelizers have chosen an entry point to rue Droite to share their Arabic-language religious literature demonstrates their singling out of a particular population, one located in a particular space, as other.

---

5   Note the metalinguistic message produced here in a minoritized language/script.
6   The Arabic translation of the title of the Jehovah's Witness pamphlet publication *The Watchtower*.
7   I am grateful to Lamia Mezzour-Hodson for her kind help in providing translations from the Arabic.

During my time on Corsica, I attended events based in the widespread Roman Catholic tradition, and overheard colleagues approvingly discuss the conversion of North African immigrants to Christianity. Integration by way of conversion is seen as commendable. Heller and McElhinny (2017: ch. 2) explore the complex historical dynamics of Christian conversion as caught up with linguistic imperialism and translational practices: "Conversion, like conquest, is a process of crossing over into the domain of someone else and claiming it as one's own" (36). Heller and McElhinny explain that the project of *reducción* (reduction: "pacification, conversion, or ordering") in Spain's colonizing of the Philippines "was meant to transform space, conduct, and language" (38). Shifting beliefs also often accompany transnational mobility in our global present: "the fact of migration with its effects of dislocation, detachment from older local forms of social and cultural organization, the loss of an organic community and so forth, is a powerful moment of conversion (Maskens, 2008)" (Blommaert, 2013: 103). On Corsica, anti-Muslim sentiment reached new heights during the burkini scandal of 2016 (Chapter 1), and it is not out of the ordinary to hear of mosques being vandalized. While I do not suggest that widespread conversion to the Jehovah's Witnesses is a norm on the island, I mean to highlight that, as other work has shown, newly arrived immigrants may be attracted to evangelical groups for both social and linguistic benefits (Blommaert, 2013: ch. 6). The Jehovah's Witnesses on rue Droite attempt a kind of *reducción* wherein those perceived as different in language or beliefs are to be brought "into the fold" (Heller & McElhinny, 2017: 29). Linguistic transformation by way of conversion is visible in the pamphlets in the transition from Arabic to French, and the recompense of obliging immigrant converts is, apparently, happiness. Sadness is paired with Arabic, and happiness with French. The drives for immigrants to integrate religiously and linguistically are linked.

The perspectives that these pamphlets represent are that of Arabic as the assumed language of immigrant groups and Franco-Corsican society as one that does not valorize these groups' assumed religious practices. Other orientations, religious and linguistic, are erased (Irvine & Gal, 2000): Corsican and Tamazight, for example, are nowhere to be found. The assumed linguistic difference—that residents of rue Droite speak Arabic—is an interesting question. While there are certainly many who do, thousands of North African immigrants to Corsica have been on the island for several generations and may be French-dominant. Among the more recently arrived, a large portion are Imazighen who wish to dissociate from Arabic sociolinguistic practices, seen as an imposition. When acknowledged at all, the Tamazight-Arabic divide on Corsica is largely left unattended, at least in the LL (see also Géa, 2005, 2006; Mahdi, 2014).

Jehovah's Witness evangelists came through the rue Droite neighborhood twice during my fieldwork period, going door-to-door to speak with residents, distribute literature, and read verses from the Bible. One woman recognized me from the Corsican class I attended and boasted that they had materials in all different languages and offered to bring me the English and Corsican versions. Aside from the one afternoon at rue Droite and Place Prelà, I have never seen religious literature in any language publicly displayed on Corsica.

§5.2.3 Multilingual Fragments

Moving from the northern and southern ends toward the center of the street, this section presents a brief overview of signage in other languages on rue Droite. This is not an exhaustive survey; rather my goal is to provide a few representative examples illustrating the diversity of other languages, sign types, and kinds of messages present in the LL of the street.

In the foyer of my building, there was a Corsican-language flyer which read, "Rispettu, pulizia, circulazione, u vulemu fà u primu passu? A mo cità, a tengu cara" (Respect, cleanliness, mobility. Do we want to take the first step? My city, I love it) (Image 5.4). The flyer promotes a neighborhood clean-up of sorts, and the trademark emblem of the city of Bastia appears in the bottom right corner. Next to this flyer was another, printed completely in French, detailing the local recycling system, complete with photos of what kinds of materials are recycled together. I posit that this highlights an orientation to care of the local space, observable in other efforts throughout the island in ads for beach clean-ups, signs protecting historic sites, and recycling receptacles. This use of Corsican can be interpreted as symbolically aligning with the goals of preserving the Corsican *patrimoine* (cultural heritage/legacy); respect toward the natural and built environments on the island is expressed in Corsican (Mendes, 2020).

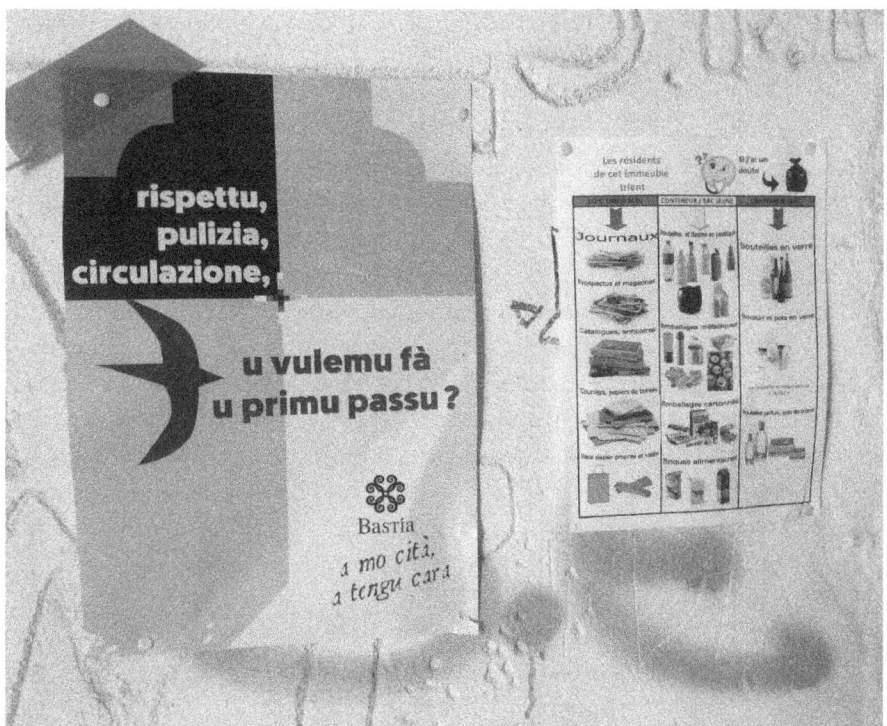

Image 5.4 Corsican-language clean-up flyer, "Rispettu, pulizia, circulazione, u vulemu fà u primu passu? A mo cità, a tengu cara." (Respect, cleanliness, mobility. Do we want to take the first step? My city, I love it.). Photo credit: Author.

On the corner of another building, a plaque reads "Ex rue Droite rue Chanoine Letteron" (Image 5.5).[8] The street was previously named rue Droite. Today, it has been officially renamed rue Chanoine Letteron. The official name honors a local figure, Lucien Auguste Letteron, a French priest who was appointed Professeur agrégé[9] de Lettres (Professor of Literature) at the local high school from 1878 until he retired in 1905. He was a passionate historian of Corsica and worked with several local societies to study, promote, and publish on the Corsican *patrimoine*. It is perhaps not at all coincidental, then, that

---

8   *Chanoine*, a "canon," is a religious title for a member of a cathedral community.
9   An *agrégation* is an advanced teaching credential in France.

a street assumed to be full of foreigners be named after an "outsider" (a Frenchman) who dedicated much of his life to Corsica (Lahlou, 2017). This renaming can be interpreted as an attempt to refashion the poor reputation of the street in the eyes of the public—the example of Canon Letteron being one that demonstrates that outsiders can, in fact, become devoted members of the Corsican community and cause. However, most locals do not know the street by anything other than rue Droite; the change has not taken hold in day-to-day life, as people still refer to the street as rue Droite verbally and even in the news (Ferrer, 2016). The existence of the plaque stating that the street was formerly known by one name and supposedly now bears another attests to an attempt at a kind of rebranding. Like the next sign I present, this example highlights the LL's dynamic, changing nature.

Toward the northern end of the street next to the stairs leading to *Église* Saint-Charles Borromée, there is a plaque in Latin above an old public fountain which reads "Fons urbis praefecto Petro Giovellina restitutus anno domini MDCCCVI imperj Napoleonis Magni secondo" (City fountain restored by mayor Petru Giovellina in the year of our Lord 1806 and in the second year of Emperor Napoleon the Great) (Image 5.6).[10] This inscription illustrates the use of Latin in imperial commemorative plaques in the region dating to the early 1800s; other similar inscriptions in Latin on the same wall date to almost a century earlier. The plaque establishes a loose tie with Napoleon, who was born on Corsica, a further connection between the local and the empire. As with the "Ex rue Droite" inscription, this plaque illustrates how "Every sign tells a story about who produced it, and who is selected to consume it" (Blommaert, 2013: 44). The former was produced by those clarifying the renaming of the street, presumably city authorities, and is addressed to a public who may or may not still refer to the space by its other name. The latter likewise gestures to a governmental source, and addresses the subjects of the empire, the general public, though in a language they likely did not read, write, or speak. Blommaert (2013: 51) explains that the LL is historical, not synchronic; it points forward and backward, temporally mediating discourses between interlocutors (17). Similarly, Pavlenko and Mullen (2015) emphasize the importance

---

10 I am grateful to Noah Guynn for his kind assistance with the Latin translation.

Image 5.5 Street name plaque, "Ex rue Droite rue Chanoine Letteron" (Former Right Street Canon Letteron Street). Photo credit: Author.

of understanding the LL diachronically, asserting that signage is very much contingent upon the preceding textual and sociopolitical context.

Above a west-facing door, an old storefront sign reads "(R)égal'Ad Snack 95.32.59.88." (Image 5.7). The "R" has all but worn away, leaving a trace of the shape of the letter. The print on the sign gives us a bit more information than meets the eye. "Régal'Ad" is a playful spelling of the word *régalade* (French: feast). *Snack* has been adopted from English into French to mean "snack bar." The format of the phone number indicates that the sign dates from before October 1996, when phone numbers in France changed from an eight- to ten-digit format; it is outdated and thus displays "diminished indexical power" (Symes, 2021: 67). The use of English here, a term adopted into everyday French, contributes to the multilingualism of the local LL in a mundane way, not in a dominant, globally hegemonic sense. Blackwood and Tufi (2015) have found "a clear trend to hybridity involving an English and a French element to business names in these coastal Mediterranean towns," such

154 *Countervocalities*

Image 5.6 Jesuit fountain plaque, "Fons urbis praefecto Petro Giovellina restitutus anno domini MDCCCVI imperj Napoleonis Magni secondo" (City fountain restored by mayor Petru Giovellina in the year of our Lord 1806 and in the second year of Emperor Napoleon the Great). Photo credit: Author.

Image 5.7 Old shop sign, "Régal'Ad Snack" (Feast Snack Bar). Photo credit: Author.

as *Happy Croq*, *Canilook*, and *Le Number One* (197). They go on to explain that linguistic "cosmopolitanism in France's Mediterranean LL is performed by the English language more often when the value of [a] product is lower than a French equivalent" (213). So, in this instance, we can read the use of English as rather commonplace and indicative of a product whose value is modest.

Though several languages reside in the Corsican LL, the mere presence of a language in a space does not necessarily indicate the presence of (fluent) speakers. For example, the presence of English on rue Droite is minimal and rather mundane. Extending from the notions of banal cosmopolitanism (Beck, 2003, 2006) and banal globalization (Thurlow & Jaworski, 2011), Blackwood and Tufi (2015) propose the idea of banal multilingualism: "multilingualism [is] a widespread feature of the public space, but this multilingualism does not refer to plurilingual individuals, but to the emplacement of several languages in a given LL as a consequence of globalization" (202). The authors conclude that despite its incomparable hegemonic influence,

English does not displace other languages in any seriously threatening way in the public space of the French and Italian coastal Mediterranean (203). From this perspective, with regard to the appearance of English for example, the LL of rue Droite displays trends happening elsewhere in the Mediterranean, if not the entire world.

From these examples, we see several things happening along the street in several languages: clean-up efforts, place-naming, advertisements, and historic markers. Aside from these, there are other signs that contribute to the multilingual make-up of the space such as inscriptions commemorating locals who fought in World War II, Christian religious phrases above entryways, graffiti mocking police authorities, and other commercial flyers. These vary in shape and material, and contribute to an assemblage of texts within the built environment of the street (Mendes, 2020). Rue Droite is decked with linguistic-graphic multiplicity.

§5.2.4 *Arabi forza*

Toward the very center of the street, there is an unkempt courtyard on the western side with a graffito along the walls. At first glance, one might not catch that the message differs from those that appeared on the bus stop in permanent marker. What appears on the wall is in fact a palimpsest of a graffitied message which someone then attempted to paint over. The words bleed through nonetheless and read in Corsican *arabi forza* (literally, "Arabs strength," here understood as an imperative along the lines of "Let's go, Arabs!" or "Onward, Arabs!") (Image 5.8).

With a minor change in a clichéd expression (*arabi fora* → *arabi forza*), transgressive meaning bursts forth—or rather, remains hidden in plain sight. This transformation illustrates two competing ideologies in the local LL: expelling versus encouraging "Arabs." The phrase is bivalent and indeed could be read as Italian.[11] This bivalency dodges strict, bounded notions of language to help us think to move between the many moving parts in a holistic repertoire of codes, as in a translanguaging approach. At the lexical level, one could imagine that *forza*

---

11 Pietikäinen et al. (2017) point to another instance of bivalency in the phrase "Made in Corsica" where "in Corsica" could be read as either English or Corsican (104); "in Corsica" could also, for that matter, be read as Italian.

Image 5.8 Graffiti palimpsest, "Arabi forza" (Arabs strength).
Photo credit: Author.

was easily borrowed from other expressions in Corsican or Italian, for example the slogan cheering on the local soccer team, *Forza Bastia* (Let's go, Bastia!). It would seem, then, that widely available words in a minority language can fuel this kind of language play, which does not necessarily require advanced proficiency (Benor, 2019; Mendes, 2020). That is, the LL, as a kind of "public pedagogy" (Cotnam-Kappel, 2014: 67), is kindling and canvas for novel appropriations and transformations of Corsican, illustrating minority codes' powerful potential in transgressive linguistic landscaping.

Transgression, the navigating, challenging, and changing of boundaries, "cannot 'succeed' without reference to norms" (Pietikäinen et al., 2017: 152; Foucault, 1977; Pennycook, 2008). Via a kind of appropriation and (rather cunning) transformation of a Corsican maxim, a new message is produced. The fact that someone has attempted to cover up this particular message sets it apart from other graffiti in the immediate area, perhaps calling even more attention to it. However, if one were to miss the addition of the letter *z*, especially considering that proficiency or "literacy" in Corsican cannot be taken for granted, and given that certain elements of the LL are often seen rather than read (Abdelhay et al., 2016: 55), the drastically distinct message would be lost on those wo see it Indeed, not everyone who walks down the street of an urban area "has the requisite multilingual competence to appreciate subtle nuances" in signage script (Das, 2016: 147). As Gal and Irvine (2019) similarly assert of their work on messages on benches, "the [...] text can address only people who can already read" (193). Pietikäinen et al. (2017) explain that "linguistic and semiotic tools of transgressive practices may include violations of genre expectations, subversions of language-ideological hierarchies, and playful distortions of boundaries" (156). The expectation that has been violated in this example is one in which the Corsican language is used to express disdain for or exclusion of outsiders; *arabi forza* is a subversive use of a conventional Corsican expression.

Arabi fora versus *arabi forza* attests to a dynamic coexistence of different kinds of users of Corsican relatively close together. These graffiti reveal a multiplicity of linguistic-ideological orientations at play, writers using Corsican to different ends. *Arabi forza* can be interpreted as a reappropriation much like that of the expression *la valise ou le cercueil* (the suitcase or the coffin) seen at the bus stop. Originally a message directed at those of French descent in newly liberated Algeria, *la valise ou le cercueil* in graffiti on Corsica is drummed up and redirected to deliver an old threat in a new place. *Arabi forza* similarly refashions a widespread ideology of exclusion in a specific local context (Abdouni, 2016; Fourquet, 2017).[12] As Pietikäinen et al. (2017) assert, "Transgressive acts do not deny boundaries but rather exceed them, and in the process, render them visible objects of reflection" (154–5). In this example, *forza* in place of *fora* blurs ideological divisions by encouraging strength in the "Arab" community expressed in the Corsican language. *Arabi forza* engages an exclusionary discourse in a minoritized language as it simultaneously refers to and warps the original message (Blommaert's layered simultaneity), signaling an

---

12   As Gal and Irvine (2019) say of a widespread message publicly displayed in Baltimore reflecting the city's mayoral campaigns and wider political dynamics, "The slogan takes its place within a system of intertextual relations" (193).

ideological shift with regard to potential uses of the Corsican language and fluidities between linguistic and cultural barriers.

Translanguaging in the LL involves holistic considerations of the various linguistic resources that make up a neighborhood's "own multilingual character" (Gorter & Cenoz, 2015: 69). *Arabi forza* helps us to think about compositional processes involved in translanguaging (Canagarajah, 2011: 6) such as drawing from widely circulated vocabulary or maxims in minoritized languages to remix (Cotnam-Kappel, 2014) or decreate (Phipps, 2019). In the *fora* → *forza* transformation, we may read what Li Wei (2018) has called a "translanguaging instinct," which "drives humans to go beyond narrowly defined linguistic cues and transcend culturally defined language boundaries" (24). Indeed, "translanguaging is a transformative resemiotization process, whereby language users display the best of their creativity and criticality" (22). Relatedly, a spatial orientation to translanguaging considers the "diverse semiotics and spatial resources" deployed in meaning-making, such as the "strategic emplacement" of *arabi forza* on rue Droite (Canagarajah, 2018: 49–50).

We need not know the authorship of *arabi forza* to observe that there are processes of erasure (Irvine & Gal, 2000) at play in the layer of paint which covers it over and represents an attempt to snub the ideological orientation that would somehow pair the Corsican language and "Arabs" in an encouraging light. The layering (literally) of the co-occurring text and palimpsest helps construct "political and socioculturally dynamic and polycentric space" (Blommaert, 2018: 85), and by way of its attempted erasure underscores the temporally sensitive and ephemeral nature of peripheral multilingualism in the LL (Pietikäinen et al., 2017: 203–4). Gal and Irvine (2019) remind us in their work on shifting signs in Baltimore that a change of signage does not simply solve wider sociopolitical issues: "racial tensions could not just be painted over" (198). The acts of writing and attempting to erase the message within the demarcated (Blommaert, 2018: ch. 7) area of rue Droite are telling of local struggles as to who can legitimately claim space there and in what language(s).

Rue Droite is home to a cacophony in its marked space, which includes both "local" and "foreign" elements. The various messages that appear in the LL, particularly the Corsican-Arabic-Corsican rejoinders I have highlighted, help constitute a central facet of the multilingual character of the neighborhood, its own special local characteristics (Gorter & Cenoz, 2015: 69). This linguistic-ideological tension attests to the dynamism of the urban Corsican periphery.

§5.3 For(z)a

In their study of public displays of peripheral multilingualism, Pietikäinen et al. (2017: 44) assert that "Linguistic landscapes [...] have the potential to represent and to 'perform' language-ideological conditions, whether actual or imagined" (Pietikäinen & Kelly-Holmes, 2013: 223; see also Blackwood & Tufi, 2015: 76). The combinations of languages and their divergent messages on rue Droite help constitute the area's local multilingualism: Arabic-language proselytizing, Corsican-language clean-up efforts, anti-immigrant sentiments in French—all contribute to a multiplicity of linguistic and social orientations. Languages do different things on the street, and this chorus suggests an understanding of the local character of rue Droite as liminal.

The destabilization of center-periphery dynamics (Pietikäinen et al., 2017) and polycentricity (Blommaert, 2010) underscore competing centers of influence, centripetal and centrifugal forces (Ottavi, 2013: 140). This is particularly evident in the Corsican context, constituted by multiple institutional and cultural authorities (Mendes, 2021). Rue Droite represents an immigrant, allophone context torn between these. The street can be understood with a "notion of liminality, the multiplicity of voices that compose the local LL are those of 'a people in the process of becoming other' (Deleuze & Guattari, 1988: 106), therefore capturing [the] state of in-betweenness" (Tufi, 2017: 92). This liminality is potent in the same ways in which the indeterminacy (Jaffe, 1999) and ambiguity (Candea, 2010) of "small languages" aptly demonstrate in their evasion of boundaries and categorization. Rue Droite is a manifestation of the peripheral, on the outskirts of central authorities, and of the liminal, a "'creative in-betweenness' (Hess, 1996) where social norms and power dynamics can be challenged and changed" (Stanford et al., 2018: 197). This colorful gray area is its power.

Rue Droite's LL illustrates language dynamics that are more complicated than the static French-Corsican binary that dominates wider conceptualizations of the contemporary sociolinguistic situation on the island. It is also crucial to interrogate the absence of certain languages in the LL, its "invisible or silenced linguistic dynamics" (Blackwood & Tufi, 2015: 205; Pavlenko & Mullen, 2015: 129). Immigrant languages on Corsica that are visually absent from rue Droite, supposedly densely inhabited by foreigners, include Portuguese, Romanian, and Tamazight, not to mention tourist languages like German. In their survey of Mediterranean LLs, Blackwood and Tufi (2015) found the absence of Arabic and Tamazight in Corsica's LL "particularly conspicuous" (138–9). Additionally, in the near total lack of Portuguese in the cities they studied, they see a glossing over of Portuguese immigrants as "white Roman Catholic Europeans, indistinguishable from the French" (212). Although the Portuguese are among the three largest groups of immigrants on Corsica, alongside Romanians and Moroccans, it is often North African immigrants who are the recipients of particularly negative attention as foreigners. In her work on Arabic as a minoritized language of Israel, Suleiman (2017) asserts that its erasure points to the idea that "Arabic and its people need not be a part of the landscape" (84–5). These speakers (or writers) are kept from participating in public space in this way.

Recent work (Pietikäinen et al., 2017) has argued that Corsican spaces "are *not* 'superdiverse' (Blommaert, 2015; Reyes, 2014). They do *not* show accumulations of multilingual and multi-ethnic migrant groups who form dense and complex communities of practice and *rework linguistic and cultural boundaries and norms*" (30; emphasis added).[13] Similarly, Blackwood and Tufi (2015) assert that "the LL do[es] not often bring to the fore voice and agency for […] those who are silenced in their written universe. In these instances, the LL does not account for social disparities as they are revealed in written language practices" (207). *Arabi forza* is an instance of both appropriation (see Chapter 3) and transgression and helps us to pivot, even slightly, from the above claims. Urla and Helepololei (2014), in their work on political protest in Spain, rightly observe the difficulty in inferring intention when ethnographically studying what can be interpreted as resistance, "actions by subordinate classes that aim to mitigate or deny the material

---

13 I do not categorize Corsica as superdiverse or not (see Pavlenko, 2018; Jaffe, 2016). Rather, my goal is to address the coexistence of minoritized languages in the LL in what has been conceptualized as a peripheral multilingual space (Pietikäinen et al., 2017).

and symbolic claims the dominant classes made upon them" (Scott, 1986: 22–31). I read *forza* as resisting *fora*, a resistance to racism, to the imposition of particular languages and their concomitant ideologies. Even if this is a singular example, I contend that *arabi forza* is an attempt at reworking boundaries—linguistic, ideological, cultural, and political. The LL of rue Droite challenges the insular French-Corsican binary at the same time that *arabi for(z)a* destabilizes—or perhaps bridges—the Corsican-other divide.

Lombardi's (2014) notion of the "postlocal" offers one lens through which to read the Corsican LL with regard to local-global dynamics (Chapter 1). The postlocal is "the experience of immediate, immanent placement that is nevertheless globally connected" (41).[14] The postlocal puts "the concept of deterritorialization in tension with the embodied practice and proximal, everyday experience of banal cosmopolitans. […] To say 'postlocal' is to approach a given text with an enmeshed understanding of local/regional/global always in mind, but also to suggest that places retain a resilient 'thickness' in everyday life" (43). In the context of peripheral multilingualism on Corsica, I take this to mean that despite (or simply, along with) global influences, the urban need not be considered drained of its "Corsicanness" (Blackwood & Tufi, 2015: 134), as attested by the cultural artifacts produced therein, like the LL, which display both "local" and "foreign" elements. In this way, I interpret the postlocal as engaged with the concept of mobility and transnationalism (cf. "deterritorialization" per Tufi, 2017), which makes urban Corsican multilingualism ("local/regional/global") possible.

Arabi forza is the postlocal epicenter of rue Droite's multilingual marked space. In this phrase, we read "the intersection of the transient and the familiar" (Blackwood & Tufi, 2015: 73) that is at once "highly localized *and* radically decentered" (Lombardi, 2014: 51; original emphasis). Cotnam-Kappel's (2014) discussion of Corsican-language graffiti argues that "the messages attempt to obstruct the obstacles to

---

14 Lombardi, an ecocritic who developed this term in his work on regional literature of California, clarifies, explaining that "A postlocal ecocriticism would balance critical regionalism—which in its many varieties analyzes but is not limited to the discursive production, accommodation, resistance, and flow of cultural imaginaries, artifacts, and spaces—with ecocriticism's attention to the study of culturally produced artifacts and the environment" (2014: 41–2).

language legitimization on the island" (59); the tags are bold and run rampant. Ottavi (2013: 153) observes the systematic nature of Corsican-language graffiti with content that discriminates against the Maghrebi community on the island (as in *arabi fora*, cf. Pietikäinen et al., 2017: 185; Abdouni, 2016; Fourquet, 2017). His pondering of Corsican-other dynamics is certainly fitting in an attempt to read *arabi for(z)a*:

> on peut se demander si, dans l'économie des échanges sociaux, n'est pas à l'œuvre une sorte de mimétisme conduisant certains ressortissants de chaque communauté à construire une image négative de l'Autre par crainte anomique de l'anéantissement par disparition de ses propres valeurs d'appartenance. (153)
>
> (one wonders if, in the economy of social exchanges, a kind of mimicry isn't at play, driving certain members of each group to construct a negative image of the Other by anomic fear of destruction through the disappearance of one's values of belonging)

As the representations of multilingualism visible on rue Droite suggest an intense engagement with "semiotics of participation and belonging" (Blackwood & Tufi, 2015: 120), *arabi for(z)a* as an epitome of the postlocal in urban Corsican space reveals "threads of nostalgia and critique that are at once ambivalent and provocative—the very essence of counter culture cache, and, therefore, an elemental site for a more engaged emplacement" (Lombardi, 2014: 51). *Arabi for(z)a*, as a "multivoiced sign" (Pietikäinen et al., 2017: 124), demonstrates novel uses of Corsican and signals a postlocal orientation to language and place.

The LL is a moving target of sorts, as it may change drastically from one date to another (Blackwood & Tufi, 2015: 59) (see also the Coda). Change is visible on rue Droite in the examples of temporary flyers for the city-wide clean up, the indication of the street's former name (*ex rue Droite*), and the Régal'Ad sign whose business is no longer operating. This impermanence is most clearly attested by the fact that two of the central signs in my analysis were either erased after a few days (*arabi fora*) or painted over (*arabi forza*), underscoring the importance of analyzing the LL diachronically, with attention to its ever-changing dynamics (Pavlenko & Mullen, 2015). The multiple manifestations of signs are evident in the preceding analyses of handwriting (Chapter 2), digital and print ABC texts (Chapter 3) and here in the shifting LL, each sign type susceptible to various kinds of transformation, layering, decay, erasure, approval, and contestation.

On rue Droite, multiplicity is attested in linguistic, cultural, political, spatial, and religious orientations. The Corsican context, as encapsulated by Metropolitan France, is a meso-level (Mendes, 2021), an in-between whose minoritized language context also experiences language from above (French) and sideways (transnational languages of immigrants and tourists), reminiscent of what Gadet calls the "Francophonia discontinua" (2014: 11). The linguistic and cultural multiplicity legible on rue Droite reveals the "results of alliances that offer alternate histories and strategies of engagement with dominant culture" (Lombardi, 2014: 52). The postlocal is evident in rue Droite's simultaneous construction of the local (clean-up efforts in Corsican), the regional (Corsican and French graffiti), and the foreign (proselytizing in Arabic): the postlocal "local/regional/global" (43). These collapse in *arabi forza*, wherein the transnational and local are brought to the fore with the addition of a single letter—political protest in a Corsican axiom within an otherwise dominantly francophone space. Corsicanness is "resilient" (Lombardi, 2014: 43) in urban spaces on the island, intact despite—or perhaps even fueled by—its coexistence with other languages and messages there. Indeed, "'small' languages are powerful tools" (Jaffe & Oliva, 2013: 114).

Rue Droite is an "internal periphery" (Blackwood & Tufi, 2015: 101). The street is actively avoided by some locals. Who is reading (writing, erasing) its signs? Rue Droite's LL should not be understood as representative. Indeed, my reading admittedly only analyzes a handful of texts in an attempt at interpreting local language-ideological orientations. Nevertheless, I understand the street as home to a kind of multilingualism from below (Phipps, 2013), a space in which new multilingual subjectivities emerge (Kramsch, 2009). *Arabi for(z)a* can be read at the intersection of political voice on one hand and minoritized-language literacy on the other. In urban spaces, immigrant/diasporic populations indeed "partially emerge through the material sedimentation of literacy practice" (Das, 2016: 146). By establishing a visual presence in local signage, the neighborhood can thus "speak" (148–9). *Arabi for(z)a* points to new ways in which societal participation can be achieved, even minimally in marking the public space, by those linguistically (orally or graphically) navigating multiple languages and forging new multilingual repertoires. The absence of certain codes (Portuguese, Arabic) echoes the disappearing languages of newly arrived immigrants to the island (Chapter 2). As with the appropriation of the Corsican language and space proffered in the ABC texts (Chapter 3), on rue Droite we see Corsican taken up for novel kinds of sociopolitical messaging. In *arabi forza*, we read a new way of talking back to franco- and corso-hegemonies. The creative deployment of a minoritized code calls us to carefully consider how resistance and appropriation are mobilized or erased. Rue Droite is not a privileged, central, or homogenous space. What we read on the street challenges us to reconsider how peripheries (Corsica) interact with still other peripheries (immigrant contexts therein) and how peripherality and multiplicity are linguistically and spatially configured as well as how we physically navigate such liminal spaces. *Arabi for(z)a* demonstrates the powerful potential of Corsican in urban settings with nascent linguistic, cultural, and political subjectivities in tow—if at times barely visible.

This chapter has attempted to show how languages marked in the urban Corsican space illustrate competing ideological orientations to multilingual coexistence. This foray into LL analysis has allowed for a consideration of linguistic and spatial semiotic tools and how they are used in public meaning-making on the island. By way of closing, I now turn to broader reflections on countervocalities as they appear outside of Corsica and what they might have to teach us about language and communication in other situations.

Coda

Les micro-réalités peuvent se faire leurs places parmi ce grand concert où on ne comprend rien.

(Micro-realities can make their place amidst this great concert where you can't understand anything)

—Livia, Corsican teacher, author, and activist (interview, May 19, 2016)

Language teaching and learning on Corsica are as dynamic as ever. The assistantship program, which has brought international assistants to teach languages in French schools for over 100 years, has expanded to include more participating countries: the Corsican school district recently hosted an English assistant from Kenya. In addition, the association Practicalingua has created *case di lingue*, immersion centers that host Corsican classes as well as other language classes (English, Italian, Spanish) and art and music classes in which Corsican is the medium of instruction.

During my most recent visit to Corsica in 2022, graffiti again painted a picture of current events. Yvan Colonna, an icon of Corsican nationalist politics, had been violently attacked and died in a Marseille prison earlier in the year. He had been serving a life sentence for the 1998 murder of a prefect appointed by the French State. His death sparked demonstrations throughout Corsica and found expression in the LL, for example in a graffito of his likeness accompanied by the

Image C.1 Yvan Colonna graffito, "omu eri populu ti si fattu" ([you] were a man made of [your] people). Photo credit: author.

Corsican text "omu eri populu ti si fattu" ([you] were a man made of [your] people) (see Image C.1).

The *vieux port* neighborhood, home to rue Droite, seems, in a word, to be gentrifying. Buildings are being renovated, an amphitheater at the citadel overlooks a boardwalk which stretches along the port

Image C.2 Graffiti palimpsest revisited, a new "A" for "for(z)a."
Photo credit: author.

and shore. All the while, the exterior of one of the main jetties reads "Corsica is not France." Rue Droite itself has had a facelift, façades repainted in bold oranges, yellows, and reds with neat trim. As of May 2022, the *arabi forza* palimpsest was still emblazoned on the unkempt courtyard wall, though not undisturbed: it would seem that some disagreement has persisted. Even more white paint has been added to the *arabi forza* graffito to try to further cover over the *-za*, with the addition of a large black capital A to insist on *fora* (out) (see Image C.2). The *for(z)a* message is still unresolved, but will apparently be built over soon. A sign announces there will be nine new residences built in the courtyard, while graffiti on the sign protest that this construction will destroy a green space. Further down the street, a lighthearted new multilayered tag of the phrase "Bastia è basta" (Bastia and that's it) has placed "Bastia" in purple brackets and added the word "pulenta" (polenta, a classic Corsican dish): "polenta, and that's it." Expression in Corsican remains both serious and playful.

170 *Countervocalities*

Image C.3 "Bastia è basta" (Bastia and that's it) → "Pulenta è basta" (Polenta and that's it). Photo credit: author.

This book has offered ruminations on multiplicity, things that are not the same, conflict, and erasure—but also on coexistence, attempts at harmony, and ideas about what an ensemble is and does. In the spirit of concluding, here I will try to reach up and out from the Corsican situation toward other issues—theoretical and practical, varied and perhaps seemingly disparate—in order to illustrate the wider implications of this work and the stakes of living in plurality and unity. In this gesture, I am keeping in mind core concepts that have grounded this work as a whole, such as language hierarchies, place and mobility, globalization, and homogenization/heterogenization. What do these have to teach us in other circumstances?

Countervocalities, competing conceptualizations of linguistic multiplicity and shifting language hierarchies, are all around us. Language attitudes are important in our day-to-day and inform what goes on in classrooms, how the census is conducted, in hiring practices, for immigration. Language is one factor among many in our collective grappling with multiplicity, and contributes to the ways in which we agree and disagree. One telling example: "_____ Lives Matter." Choose your qualifier. With the rise of "alternative facts," we have seen that concepts supposedly at the core of modern democratic institutions like "justice" mean radically different things to different people. The mechanisms by which we even consider multiple viewpoints are failing: widespread voter suppression is alive and well amongst historically marginalized populations, a sweeping erasure of voices in the life of the American nation and the wider world (Anderson, 2018; Bracken & Eaton, 2020; Fausset et al., 2021; Wines, 2021). Civic discourse (Komska et al., 2018), akin to multilingual dynamics as a site in which power is established, navigated, and contested, merits our attention for the role it has to play therein.

In 2021, French President Emmanuel Macron launched investigations of American universities, accusing them of fomenting radical political ideologies seen as threats to French Republican ideals (Onishi, 2021; Onishi & Méheut, 2021). This move to supposedly protect national unity is, I would argue, one of the latest guises of what I have been calling francohegemony. Amidst the shifting combinations of languages in use in various contexts on Corsica, French and its concomitant national ideologies maintain an ironclad grip on the hearts and minds of speakers as the ideal language in which to live one's life. Elsa recalls her childhood dream of learning French, a beautiful and sexy language (Chapter 4), while Emmanuelle suggests to her students that forgetting one's native language, though perhaps bizarre, is not necessarily a bad thing as it is proof of integration (Chapter 2). Yet, as Hamid and Diana recount (Chapter 4), French is also an oppressive presence, one that crushes everything else and from which it is impossible to escape. Francohegemonic ideology is so pervasive that it invades other languages: Republican *laïcité* and *fraternité* appear in the ACF as their Corsican counterparts *laicità* and *fraternità* (Chapter 3). That is, even in cultural orientations fueled by opposing themselves to French and France, like on Corsica, francohegemony takes root and is seen to flourish as seemingly good and natural. Challenges to francohegemony are sticky: rejections of a francocentric sociopolitical orientation, as in "Français de merde" (shitty French) (Chapter 5), are ironically rendered in French, the language of the (former) colonizer. French can be seen to resonate from various centers (policies, curricula, attitudes); the hard-to-pinpoint nature of the source of its authority attests to its ubiquity. Even as this book has attempted to push past the central periphery to analyze multilingual dynamics beyond the maintenance and revitalization of Corsican and the French-Corsican binary, francohegemony persists.

The various contexts I have analyzed in contemporary Corsican society have allowed for the exploration of multiple heritage dynamics at play amid globalizing surges, global forces out of our control. These cases have the potential to inform policymaking related to school curricula and standardized testing, teacher training and teaching praxis, immigration law, media/journalism and publishing, access to social services, and the capacity for civic participation more generally. Participation can mean speaking (and being heard), working, studying, voting, and even things like recycling. Corsican and other languages on the island have a role to play in mediating the place of humans among shared built and natural environments (Mendes, 2020). Discourses of environmental activism that make use of Corsican and other minoritized languages have the potential to shape the future of the island, home to important nature reserves and endemic and endangered species facing habitat destruction and rising sea levels.

Working across languages in civic and political discourse, as in Diana's students' experience at the Corsican Assembly (Chapter 4), indeed plays out in political arenas for such goals as environmental protection. Minoritized languages are being used in some of the most powerful spaces in government today, including in the United States Congress. For example, in her confirmation hearing as Secretary of the Interior, Senator Deb Haaland of New Mexico used the Diné (Navajo) word *nihimá* ("our mother") to describe her motivation to protect the country's nature and wildlife.[1] A word in a minoritized language was at the crux of her argument as she explained that the Navajo code-talkers who fought in World War II had chosen *nihimá* to refer to the United States. Haaland drew from indigenous language knowledge and US history across languages in forging her discourse, critical translingual praxis at the American capitol. Caring for community, nature, and place can be inclusive of "small" languages. Conviviality—living well together—can be wide and deep.

Throughout the chapters here, translingual praxis has proven to be a fruitful way in which diverse semiotic systems (named languages,

---

1 See https://www.instagram.com/tv/CLu6aeiDwoR/?igshid=1gnyhnjv7f2jz

handwriting, physical materials, images, the built environment) combine in multimodal meaning-making. This conscious, committed practice has played out in various contexts: students drawing from diverse languages in their learning of French (Chapter 2), hybrid Corsican-French alphabet books (Chapter 3), teachers actively working within/across several languages in their instruction (Chapter 4), and in the multilingual messaging of one neighborhood's linguistic landscape (Chapter 5). Beyond the classroom, translingual praxis has an important role to play in community building, informing ideas about citizenship, in political arenas, in leadership and activism. As we understand various semiotic repertoires implicated in the many facets of human communication, we see that translingual praxis affirms emergent multilingual subjectivities. Minoritized languages are emboldened to find expression in such constellations.

As I have shown, transnational mobility to and from Corsica may consist of one's own travels or be experienced in a received manner by residents, for example via tourism. Mobility can also be imagined or aspirational: Elsa (Chapter 4) observes some locals' fictional worldliness reflected by flashy accessories worn to index international hubs of *haute couture* like Milan and Paris. Corsican educators have also underscored the advantages of teaching with virtual mobility, as in online exchanges with international pen pals, for example with the platform ETwinning, particularly when international travel became more difficult during the COVID pandemic. Mobility, and by extension places, can also be inherited. Hamid's daughter (Chapter 4) has grown up on Corsica in a household in which there is constant reference to her father's home country of Morocco. Our physical place in the world can be one that we carefully plan and agentively navigate, or it can be decided for us. Miquela chose Corsica for her adventure as an au pair (Chapter 4), while some students in the Sud FLE class (Chapter 2) were sent to Corsica after multiple border crossings and travails. Changing one's locale can endure, as in Hamid's more than 30-year residence on Corsica, or be fleeting as in Giorgia's stint in Paris and school year on the island (Chapter 4). The temporal dimension of transnational trajectories is almost as variable as the geographic; there is more to place than our immediate surroundings or the setting in which a discourse emerges. I have tried to show how Corsica can be understood as a kind of postlocal *francophonie* in which we see a simultaneity of here-and-there: the local remains resilient in encounters with the other. Even small corners of the world, micro-realities as Livia calls them in the epigraph above, have their place and help us make sense of things. The places we carry with us lead us to our understandings of the places we find ourselves in.

Tolérance (tolerance) is a core civic value in contemporary French society often accompanied by discourses of *le bien vivre ensemble* (living well together) (Mendes, 2018b, 2021). By extension, the Corsican equivalent *tullerenza* is also touted by the ACF (Chapter 3) as an important value in the island society today. *Le bien vivre ensemble* can be interpreted as a well-mannered fitting-in that plays out socially in a number of ways, including through language. Etymologically, one might interpret *le bien vivre ensemble* as akin to conviviality:

> a form of order [which we should see] as *very* relevant, as a really important *structure* of social life through which people manage to agree and get on with each other in spite of deep inequalities and bewildering diversity. Conviviality is the attitude that enables people to accept different trajectories of life and different ways of going about things within the same space, and creates a level of sharedness that can generate solidarity and sympathy with others. It is not a detail, therefore, and not trivial and meaningless, but a highly meaningful mode of conduct. (Blommaert, 2013: 89; original emphasis)

In an age of ever-increasing vitriol and violence, sympathy—even just the potential for it—is more important than ever. How do we get there? As a colleague once poignantly (exasperatedly) summarized: "On parle plus sur le corse qu'on ne le parle" (We[2] speak more about Corsican than we actually speak it). Lest this study and future work fall into a similar trap, I wonder if our fostering of multilingual dynamics, in all their many forms, could be more explicitly accompanied by better, conscious, compassionate listening. As we navigate multimodal meaning-making, we also navigate and manipulate silences, including our own. In order to speak across linguistic, cultural, and political divides, we must also be willing to listen and move toward better "civic listenership" (Gramling, 2021: 57). Could more generous listening help us move toward more equitable futures? The cases explored throughout

---

2 Here, *on* could also be understood as "people."

this book have shown that tensions need not be paralyzing; perhaps listening better is a first step to addressing seemingly irreconcilable conflicts.

Shifting language hierarchies and various orientations to place represent powerful linguistic and spatial ambiguity to be drawn from in discourse. When creatively engaged, these ambiguities have the potential to challenge and destabilize sociopolitical domination. Future work on marginalized voices and minoritized languages should continue to analyze the seepage of linguistic hegemonies into our day-to-day lived experience. We must continue to strive to foster language reclamation and translingual praxis in order to speak truth to power—in small languages, in new ways.

Bibliography

Abdelhay, A., Mahgoub, A., & Mohamed, E. (2016). "The Semiotic Landscaping of Heritage: Al-Mantiqa al-Tarkhiyya in Jeddah." *Linguistic Landscape*, 2(1): 52–79.

Abdouni, A. (2016, March 26). "A l'épreuve de la Corse: 'Arabi Fora'." *Huffington Post Maghreb*. Retrieved from: https://www.huffpostmaghreb.com/ahmed-abdouni/a-lepreuve-de-la-corse-arabi-fora_b_9547854.html.

Abello-Contesse, C. (2009). "Age and the Critical Period Hypothesis." *ELT Journal*, 63(2): 170–2.

Académie de Corse. (2016). *Présentation du Collège de Montesoro (2015/2016)*. Bastia: Académie de Corse.

Adams, T.E., Holman Jones, S., & Ellis, C. (2015). *Autoethnography: Understanding Qualitative Research*. New York: Oxford University Press.

Adrey, J.-B. (2009). *Discourse and Struggle in Minority Language Policy Formation: Corsican Language Policy in the EU Context of Governance*. New York: Palgrave MacMillan.

Agenzia Nazionale Stampa Associata. (2019, July 1). "Italy Allocates 647,000 Euros for Italian-Language Teaching." Retrieved from: https://www.infomigrants.net/en/post/14326/italy-allocates-647000-euros-for-italianlanguage-teaching.

Albertini, A. (2018). *Les Invisibles*. Paris: Points.

Alexander, R. (2006). *Bosnian, Croatian, Serbian: A Grammar with Sociolinguistic Commentary*. Madison: University of Wisconsin Press.

Anderson, C. (2018). *One Person, No Vote: How Voter Suppression Is Destroying Our Democracy*. New York: Bloomsbury.

Aronin, L. & Jessner, U. (2016). "Spacetimes of Multilingualism." In *Researching Second Language Learning and Teaching from a Psycholinguistic Perspective: Studies in Honor of Danuta Gabrys-Barker*. In D. Galajda, P. Zakrajewsky, & M. Pawlak, eds. Berlin: Springer. pp. 23–35.

Aronin, L. & Ó Laoire, M. (2012). "The Material Culture of Multilingualism." In *Minority Languages in the Linguistic Landscape*. D. Gorter, H.F. Marten, & L. Van Mensel, eds. New York: Palgrave MacMillan. pp. 299–318.

Aronin, L. & Politis, V. (2015). "Multilingualism as an Edge." *Theory and Practice of Second Language Acquisition*, 1(1): 27–50.
Bakhtin, M.M. (1981). *The Dialogic Imagination: Four Essays*. M. Holquist, ed. Austin: University of Texas Press.
—. (1986). *Speech Genres and Other Late Essays*. V. W. McGee, trans.; C. Emerson & M. Holquist, eds. Austin: University of Texas Press.
Barni, M. & Bagna, C. (2015). "The Critical Turn in LL: New Methodologies and New Items in LL." *Linguistic Landscape*, 1–2: 6–18.
Beck, U. (2003). "Toward a New Critical Theory with a Cosmopolitan Intent." *Constellations*, 10(4): 453–68.
—. (2006). *The Cosmopolitan Vision*. C. Cronin, trans. Cambridge: Polity.
Benor, S. (2019). "Ethnolinguistic Infusion at Sephardic Adventure Camp." In *The Routledge Companion to the Work of John Rickford*. R. Blake & I. Buchstaller, eds. New York: Routledge, pp. 142–51.
Ben-Rafael, E., Shohamy, E., Amara, M., & Trumper-Hecht, N. (2006). "Linguistic Landscape as Symbolic Construction of the Public Space: The Case of Israel." *International Journal of Multilingualism*, 3(1): 7–30.
Benwell, B. & Stokoe, E. (2006). *Discourse and Identity*. Edinburgh: Edinburgh University Press.
Bertrand, F. (2015). *Abbiccì dì*. Bastia: Centre culturel Una Volta.
Blackwood, R. (2004). "Compulsory Corsican Language Classes in School as a Method for Reversing the Language Shift to French?" *Transactions of the Philological Society*, 102(3): 207–333.
—. (2008). *The State, the Activists, and the Islanders: Language Policy on Corsica*. New York: Springer.
—. (2015). "LL Explorations and Methodological Challenges: Analysing France's Regional Languages." *Linguistic Landscape*, 1–2: 38–53.
Blackwood, R. & Tufi, S. (2015). *The Linguistic Landscape of the Mediterranean: French and Italian Coastal Cities*. London: Palgrave Macmillan.
Blanchet, P. (2020). "'Corsican Sociolinguistics': Keywords and Concepts of a Cross-Linguistic Theory." *International Journal of the Sociology of Language*, 261: 9–26.
Block, D. (2014). "Moving Beyond 'Lingualism': Multilingual Embodiment and Multimodality in SLA." In *The Multilingual Turn: Implications for SLA, TESOL, and Bilingual Education*. S. May, ed. New York: Routledge, pp. 54–77.
Blommaert, J. (2004). *Discourse: A Critical Introduction*. Cambridge: Cambridge University Press.
—. (2008). *Grassroot Literacy: Writing, Identity, and Voice in Central Africa*. New York: Routledge.
—. (2010). *The Sociolinguistics of Globalization*. Cambridge: Cambridge University Press.
—. (2012). "Complexity, Accent and Conviviality: Concluding Comments." *Tilburg Papers in Culture Studies*, Paper 26. Retrieved from: https://www.tilburguniversity.edu/upload/e616b261-9170-4579-b326-cac354b8678d_tpcs%20paper26.pdf.

—. (2013). *Ethnography, Superdiversity and Linguistic Landscapes: Chronicles of Complexity*. Bristol: Multilingual Matters.

—. (2014). "From Mobility to Complexity in Sociolinguistic Theory and Method." *Working Papers in Urban Language and Literacies*, Paper 135. Retrieved from: https://www.tilburguniversity.edu/upload/5ff19e97-9abc-45d0-8773-d2d8b0a9b0f8_TPCS_103_Blommaert.pdf.

—. (2015). "Commentary: Superdiversity Old and New." *Language & Communication*, 44(1): 82–9.

—. (2016). "From Mobility to Complexity in Sociolinguistic Theory and Method." In *Sociolinguistics: Theoretical Debates*. N. Coupland, ed. Cambridge: Cambridge University Press, pp. 242–60.

—. (2018). *Dialogues with Ethnography: Notes on Classics and How I Read Them*. Bristol: Multilingual Matters.

Blommaert, J. & Jie, D. (2010). *Ethnographic Fieldwork: A Beginner's Guide*. Bristol: Multilingual Matters.

Bonacina, F. (2011). *A Conversation Analytic Approach to Practiced Language Policies: The Example of an Induction Classroom for Newly-Arrived Immigrant Children in France*. (Doctoral dissertation). University of Edinburgh.

Bourdieu, P. (1977). *Outline of a Theory of Practice*. Cambridge: Cambridge University Press.

—. (1990). *The Logic of Practice*. Stanford: Stanford University Press.

Bracken, K. & Eaton, A. (2020, September 27). "How Could Voter Suppression Affect the Presidential Election? Look at Georgia." *The New York Times*. Retrieved from: https://www.nytimes.com/2020/09/27/us/elections/voting-rights-georgia.html.

Breeden, A. (2022, March 22). "Yvan Colonna, Corsican Jailed for French Prefect's Murder, Dies at 61." *The New York Times*. Retrieved from: https://www.nytimes.com/2022/03/22/world/europe/yvan-colonna-dead.html.

Bucholtz, M. & Hall, K. (2016). "Embodied Sociolinguistics." In *Sociolinguistics: Theoretical Debates*. N. Coupland, ed. Cambridge: Cambridge University Press, pp. 173–97.

Burawoy, M. (2003). "Revisits: An Outline of a Theory of Reflexive Ethnography." *American Sociological Review*, 68(5): 645–79.

Butler, J. (2011). "Bodies in Alliance and the Politics of the Street." European Institute for Progressive Cultural Policies. Retrieved from: https://pdfs.semanticscholar.org/9cf5/3d72261800bc7ac2f7353270a8f59287a9be.pdf?_ga=2.112978755.650196991.1614804964-1524281117.1614804964.

Buzard, J. (2003). "On Auto-Ethnographic Authority." *The Yale Journal of Criticism*, 16(1): 61–91.

Camus, A. (1957). "L'hôte." In *L'Exil et le royaume*. Paris: Éditions Gallimard, pp. 79–99.

Canagarajah, S. (2011). "Translanguaging in the Classroom: Emerging Issues for Research and Pedagogy." *Applied Linguistics Review*, 2: 1–28.

—. (2013). *Translingual Practice: Global Englishes and Cosmopolitan Relations*. New York: Routledge.

—. (2018). "Translingual Practice as Spatial Repertoires: Expanding the Paradigm beyond Structuralist Orientations." *Applied Linguistics*, 39(1): 31–54.
Candea, M. (2010). *Corsican Fragments: Difference, Knowledge, and Fieldwork.* Bloomington: Indiana University Press.
Carlotti, S. (2016, June 8). *L'abécédaire photo des collégiens de Montesoro.* Retrieved from: https://www.corsematin.com/article/article/labecedaire-photo-des-collegiens-de-montesoro.
CASNAV de Bastia. (2015). *Les enjeux de l'accueil par l'institution.* Bastia: CASNAV de Bastia.
Catalano, T. (2016). *Talking about Global Migration: Implications for Language Teaching.* Bristol: Multilingual Matters.
Centre Méditerranéen de la Photographie (CMP). (2016). *Abicidì fotogràficu corsu-francese.* Retrieved from: https://en.calameo.com/books/0048204251dc4a4df0ddd.
Chouliarki, L. & Fairclough, N. (1999). *Discourse in Late Modernity: Rethinking Critical Discourse Analysis.* Edinburgh: Edinburgh University Press.
Collas, A. (12 February 2016). "Les enseignements de langues d'origine vont disparaître." Retrieved from: https://www.lemonde.fr/education/article/2016/02/13/les-enseignements-de-langues-dorigine-vont-disparaitre_4864741_1473685.html.
Colonna, R. (2020a). "Introduction: The Corsican Language: A Singular, Concerning and Uncertain Situation. Assessment and Future Challenges." *International Journal of the Sociology of Language*, 261: 1–7.
—. (2020b). "Réévaluer le conflit diglossique en Corse: apports et dépassements de la sociolinguistique du conflit." *International Journal of the Sociology of Language*, 261: 85–102.
Coluzzi, P. (2004). *Regional and Minority Languages in Italy: A General Introduction on the Present Situation and a Comparison of Two Case Studies: Language Planning for Milanese (Western Lombard) and Friulian* (Working Paper 14). Barcelona: Escarré International Centre for Ethnic Minorities and Nations.
—. (2008). "Language Planning for Italian Regional Languages ('Dialects')." *Language Problems & Language Planning*, 32(3): 215–36.
Comiti, J.-M. (2011). *A Pratica è a Grammatica.* Ajaccio: Albiana/CCU.
Copland, F. & Creese, A., eds. (2015). *Linguistic Ethnography.* London: Sage.
Cotnam, M. (2012). "Pour exercer son droit d'apprendre sa langue minoritaire: éléments de comparaison des systèmes d'éducation en contexte minoritaire ontarien et corse." In *La langue corse dans le système éducatif: enjeux sociaux, curriculaires et didactiques du bi-plurilinguisme.* P. Ottavi, ed., Ajaccio: Albiana, pp. 67–86.
Cotnam-Kappel, M. (2014). "Reflexive Graffiti Remixing: Curriculum, Corsican Language, and Critical Pedagogy." *Journal of the Canadian Association for Curriculum Studies*, 11(2): 44–74.
Coupland, N. (2012). "Bilingualism on Display: The Framing of Welsh and English in Welsh Public Spaces." *Language in Society*, 41: 1–27.

Culioli, A.-L., Culioli, G.-X., Paoli, G.H.J.-B., & Weber, G.H.J.-M. (2010). *U Minò: petit dictionnaire français-corse corse-français*. Ajaccio: DCL.
Dalpvia, N.A. (2016, July 2). "Marine Le Pen et Louis Alliot refoulés d'un restaurant en Corse." *Le Gossip*. Retrieved from: https://www.legossip.net/marine-pen-louis-alliot-corse/270582/.
Daly, N. (2019). "The Linguistic Landscape of Multilingual Picturebooks." *Linguistic Landscape*, 5(3): 281–301.
Das, S. (2016). *Linguistic Rivalries: Tamil Migrants and Anglo-Franco Conflicts*. Oxford: Oxford University Press.
Deleuze, G. & Guattari, F. (1988). *A Thousand Plateaus: Capitalism and Schizophrenia*. London: Athlone.
Département des statistiques, des études et de la documentation. (2016, April 20) "En 2010 comme en 1990, des disparités régionales de la présence et de l'origine des immigrés." *Infos migrations*, 82–3. Retrieved from: https://www.immigration.interieur.gouv.fr/Info-ressources/Actualites/Focus/En-2010-comme-en-1990-des-disparites-regionales-de-la-presence-et-de-l-origine-des-immigres.
Di Meglio, A. (2020). "La langue polynomique, le concept phare de l'appareil critique corse." *International Journal of the Sociology of Language*, 261: 45–65.
Duchêne, A. (2020). "Multilingualism: An Insufficient Answer to Sociolinguistic Inequalities." *International Journal of the Sociology of Language*, 263: 91–7.
Evers, C. (2018). "Not Citizens of a Classical Mediterranean: Muslim Youth from Marseille Elude a Linguistic Gentrification by the French State." *Signs and Society*, 6(2): 435–74.
Fairclough, N. (1989). *Language and Power*. London: Longman.
—., ed. (1992). *Critical Language Awareness*. London: Longman.
—. (1995). *Critical Discourse Analysis: The Critical Study of Language*. London: Longman.
—. (1999). "Global Capitalism and Critical Awareness of Language." *Language Awareness*, 8(2): 71–83.
Faucheux, C. (2006). *Language Classification and Manipulation in Romania and Moldova*. (Master's Thesis). Louisiana State University, Baton Rouge.
Fausset, R., Corasaniti, N., & Leibovich, M. (2021, March 3). "Why the Georgia G.O.P.'s Voting Rollbacks Would Hit Black People Hard." *The New York Times*. Retrieved from: https://www.nytimes.com/2021/03/03/us/politics/georgia-voting-laws.html.
Fazi, A. (2020). "How Language Becomes a Political Issue: Social Change, Collective Movements, and Political Competition in Corsica." *International Journal of the Sociology of Language*, 261: 119–44.
Ferrer, C. (2016, March 1). *Corsica Sera: Michel Barat tire sa révérence, il est l'invité du journal*. Retrieved from: http://france3-regions.francetvinfo.fr/corse/corsica-sera-michel-barat-tire-sa-reverence-il-est-l-invite-du-journal-940545.html.
Feyfant, A. (2012). "Le Français langue d'intégration." Éduveille: autour des recherches en education et *formation*. Retrieved from: https://eduveille.hypotheses.org/4276.

Foucault, M. (1977). *Language, Counter-Memory, Practice: Selected Essays and Interviews by Michel Foucault*. D.F. Bouchard, ed. New York: Cornell University Press.

Fourquet, J. (2017). *La nouvelle question corse: nationalisme, clanisme, immigration*. La Tour d'Aigues: L'aube.

Freire, P. (2005). *Pedagogy of the Oppressed: 30th Anniversary Edition*. M. Bergman Ramos, trans. New York: Continuum.

Fr.soc.politique. (2016, July 4). *Marine Le Pen et Louis Alliot refoulés d'un restaurant en Corse*. [Google Group]. Retrieved from: https://groups.google.com/forum/#!topic/fr.soc.politique/ZMGyRzvCFPc.

Gadet, F. (2014). "French Language(s) in Contact Worldwide: History, Space, System, and Other Ecological Factors." *Journal of Language Contact*, 7: 3–35.

Gaggioli, GHJ. (2012). *La langue corse en 23 lettres*. Ajaccio: Albiana.

Gal, S. & Irvine, J.T. (2019). *Signs of Difference: Language and Ideology in Social Life*. New York: Cambridge University Press.

García, O. (2009). "Education, Multilingualism, and Translanguaging in the 21st Century." In *Social Justice through Multilingual Education*. T. Skutnabb-Kangas, R. Phillipson, A.K. Mohanty, & M. Panda, eds. Bristol: Multilingual Matters, pp. 140–58.

Géa, J.-M. (2005). "Immigration et contacts de langues en Corse: l'exemple de deux familles marocaines." *Langage et société*, 112 (June): 57–78.

—. (2006). "Marocains de Corse: entre deux pays et trois langues." *Langues et cite*, 8 (December): 5.

—. (2016). "L'acculturation linguistique (français/langue régionale) des enfants de migrants en Corse: représentations et dimensione socio-identitaire." *Langage et société*, 157(3): 99–118.

Gee, J. (1990). *Social Linguistics and Literacies: Ideologies in Discourses*. New York: Routledge.

Goldschmidt, W. (1977). "Anthropology and the Coming Crisis: An Autoethnographic Appraisal." *American Anthropologist*, 79(2): 293–308.

Goodall, H.L. (2000). *Writing the New Ethnography*. Walnut Creek, CA: AltaMira.

Gorter, D. (2006). "Introduction: The Study of the Linguistic Landscape as a New Approach to Multilingualism." *International Journal of Multilingualism*, 3(1): 1–6.

Gorter, D. & Cenoz, J. (2015). "Translanguaging and Linguistic Landscapes." *Linguistic Landscape*, 1(1–2): 54–74.

Gramling, D. (2016). *The Invention of Monolingualism*. London: Bloomsbury.

—. (2021). *The Invention of Multilingualism*. Cambridge: Cambridge University Press.

Gramsci, A. (2007 [1948]). *Quaderni del carcere*. Turin: Einaudi.

Groff, C. (2017). "Language and Language-in-Education Planning in Multilingual India: A Minoritized Language Perspective. *Language Policy*, 16: 135–64.

Hartigan, Jr., J. (2015). "Plant Publics: Multispecies Relating in Spanish Botanical Gardens." *Anthropological Quarterly*, 88(2): 481–507.

Heller, M. (2011). *Paths to Post-Nationalism: A Critical Ethnography of Language and Identity*. Oxford: Oxford University Press.
Heller, M. & McElhinny, B. (2017). *Language, Capitalism, Colonialism: Toward a Critical History*. Toronto: University of Toronto Press.
Heller, M., Pietikäinen, S., & Pujolar, J. (2018). *Critical Sociolinguistic Research Methods: Studying Language Issues that Matter*. New York: Routledge.
Hélot, C. (2003). "Language Policy and the Ideology of Bilingual Education in France." *Language Policy*, 2: 255–77.
Hélot, C. & Young, A. (2006). "Imagining Multilingual Education in France: A Language and Cultural Awareness Project at the Primary Level." In *Imagining Multilingual Schools: Languages in Education and Glocalization*. O. García, T. Skutnabb-Kangas, & M.E. Torres Guzmán, eds. Bristol: Multilingual Matters, pp. 69–90.
Hess, N. (1996). "Code Switching and Style Shifting as Markers of Liminality in Literature." *Language and Literature: International Journal of Stylistics*, 5(1): 5–18.
Huidobro, V. (2003). *Altazor, or A Voyage in a Parachute: Poem in VII Cantos (1919)*. E. Weinberger, trans. Middletown, Connecticut: Wesleyan University Press.
Institut national de la statistique et des études économiques (INSEE). (2015, June 25). "Population immigrée: une main-d'oeuvre plus européenne." *Insee Flash: Corse*, 6(June). Retrieved from: https://www.insee.fr/fr/statistiques/1288147.
—. (2017). "Bilan annuel du tourisme—2016." *INSEE Corse Dossier*, 7(May). Retrieved from: https://www.insee.fr/fr/statistiques/2854071.
Irvine, J.T. & Gal, S. (2000). "Language Ideology and Linguistic Differentiation." In *Regimes of Language: Ideologies, Polities, and Identities*. P. Kroskrity, ed. Santa Fe: School of American Research Press, pp. 35–83.
Jaffe, A. (1996). "The Second Annual Corsican Spelling Contest: Orthography and Ideology." *American Ethnologist*, 23(4): 816–35.
—. (1999). *Ideologies in Action: Language Politics on Corsica*. Berlin: Mouton de Gruyter.
—. (2010). "Critical Perspectives on Language-in-Education Policy: The Corsican Example." In *Ethnography and Language Policy*. T. McCarty, ed. London: Routledge, pp. 205–29.
—. (2014). "Idéologies linguistiques, pratiques pédagogiques et positionnement sociolinguistiques." *Cahiers d'atelier de sociolinguistique*, 6: 149–68.
—. (2016). "What Kinds of Diversity Are Super? Hidden Diversities and Mobilities on a Mediterranean Island." *Language & Communication*, 51: 5–16.
—. (2019). "Poeticizing the Economy: The Corsican Language in a Nexus of Pride and Profit." *Multilingua*, 38(1): 9–27.
—. (2020). "Language Ideologies and Linguistic Representations: Two Lenses for a Critical Analysis of Polynomie in Corsica." *International Journal of the Sociology of Language*, 261: 67–84.
Jaffe, A. & Oliva, C. (2013). "Linguistic Creativity in Corsican Tourist Context." In *Multilingualism and the Periphery*. S. Pietikäinen & H. Kelley-Holmes, eds. Oxford: Oxford University Press, pp. 95–117.

Johnstone, B. (2011). "Language and Place." In *The Cambridge Handbook of Sociolinguistics*. R. Mesthrie, ed. Cambridge: Cambridge University Press, pp. 203–17.
Jones, J.P., Leitner, H., Marston, S.A., & Sheppard, E. (2017). "Neil Smith's Scale." *Antipode*, 49(1): 138–52.
Komska, Y., Moyd, M., & Gramling, D. (2018). *Linguistic Disobedience: Restoring Power to Civic Language*. London: Palgrave Macmillan.
Kramsch, C. (1993). *Context and Culture in Language Teaching*. Oxford: Oxford University Press.
—. (2009). *The Multilingual Subject: What Foreign Language Learners Say about Their Experience and Why It Matters*. Oxford: Oxford University Press.
—. (2018). "Trans-Spatial Utopias." *Applied Linguistics*, 39(1): 108–15.
Kramsch, C. & Zhang, L. (2018). *The Multilingual Instructor: What Foreign Language Teachers Say about Their Experience and Why It Matters*. Oxford: Oxford University Press.
Lafont, R. (1967). *La Révolution régionaliste*. Paris: Gallimard.
Lahlou, R. (2017, May 9). *Un chanoine historien dévoué à la Corse: Lucien-Auguste Letteron*. Retrieved from: http://www.corse.catholique.fr/accueil/292383-chanoine-historien-devoue-a-corse-lucien-auguste-letteron/.
Lazaridis, M. & Seksig, A. (2005). "L'immigration à l'école: evolution des politiques scolaire d'intégration." *Santé, société et solidarité*, 1: 153–63.
Leonard, W. (2011). "Challenging 'Extinction' through Modern Miami Language Practices." *American Indian Culture and Research Journal*, 35(2): 135–60.
—. (2020). "Musings on Native American Language Reclamation and Sociolinguistics." *International Journal of the Sociology of Language*, 263: 85–90.
Li Wei (2018). "Translanguaging as a Practical Theory of Language." *Applied Linguistics*, 39(1): 9–30.
Linares, E. (2019a). "Introduction to the Special Issue: Practicing Multilingual Research." *Critical Multilingualism Studies*, 7(1): 1–10.
—. (2019b). "Afterword: Socialization to the Practice of Multilingual Research." *Critical Multilingualism Studies*, 7(1): 124–9.
Lippi-Green, R. (1997). *English with an Accent: Language, Ideology, and Discrimination in the United States*. New York: Routledge.
Litaudon, M.-P. (2014). *Les abécédaires de l'enfance: verbe et image*. Rennes: Presses universitaires de Rennes.
Lombardi, W.V. (2014). "Global Subcultural Bohemianism: The Prospect of Postlocal Ecocriticism in Tim Winton's *Breath*." In *New International Voices in Ecocriticism*. S. Oppermann, ed. Lanham, MD: Rowan & Littlefield, pp. 41–54.
Luciani, M.-P. (1995). *Immigrés en Corse: minorité de la minorité*. Paris: L'Harmattan.
Ludwig, B. (2016). "The Different Meanings of the Word Refugee." In *Refugee Resettlement in the United States: Language, Policy, Pedagogy*. E.M. Feuerherm & V. Ramanathan, eds. Bristol: Multilingual Matters, pp. 35–53.
Luke, A. (2004). "Teaching After the Market: From Commodity to Cosmopolitan." *Teachers College Record*, 106(7): 1422–43.

Madison, D.S. (2012). *Critical Ethnography: Method, Ethics, and Performance*. Los Angeles: Sage.
Mahdi, M. (2014). "Les conditions de l'insécurité linguistique chez les berbérophones d'origine marocaine nouvellement arrivés en France, d'après une étude en Haute Corse." *Revue de dialectologie des langues-cultures et de lexiculturologie*, 175(3): 343–59.
Marchetti, P. & Geronimi, D. A. (1971). *Intricciate è cambiarine: manuel pratique d'orthographe corse*. Paris: Beaulieu.
Mari, N. (2016, October 11). "Le statut de la Corse—île montagne a été adopté à l'Assemblée nationale." *Corse Net Infos*. Retrieved from: https://www.corsenetinfos.corsica/Le-statut-de-la-Corse-ile-montagne-a-ete-adopte-a-l-Assemblee-nationale_a23693.html.
Martinet, L. (2015, December 28). "Corse: 'Arabi fora' ne peut pas être considéré comme un slogan nationaliste." *L'Express*. Retrieved from: https://www.lexpress.fr/actualite/societe/corse-arabi-fora-ne-peut-pas-etre-considere-comme-un-slogan-nationaliste_1749157.html.
Maskens, M. (2008). "Migration et pentecôtisme à Bruxelles: expériences croisées." *Archives de sciences sociales des religions*, 143: 49–68.
Menard-Warwick, J. (2005). "Transgressive Narratives, Dialogic Voicing, and Cultural Change." *Journal of Sociolinguistics*, 9(4): 533–56.
—. (2014). *English Language Teachers on the Discursive Faultlines: Identities, Ideologies, and Pedagogies*. Bristol: Multilingual Matters.
Mendes, A. (2018a). *On Multilingual Corsica: Language, Multiplicity, and Globalization*. (Doctoral dissertation). University of California, Davis.
—. (2018b). "Granite Island Pearls: 'Unaccompanied Foreign Minors' in a Corsican FLE Class." *Critical Multilingualism Studies*, 6(1): 190–214.
—. (2020). "Verdant Vernaculars: Corsican Environmental Assemblages." *Journal of Linguistic Anthropology*, 30(2): 156–78.
—. (2021). "Forging Multilingualism: Teleological Tension in French and Corsican Middle School Curricula." *Language Policy*, 20(2): 173–92.
—. (2022). "*Je la veux … cuite*? Francohegemony, Steak, and FLE in French Cultural Contexts." *The French Review*, 95(3): 139–56.
Mendonça Dias, C. (2013). "Les progressions linguistiques et scolaires des collégiens nouvellement arrivés, non ou peu scolarisés antérieurement." *Recherches en didactique des langues et des cultures: Les cahiers de l'Acedle*, 10(1): 159–75.
Mestersheim, A. (2002). *Corse-colonies*. Ajaccio: Albiana.
Ministère de l'éducation nationale. (2012). "Les élèves nouveaux arrivants non-francophones en 2010–2011." *Note d'information*, 12(1): 1–6.
—. (2015). "Année scolaire 2014–2015: 52 500 élèves allophones scolarisés dont 15 300 l'étaient déjà l'année précédente." *Note d'information*, 15 (October): 1–4.
Muncey, T. (2010). *Creating Autoethnographies*. Los Angeles: Sage.
Mura, P. (2019a). "Language Policy and Language Beliefs in Sardinia: A Case Study." *Linguistica Online*, 22: 1–24.

—. (2019b). "Macro-Policy vs. Micro-Policy: A Study on Two Italian-Sardinian Websites." *Linguistica Online*, 22: 25–35.

Nannipieri, L. (2016, August 7). "VIDÉO. Opération de police 'choc' à Bastia: 'C'est du n'importe quoi, c'est un show!'" Retrieved from: https://www.corsematin.com/article/bastia/video-cest-du-nimporte-quoi-cest-un-show.

Newberry Library. (September 9–December 30, 2022). Hanging Text. *A Show of Hands*. Newberry Library, Chicago, IL.

Nirayan, K. (1993). "How Native Is a 'Native' Anthropologist?" *American Anthropologist*, 95: 671–86.

Onishi, N. (2021, February 9). "Will American Ideas Tear France Apart? Some of Its Leaders Think So." *The New York Times*. Retrieved from: https://www.nytimes.com/2021/02/09/world/europe/france-threat-american-universities.html.

Onishi, N. & Méheut, C. (2021, February 18). "Heating Up Culture Wars, France to Scour Universities for Ideas that 'Corrupt Society.'" *The New York Times*. Retrieved from: https://www.nytimes.com/2021/02/18/world/europe/france-universities-culture-wars.html.

OECD. (2014). *Perspectives de politiques de l'éducation: France*. Retrieved from: http://www.oecd.org/edu/EDUCATION%20POLICY%20OUTLOOK%20FRANCE_F.pdf.

Ottavi, P. (2008). *Le bilinguisme dans l'école de la République? Le cas de la Corse*. Ajaccio: Albiana.

—., ed. (2012). *La langue corse dans le système éducatif: enjeux sociaux, curriculaires et didactiques du bi-plurilinguisme*. Ajaccio: Albiana.

—. (2013). "Corse: la construction problématique d'une identité collective dans une société multiculturelle." *Cahiers internationaux de sociolinguistique*, 2(4): 139–58.

Parry, M. (2002). "The Challenges to Multilingualism Today." In *Multilingualism in Italy: Past and Present*. A.L. Lepschy & A. Tosi, eds. Routledge, pp. 47–59.

Pavlenko, A. (2018). "Superdiversity and Why It Isn't: Reflections on Terminological Innovations and Academic Branding." In *Sloganizations in Language Education Discourse*. S. Breidbach, L. Küster, & B. Schmenk, eds. Bristol: Multilingual Matters, pp. 142–68.

Pavlenko, A. & Mullen, A. (2015). "Why Diachronicity Matters in the Study of Linguistic Landscapes." *Linguistic Landscape*, 1–2: 114–32.

Pavlenko, A. & Norton, B. (2007). "Imagined Communities, Identity and English Language learning." In *International Handbook of English Language Teaching*. J. Cummins & C. Davidson, eds. New York: Springer, pp. 669–80.

Pennycook, A. (1999). "Introduction: Critical Approaches to TESOL." *TESOL Quarterly*, 33: 329–48.

—. (2008). "Linguistic Landscapes and the Transgressive Semiotics of Graffiti." In *Linguistic Landscape: Expanding the Scenery*. E. Shohamy & D. Gorter, eds. London: Routeledge, pp. 302–12.

—. (2018). *Posthumanist Applied Linguistics*. New York: Routledge.

Pennycook, A. & Otsuji, E. (2015). *Metrolingualism: Language in the City.* New York: Routledge.
Phipps, A. (2011). "Travelling Languages? Land, Languaging and Translation." *Language and Intercultural Communication*, 11(4): 364–76.
—. (2013). "Unmoored: Language Pain, Porosity, and Poisonwood." *Critical Multilingualism Studies*, 1(2): 96–118.
—. (2019). *Decolonising Multilingualism: Struggles to Decreate.* Bristol: Multilingual Matters.
Pietikäinen, S. & Kelly-Holmes, H. (Eds.). (2013). *Multilingualism and the Periphery.* Oxford: Oxford University Press.
Pietikäinen, S., Kelly-Holmes, H., Jaffe, A., & Coupland, N. (2017). *Sociolinguistics from the Periphery: Small Languages in New Circumstances.* Cambridge: Cambridge University Press.
Piller, I. (2016). *Linguistic Diversity and Social Justice: An Introduction to Applied Linguistics.* Oxford: Oxford University Press.
Pomponi, F. (1979). *Histoire de la Corse.* Paris: Hachette.
Quenot, S. (2010). *Structuration de l'école bilingue en Corse: processus et stratégies scolaires d'intégration et de différenciation dans l'enseignement primaire.* (Doctoral dissertation.) Università di Còrsica Pasquale Pàoli.
—. (2012). "Les familles et les écoles bilingues. L'école publique en mutation: la langue corse investit le 'bocal' scolaire." In *La langue corse dans le système éducatif: enjeux sociaux, curriculaires et didactiques du bi-plurilinguisme.* P. Ottavi, ed. Ajaccio: Albiana, 199–214.
—. (2020). "Public Policy for the Corsican Language: From Revitalization to Normalization?" *International Journal of the Sociology of Language*, 261: 145–62.
Ramanathan, V. (2013a). "Introduction: Language Policies and (Dis)citizenship: Access, Rights, Pedagogies." In *Language Policies and (Dis-)Citizenship: Rights, Access, Pedagogies.* V. Ramanathan, ed. Bristol: Multilingual Matters, pp. 1–16.
—. (2013b). "Afterword." In *Language Policies and (Dis-)Citizenship: Rights, Access, Pedagogies.* V. Ramanathan, ed. Bristol: Multilingual Matters, pp. 253–55.
Rampton, B. (1995). *Crossing: Language and Ethnicity among Adolescents.* London: Longman.
Reed-Danahay, D. (2009). "Anthropologists, Education, and Autoethnography." *Reviews in Anthropology*, 38: 28–47.
Reyes, A. (2014). "Linguistic Anthropology in 2013: Super-New-Big." *American Anthropologist*, 116(2): 366–78.
Romano, A., Boula de Mareüil, P., Lai, J.-P., & Mairano, P. (2011). "Quelques patrons intonatifs du corse dans le cadre de l'AMPER." *Bollettino dell'Atalante Linguistico Italiano*, 35 (III Serie): 25–42.
Rovera, S. (2013). *Mineurs isolés étrangers: l'essentiel sur l'accueil et la prise en charge en France.* Retrieved from: https://www.france-terre-asile.org/images/stories/mineurs-isoles-etrangers/MIE_web.compressed1.pdf.
Rozenholc, C. (2014). "Sens du lieu, identifications et *méditerranéité* à Tel-Aviv et Marseille." *Géographie et cultures*, 89–90: 261–82.

Saldaña, J. (2016). *The Coding Manual for Qualitative Researchers* (3rd ed.). London: Sage.
Schjerve, R.R. (2017). "Sociolinguistica e vitalità del sardo." In E. Blaco Ferrer, P. Koch, & D. Marzo, eds. *Manuale di linguistica sarda*. Berlin: De Gruyter, 31–44.
Schulte, K. (2018). "Romance in Contact with Romance." In *Manual of Romance Sociolinguistics*. W. Ayres-Bennett & J. Carruthers, eds. Berlin: De Gruyter, 587–618.
Scollon, R. & Scollon, S.W. (2003). *Discourses in Place: Language in the Material World*. London: Routledge.
Scott, J.C. 1986. "Everyday Forms of Peasant Resistance." *Journal of Peasant Studies*, 13(2): 5–35.
Serrano, I. (2011). "The End of the Corsican Question?" In *Federalism Beyond Federations: Asymmetry and Processes of Resymmetrisation*. F. Requejo & K.J. Nagel, eds. London: Ashgate, 223–47.
Shohamy, E. (2015). "LL Research as Expanding Language and Language Policy." *Linguistic Landscape*, 1–2: 152–71.
Shohamy, E., Ben-Rafael, E., & Barni, M., eds. (2010). *Linguistic Landscape in the City*. Bristol: Multilingual Matters.
Smith, M.A. (2019). *Senegal Abroad: Linguistic Borders, Racial Formations, and Diasporic Imaginaries*. Madison: University of Wisconsin Press.
Smith, N. (1992). "Geography, Difference, and the Politics of Scale." In *Postmodernism and the Social Sciences*. J. Doherty, E. Graham, & M. Malek, eds. London: Macmillan, 57–79.
Stanford, J.N., Ito, R., & Nibbs, F. (2018). "Language Regard in Liminal Hmong American Speech Communities." In *Language Regard: Methods, Variation, and Change*. B.E. Evans, E.J. Benson, & J.N. Stanford, eds. Cambridge: Cambridge University Press, 197–217.
Suleiman, C. (2017). *The Politics of Arabic in Israel: A Sociolinguistic Analysis*. Edinburgh: Edinburgh University Press.
Symes, C. (2021). "Sitting on the Fence: A Geosemiotic Analysis of School Perimeters." *Linguistic Landscape*, 7(1): 60–85.
Talmy, S. (2011). "The Interview as Collaborative Achievement: Interaction, Identity, and Ideology in a Speech Event." *Applied Linguistics*, 32(1): 25–42.
Thiers, J. (2020). "Élaboration, distanciation, polynomie: naissance et feux croisés de la sociolinguistique corse." *International Journal of the Sociology of Language*, 261: 27–43.
Thurlow, C. & Jaworski, A. (2011). "Tourism Discourse: Languages and Banal Globalization." *Applied Linguistics Review*, 2: 285–312.
Tollefson, J. (2006). "Critical Theory in Language Policy." In *An Introduction to Language Policy: Theory and Method*. T. Ricento, ed. Oxford: Blackwell, pp. 42–59.
Toso, F. (1996). *Frammenti d'Europa: guida alle minoranze etnico-linguistiche e ai fermenti autonomisti*. Milan: Baldini & Castoldi.
—. (2008). *Le minoranze linguistiche in Italia*. Bologna: Il Mulino.

Tufi, S. (2013). "Language Ideology and Language Maintenance: The Case of Sardinia." *International Journal of the Sociology of Language*, 219: 145–60.
—. (2017). "Liminality, Heterotopic Sites, and the Linguistic Landscape." *Linguistic Landscape*, 3(1): 78–99.
Tusting, K. & Maybin, J. (2007). "Linguistic Ethnography and Interdisciplinarity: Opening the Discussion." *Linguistic Ethnography*, 11(5): 575–83.
Urla, J. & Helepololei, J. (2014). "The Ethnography of Resistance Then and Now: On Thickness and Activist Engagement in the Twenty-First Century." *History and Anthropology*, 25(4): 431–51.
Vallaud-Belkacem, N. (2016, June 5). "Langues vivantes à la rentrée 2016: un apprentissage plus précoce et la fin des ELCO—Infographies." Retrieved from: https://www.najat-vallaud-belkacem.com/2016/06/05/langues-vivantes-a-la-rentree2016-un-apprentissage-plus-precoce-et-la-fin-des-elco-infographie/.
Vertovec, S. (2007). "Super-Diversity and its Implications." *Ethnic and Racial Studies*, 30(6): 1024–54.
—. (2010). "Towards Post-Multiculturalism? Changing Communities, Conditions, and Contexts of Diversity." *International Social Science Journal*, 61(199): 83–95.
Wines, M. (2021, January 30). "After Record Turnout, Republicans Are Trying to Make It Harder to Vote." *The New York Times*. Retrieved from: https://www.nytimes.com/2021/01/30/us/republicans-voting-georgia-arizona.html.
Wong Fillmore, L. (2000). "Loss of Family Languages: Should Educators Be Concerned?" *Theory into Practice*, 39(4): 203–10.
Woolard, K. (2016). *Singular and Plural: Ideologies of Linguistic Authority in 21st Century Catalonia*. Oxford: Oxford University Press.

Index

Abdouni, A. 145
Académie de Corse (Corsican School District) 29n2–30, 31n4–32, 47, 48
alphabet books 61–89, 135, 173
   Abbiccì dì (Bertrand) 62, 65–71, 73, 75, 77, 81, 84, 89
   abécédaires 62, 63–64
   Abicidì fotogràficu corsu-francese (ACF) 71–80, 81–82, 83, 84, 85–87, 89, 174
arabi fora 143–146, 169–170
arabi forza 156–165, 169–170
Arabic language 5, 11, 106, 117, 119–120
autoethnography 20–21

Bakhtin, M.M. 92, 93–94
Bertrand, Frédérique 65–71, 73, 75, 77, 81, 85, 89
bi-plurilingualism 5–7, 10, 87–88, 105, 133
Blackwood, R. 92, 141–142, 146, 153–154, 155, 161
Blanchet, P. 10
Blommaert, J. 7, 18, 70, 137, 140–141, 152, 158–159
Bourdieu, P. 21
Bucholtz, M. 136
Burawoy, M. 21

Camus, Albert 3, 17
Canagarajah, S. 88
Colonna, R. 4
Colonna, Yvan 167–168
Coluzzi, P. 13
Corsica
   diaspora and regional language 10–11n9
   language-culture-nation narrative 102–103, 131–132
   minority language communities 2, 11–12, 13–18, 28, 57, 79, 82–83, 87, 116, 157
   nationalist sentiment 15–19, 106
   perception of locals as "closed" to outsiders 99–100, 113–114, 146
   sociopolitical context 15–19
   urban-rural cultural spaces 8–9, 18, 31, 37, 74, 140–142, 162
   see also Corsican language
Corsican language 65n2–71
   binary center-periphery relationship to French 8
   diglossic divide 4–5
   educator-activist dynamics 92–93, 123–133
   graffiti 144n4–145

institutional support of language 4, 9, 13, 17, 24, 55, 57–59, 70, 97–100
language activism 123–133
linguistic diversity 1–2, 7–12, 94–95, 141–142
multilingual signage 150–156
politicization of regional language 2–4
revitalization initiatives 1–2, 4, 10–11, 31, 141–142
symbol of national culture 1–2, 4, 82, 83, 102–103
u Riacquisto ("Reappropriation") 3
see also alphabet books
Cotnam-Kappel, M. 81, 141, 144–145, 162–163
critical ethnography 21

Daly, N. 64, 71, 82
Das, S. 9
Deixonne Law (1951) 3
diglossia 2–3, 4–5, 94
see also heteroglossia
Duchêne, A. 23–24

education 6, 10, 13
language policies 14, 27–28
transfer of students to rural areas 31–32
see also ENAs (*élèves nouvellement arrivés*); FLE (*français langue étrangère*); teachers' narratives
ELCO (*l'enseignement des langues et cultures d'origine*) 116–123
ENAs (*élèves nouvellement arrivés*) 28–34
academic success inseparable from transnational mobility 30–34
admission to normal classes based on reaching A1 level 29–30, 47
conflated into remedial/ non-achieving students 29
constantly shifting nature of classes 32n6–33
integration supersedes language proficiency 29–30n2
learning of Corsican language 85n13–87
subordination of first language to French model 52–56, 119–120
transnational trajectories 33–34
English language 155–156
dominant position 110, 126
ethnography 19, 20–21, 28–34
see also autoethnography; critical ethnography
European minority language communities 2, 12, 38
Evers, C. 18, 135

FLE (*français langue étrangère*) 10, 25, 27–28, 47–53, 135
French cultural model 42–45, 81–82
gatekeeping (integration) function 32n7, 46, 52–53, 85–86, 110
socioeconomic diversity 35n10–36
see also alphabet books; ENAs (*élèves nouvellement arrivés*); ethnography
Fortini, Marcellu 71–74, 74, 80, 86–87, 87
Fourquet, J. 17, 146
France
annexation of Corsica 2
hegemony of French over regional languages 2–3, 4–5, 9–10, 17, 25, 97, 104, 133, 171–172
internal colonialism 3, 12
periods of racial tension 116, 123, 159
Republican ideals of societal integration and secularism 53, 78, 79–80, 81–82, 116–117, 171
see also Deixonne Law (1951)

Gal, S. 134, 158, 159
Gee, J. 93
Gentili, Emmanuelle de 74, 80

German language 6, 12, 98–99, 108–109, 112–114, 133–134, 137, 161
Geronimi, Dominique Antoine 75
globalization 2, 22–23
    effect on immigrant youth 56
    effect on minority groups 28
    instability of sociolinguistics 7–12, 129, 134
    integration through religious conversion 149–150
    linguistic heterogeneity 11–12, 170–171
    surges 56–59, 94–95, 129–130
graffiti 6, 19, 141, 143–146, 167–168
    anti-immigrant rhetoric 143–146, 156–160
    Corsican language 144n4–145
Gramling, D. 23, 85
Gramsci, A. 10

Haaland, Deb 172
Hall, K. 136
Hartigan, J., Jr. 18
Helepololei, J. 161–162
Heller, M. 19, 149
heritage languages 117, 120–121
heteroglossia 94

Ireland 8
Irvine, J.T. 134, 158, 159
Italy
    Friulian language 12, 13, 14
    hierarchy of regional languages and dialects 12–15, 97
    Italianate rule of Corsica 2–3
    Sardinia 13–14

Jaffe, A. 5, 7, 8, 82–83, 87, 146

Kramsch, C. 58, 95, 136, 137

Lafont, Robert 3, 12
Le Pen, Marine 16n11
Leonard, W. 82

Li Wei 6, 7n6, 137, 159
linguistic landscapes (LL) 25–26, 62, 64, 73, 82, 137–138, 140–142, 153–156
    liminality of local space 160–161
linguistics
    combinations of languages 1–2, 170–171
    "countervocalities" 10–11, 135, 170–171
    ethnographic approach 20–21
    gatekeeping characteristic 52–53, 85–86, 110
    intercultural communication 98–99, 132–133, 142–143
    language activism 3–4, 81–83, 121
    minority language communities 2, 11–12, 13–18, 28, 57, 79, 82–83, 87, 116, 157, 172–173, 175
    peripheral multilingualism 8
    see also bi-plurilingualism; monolingualism; multilingualism; polynomy; translanguaging
Litaudon, M.-P. 63n1, 73, 78, 81, 86, 88–89
Lombardi, W.V. 137, 162n15
Luciani, M.-P. 8n7

McElhinny, B. 149
Macron, Emmanuel 171
Madison, D.S. 21
Maghrebi immigrants 143–144
maisons d'enfants (children's homes) 36–37, 50, 51, 58
Marcellesi, Jean-Baptiste 4
Marchetti, Pascal 75
Mediterranean, hierarchy of geopolitical orientation 18–19, 102, 105–106, 129, 133
Menard-Warwick, J. 92, 93
MIEs (*mineurs isolés étrangers*, unaccompanied foreign minors) 36n15–37, 50n24–59

minority language communities 2, 11–12, 13–18, 28, 57, 79, 82–83, 87, 116, 157, 172–173, 175
monolingualism 4–5, 10, 23, 45, 58–59, 143n3
   surface 85
Morocco
   intergenerational divide 115–116
   tensions with France 115
Mullen, A. 152–153
multilingualism 1–2, 120–121, 173–175
   hidden by surface monolingualism 85
   not agreed-upon category 21–22, 91
   unmoored to geographic place 11–12, 22–23, 57, 133–134
Muncey, T. 20–21
Mura, P. 14–15

Oliva, C. 87, 146
orthography (handwriting) 39n17–42, 64, 75–76n5
Ottavi, P. 9, 162–163

Paoli, Pasquale 110n7, 128, 132
Parry, M. 12–13
Pavlenko, A. 7–8, 152–153
Phipps, A. 11, 57
Pietikäinen, S. 8, 38, 156n11, 158, 160
Piller, I. 148
polynomy 4–5, 17, 88
Portuguese language 5, 11, 107

religious literature 146–150
Rovera, S. 50n24
Rozenholc, C. 18, 22n12

Sámiland 8
Schulte, K. 86
Senegal 134
Simeoni, Edmond 16
Simeoni, Gilles 16, 65, 70, 85, 86
Smith, M.A. 9, 45, 97, 134
Smith, N. 17–18
sociolinguistics 19–20
   language-related element (accent/spelling/word choice) 38
   "pearl" as speech event metaphor 37–39
Spain 161–162
   Catalonia 3, 9, 12, 18
   colonialism 149
   Galicia 12
   Valencia 18, 101, 106
Spanu, Filippo 15
Suleiman, C. 161

Tamazight (Berber) language 5–6n5, 11, 119, 120, 149–150
teachers' narratives 91–138
   understanding of multilingualism and globalization 91–95, 113
Toso, F. 13–14
translanguaging 6–7, 137–138, 140, 142–143, 159
Tufi, S. 14, 141–142, 146, 153–154, 155, 161

Urla, J. 161–162

la valise ou le cercueil 158
Vallaud-Belkacem, Najat 116–117

Wales 8, 11
Woolard, K. 116

Zhang, L. 58, 95, 136

www.ingramcontent.com/pod-product-compliance
Lightning Source LLC
Chambersburg PA
CBHW060351031025
33500CB00046B/3386